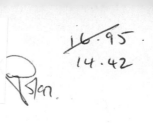

Tourism

A New Perspective

2008

Tourism
A New Perspective

Peter Burns and *Andrew Holden*

 PRENTICE HALL

London   New York   Toronto   Sydney   Tokyo   Singapore
Madrid   Mexico City   Munich

First published 1995 by
Prentice Hall International (UK) Limited
Campus 400, Maylands Avenue
Hemel Hempstead
Hertfordshire, HP2 7EZ
A division of
Simon & Schuster International Group

Typeset in 10/12 pt Baskerville
by Photoprint, Torquay, Devon

Printed and bound in Great Britain by
Hartnolls Ltd, Bodmin

Library of Congress Cataloging-in-Publication Data

Available from the publisher

British Library Cataloguing in Publication Data

A catalogue record for this book is available from
the British Library

ISBN 0-13-191552-5

---

1 2 3 4 5   99 98 97 96 95

Contents

Contents

Contents

Introduction

Studying tourism can be both enigmatic and bizarre: enigmatic, inasmuch as there remain aspects of it difficult to define, and bizarre in that it sets out to make theoretical sense of people having fun. We learn from Dean MacCannell that:

> ... tourism is a primary ground for the production of new cultural forms on a global base. In the name of tourism, capital and modernised peoples have been deployed to the most remote regions of the world, farther than any army was ever sent. Institutions have been established to support this deployment, not just hotels, restaurants, and transportation systems, but restorations of ancient shrines, development of local handcrafts for sale to tourists, and rituals performed for tourists. In short, tourism is not just an aggregate of merely commercial activities; it is also an ideological framing of history, nature, and tradition; a framing that has the power to reshape culture and nature to its own needs (MacCannell, 1992:1)

Given the power that MacCannell describes those that have any sort of responsibility for planning, managing or teaching about tourism, at any level, need to have a holistic understanding of tourism, its implications, processes and *problématique*. This, together with an awareness of the emergent planning and coping philosophies that are gaining ground within the tourism process, is the bedrock upon which the long-term sustainability of this global phenomenon will be built. While evidence indicating the sheer size of tourism is well known and extensively written about elsewhere (Burkart and Medlik, 1989; Poon, 1993; Cooper, 1989; Teare and Olsen, 1992; Edgell, 1990) straightforward statistics that demonstrate its scale are worth reiterating here (Figure 0.1). According to World Tourism Organisation analyses (WTO, 1992), international tourism receipts:

1

- grew faster than world trade in goods and services in the 1980s – the average annual growth between 1980–1990 in the current price value of merchandise exports rose 5.5%, commercial services 7.5% and international tourism 9.6%; (and)
- now rank third (after crude petroleum/petroleum products, and motor vehicles/parts/accessories) in the list of global export categories. Significantly, this places tourism ahead of electronic equipment, ores/minerals/non-ferrous metals, clothing, textiles, and iron/steel.

As Table 0.1 and Figure 0.2 indicate, this growth pattern is likely to continue. This growth has been a characteristic of all regions of the world – as illustrated by Figure 0.3.

Parallel with this has been a growth in the broader interpretation of tourism, both from a professional development perspective (Inskeep, 1991; Cooper, 1989; Ryan, 1991) and from scholarly interest (Urry, 1990; MacCannell, 1992; Burns 1994; Jafari *passim*). The World Travel and Tourism Council (WTTC, 1994), an industry-sponsored pro-tourism pressure group, claims that tourism:

- is the world's largest industry;
- the world's largest employer and creator of jobs;

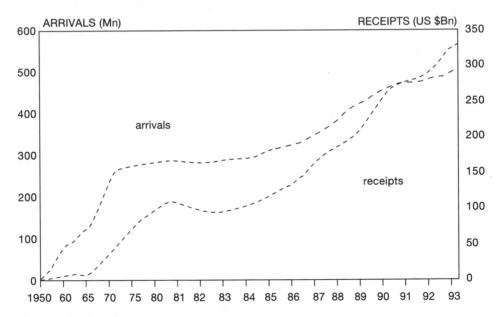

Figure 0.1 Development of international tourism arrivals and receipts* worldwide 1950–93. * Excluding international fare receipts.
Source: WTO.

Introduction

Table 0.1 World
tourism growth trends
and forecasts.

Tourist arrivals, average annual growth rate (%)	
■ 1950–70	9.9%
■ 1970–80	5.7%
■ 1980–90	4.7%
■ 1950–90	7.5%
■ 1990–5	3.2%
■ 1995–2000	4.4%
■ 1990–2000	3.8%
■ 2000–2010	3.5%

Source: WTO.

- accounts for one in nine global jobs (direct and indirect employment);
- represents ten per cent global wages;
- is responsible for 10% of world GDP;
- (and) accounts for 11% of non-food consumer retailing.

The extent to which these extraordinary claims can be backed up is debatable, especially given that the core membership of WTTC comprises chief executives of global and international tourism corporations. It depends largely on the scope of tourism within their definition and what precisely constitutes a tourism job (for a fuller discussion on this see Burns, 1994). The claims do,

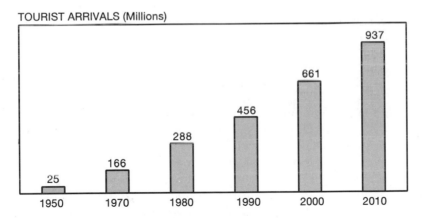

Figure 0.2 International tourist arrivals worldwide: trends and prospects 1950–2010.
Source: WTO.

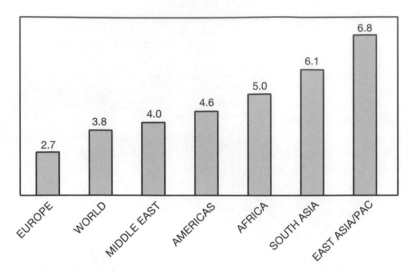

Figure 0.3   Growth of international tourist arrivals worldwide by region of origin: average annual growth rate (%) 1990–2000.
Source: WTO.

however, emphasise the sheer scale of the phenomenon, and the huge range of economic, social and political actions that can affect it and the effect it can have on the external sociopolitical environment. Two easily remembered recent examples of global events that have had an impact on tourism are *perestroika* and the invasion of Kuwait and consequential war against Iraq. The impact of (for instance) allowing all citizens of China the freedom to travel abroad or of doubling the number of US citizens who hold passports would be nothing short of dramatic.

Defining tourism

At the heart of any discourse is the notion of definition. The question then arises as to what, for the purpose of this book, is tourism? Should we define tourism as a product? But then we might include in this so-called 'product' things that, perhaps, should not be included: village life; unique religious ceremonies and other private aspects of culture and lifestyle. The word 'product' implies something that is there to be marketed, wrapped and sold. In the same way, if we define tourism as being an industry there are implications that there exists a clear entity; things may be categorised as being part of the tourist industry or not. We know that this is simply not possible. How do we categorise a restaurant that serves both a local clientèle and foreign tourists?

Introduction

Are the Amish, who for the most part want nothing to do with the twentieth century, to be counted as part of America's tourist product? We should perhaps remind ourselves (as the Killing Fields of Cambodia and the Ho Chi Min Trail inexorably find market niches in global tourism) that it was, at one time, considered amusing to visit the lunatics in Bedlam (organised trips for this activity are redundant, as 'Care in the Community' has positioned the lunatics as an integral part of contemporary Britain's urban landscape). Socialites in 1920s New York went 'slumming' to Harlem. In the 1970s they were likely to visit Haiti's resort Club Habitation Leclerc, where the sweetness of luxury was heightened by its juxtaposition with the abject, hopeless poverty of Port-au-Prince's slums (Turner and Ash, 1975:201). In more recent times, we might ask if the teenage girls from Lithuania who perform as striptease dancers in Bucharest night clubs, the pimps and prostitutes of Moscow or Seoul are to be counted as employees of this 'industry'? These uncomfortable, shadowy aspects of tourism illustrate the complexities of this global phenomenon while exposing yet another paradox: while tourism's proponents (such as WTTC and WTO) claim it promotes 'international understanding' (UNEP, 1979) the requirement of much of tourism is for a sort of zero relationship between host and guest (MacCannell, 1992:307).

The abstract nature of the concept of tourism has resulted in many and varied interpretations, evidencing its complexity and importance (Lizaso-Urrutia, 1993:3). Tourism may be defined in many ways with definitions varying according to the underlying purpose for the definition. There are generally accepted to be three aspects to defining tourism. The first concerns the purpose or motivation of the visit (such as drawing a distinction between, for instance, business and pleasure, pilgrimage and rite of passage). The second element will be concerned with *time*, making the important differentiation between day trips and voyages that involve overnight stays. Thirdly, a definition should take account of particular situations enabling categories that may or may not be counted as tourism (such as migration, transit, sea cruises) (Burkart and Medlik, 1989:42). Thus, we have Mathieson and Wall (1982:1) defining tourism as: 'the temporary movement of people to destinations outside their normal place of work and residence, the activities taken during their stay in those destinations and the facilities created to cater for their needs'. Mill and Morrison (1985) emphasise that tourism must be seen as a process rather than an industry. They write:

> Tourism is a difficult phenomenon to describe . . . all tourism involves travel, yet all travel is not tourism. All tourism involves recreation, yet all recreation is not tourism. All tourism occurs during leisure time, but not all leisure time is given to touristic pursuits . . . Tourism is an activity [taking place] when people cross a border for leisure or business and stay at least twenty-four hours . . . (Mill and Morrison, 1985:xvii)

Given, then, that we have not just one continuum concerning tourism 'from tourism as business to tourism as impact' (Buck, 1978) but at least one other, that is the tourism as agent in middle-class search for authenticity (see MacCannell, 1976) to tourism as imperialism (see Nash, 1989) we need a definition that enables us to draw together the various viewpoints. Jafar Jafari (1977: 8) defines tourism as

> . . . a study of man [sic] away from his usual habitat, of the industry which responds to his needs, and the impacts that both he and the industry have on the host socio-cultural, economic, and physical environments.

Here is a holistic definition that not only embraces the concept of tourism as business or system but implicitly acknowledges the consequential aspect (i.e. the 'cost', in human and environmental terms) of the relationship between supply and demand. Nash and Smith (1991:14) develop this theme to encompass a global perspective by saying:

> [tourism is] a pan-human touristic process that originates with the generation of tourists in some society . . ., continues as these tourists travel to other places where they encounter hosts, and ending as the give-and-take of this encounter affects the tourists, their hosts, and their home cultures . . .

Given the need (as we claim in this book) for a holistic interpretation and understanding of tourism, it is the forces and notions that arise from writers such as Jafari and Nash and Smith (cited above) that define and underpin the theoretical framework for this book.

The general approach

With the problems of definition alluded to above comes the problem of writing about tourism. The case for tourism as a distinct academic activity has been made (notably through *Annals of Tourism Research*); however, the approach to be taken is still the subject of debate. In a general sense, there has been a growing awareness of the broad range of impacts that business may have on culture and the environment (evidenced perhaps most strongly by consumer awareness of green issues and the growth of 'ethical' stock holding and the launch, in 1993, of new academic journals such as the *Journal of Sustainable Tourism*). This debate has been particularly strong in relation to tourism where the environment, community and culture are seen as prime resources, in some cases even being referred to in tourism textbooks (e.g. Middleton, 1988) as being part of the tourism 'product'.

A starting point for considering tourism's alternative perspectives and thus also for understanding its concepts and dynamics lies with recognising the continuum (noted above)   ts: one end represented by tourism as business, the other represented by tourism as problem; these two extremes have also been termed 'the business camp' and 'the impacts–externalities camp' (Buck, 1978). There is a need, as Buck identifies, to:

> bring the two together into some kind of theoretical synthesis. It might be observed that the principal preoccupation with both camps has been with factual issues, especially those relating to tourism's effects: there is a need to bring about a balance of factual and theoretical studies, to develop broad-based theories which help explain the whole phenomenon ... efforts can proceed more efficiently and collective efforts become more economical with a common base; work on the subject is likely to be more scientific; there is a formal medium for relating the body of knowledge to other academic domains, and students derive intellectual training from working with discipline-based methodologies.

The response of this book to such worthy ambition is in its attempts to reconcile the two camps. In doing this we recognise that tourism is a curiously intangible product (if it can be called a product), an industry of interlocking networks, global reservation systems, the result of which combines not only services, landscapes and culture, but also intangibles such as hospitality, customs and curiosities: 'a combination of services and enticing images' as Lanfant (1980) describes it. Mathieson and Wall (1982) offer a conceptual framework of tourism (Figure 0.4) which, while almost 15 years old, has stood the test of time and serves to illustrate what they see as the 3 major elements of tourism: the consequential; the static (and) the dynamic.

However, this framework for tourism should not be viewed in isolation. It should be remembered that tourism is just one part of a global economic system. Hoogvelt (1982:191) argues Wallerstein's notion that

> Neither the 'development' nor the underdevelopment of any specific territorial unit can be analyzed or interpreted without fitting it into the cyclical rhythms and secular trends of the world's economy as a whole.

This 'world systems' view (attributed to Wallerstein, 1980), the acknowledgement of the complex, inexorable yet unequal links that frame the global condition is a key factor in understanding tourism. This can be illustrated, for example, by the commercial aspirations and marketing of Delta Air Lines, a major US carrier, which in mid-1993, under the logo 'Global Excellence', was proclaiming a 'global alliance' with Swissair and Singapore Airlines. While the motivation for this is to enhance business, it is not only the result of advances

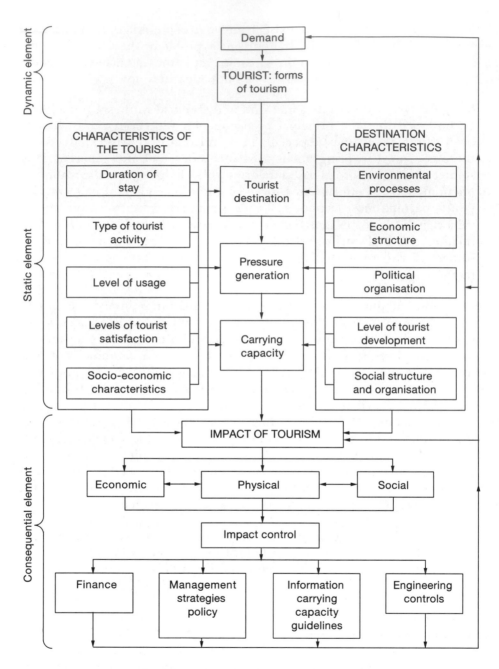

Figure 0.4 A conceptual framework of tourism.
Source: Mathieson and Wall (1982:15).

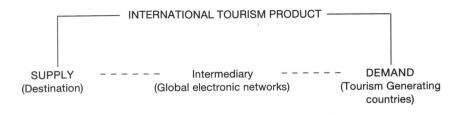

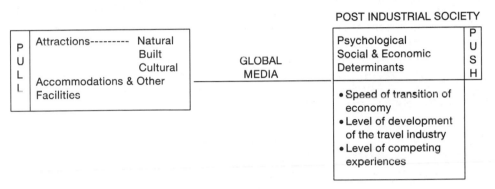

Figure 0.5 Determinants of a standardised international tourism product.

in information technology, transportation technology and deregulation, but is also due to changing attitudes to political barriers and growing consumer awareness of societies and cultures. The trading environment for a trans-national tourism or hospitality corporation is truly global in magnitude. During the same period, British Airways had a clear corporate mission to become the world's first truly global airline.

These complex issues lead us to the conclusion that we should recognise that, for purposes of analysis, tourism can be thought of as a sort of traded commodity – displaying some of the characteristics of the trade in commod-ities (such as having the prices set in metropoles and being subject to possible market manipulation, and, to some extent, only tenuous links between cost of production and selling price). This enables us to recognise that what started as pilgrimage, as education for an élite, or amusement for the masses has been transformed into a global consumer product in much the same way that Pepsi Cola, Benetton, McDonald's, etc. have all become standardised, rationalised global phenomena: as much a part of our so-called 'global village' (a theme explored by Boniface and Fowler, 1993) as the remnants of our individuality. The determinants of a standardised international tourism product are illustrated in Figure 0.5.

Mass tourism to metatourism?

A general theme and characteristic intrinsic to this book is the overt attention given to tourism in the 'North–South' debate. Given the importance we place on this a model of tourism, 'metatourism,' has been devised which helps conceptualise these particular issues. Poon defines mass tourism as 'a phenomenon of large-scale packaging of standardised leisure services at fixed prices for sale to a mass clientele' (1993:32). Poon then goes on to describe four characteristics that determine mass tourism: standardised, inflexible packaging; mass replication (or mass production); mass marketing to 'an undifferentiated clientele' (and) 'The holiday is consumed *en masse*' with little regard by the tourist to place or culture (1993:32). Poon claims that 'mass tourism certainly had its time and place' (1993:33) implying that the age of mass tourism is over; while this remains to be seen there is clear evidence (as presented by Poon) that there are changes to the consumer culture of holidays. However, the debate over mass tourism seems to focus on two aspects:

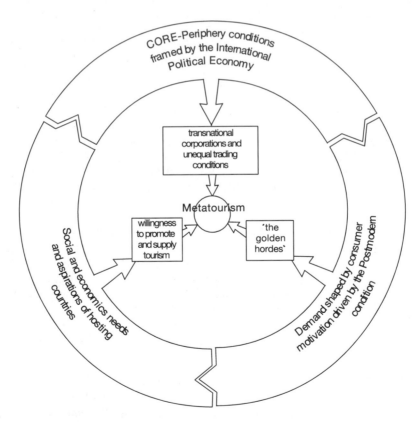

Figure 0.6 Conditions that create and shape metatourism.

the environment and the consuming tourist. Thus the phrase 'mass tourism' does not help the debate to focus on destination impacts in Third World countries. For this reason, we introduce the notion of metatourism (see Figure 0.6).

Metatourism is defined as large-scale tourism dominated by metropolitan centres, which takes place in Third World countries at the geographic, pleasure and economic peripheries of the economically advanced world. Thus we see a differentiation between 'mass tourism' (which need not take place in a 'developing' country and which can be, indeed often is, a form of domestic tourism) and metatourism. It is useful, therefore, to have a term that allows us to distinguish between these forms of tourism and focus on tourism in the 'North–South' debate where necessary. Thus we can see that while it is mass tourism that takes place at Bondi Beach, the term is not sufficient to describe the tourism which takes place in Saipan, which is dominated by Japanese ownership and control; Antigua, which has its tourism inbound monopolised by a foreign carrier; or Fiji, which has both foreign ownership and inbound air capacity constraints. It is these conditions that may be described as meta-tourism. The term 'metatourism' has its roots in postmodern discourse. Metafiction is where 'someone from outside the work steps into the novel . . . in order to raise questions about relationships . . .' (Marshall, 1992:77); thus we have the idea of outsider (in the case of metatourism the notion of outsider relates to control) and relationships (which, for metatourism refer to core–periphery relationships). Metalinguistics seem to be ascribed by McHale with characteristics that allow it to mingle or straddle worlds 'produc[ing], in short, a characteristically postmodernist text in which multiple worlds coexist in uneasy tension' (McHale, 1992:217). Again, given that the tourists who consume metatourism are from a postmodern world seeking renewal through the psychological comfort of (as they see it) the easier, less frenetic liminality of undeveloped Third World destinations, we find the term metatourism helps us to describe the condition.

Terms like 'Developing Countries', 'Third World' and 'North–South' are all unsatisfactory in their own ways. The phrases which include the word 'developing' are a generalisation that arrives out of the theories of development which emerged in the 1950s and 1960s. 'Third World' carries a sort of negative connotation (and is anyway redundant following the political upheavals of the Eastern Bloc 'Second World'), and 'North–South' is geographically innaccurate.

However, such phrases do carry meaning, and are part of a common vocabulary. Under these circumstances, we reluctantly use all three terms in this book.

Tourism and consumerism

Tourism is inexorably linked to consumerism, a constituent of what Vance Packard in *The Hidden Persuaders* (1956) negatively termed 'consumer society'.

Bayley (1991:47) relates the history of the word 'consumer' to the development of Western economy. He notes:

> Mass production and all that it entails – investment, long lead-times, low unit costs and ready availability – replaced a system where simple makers could articulate and satisfy needs; the new distant customers alienated from the production process became consumers.

How easy it is to apply this to contemporary tourism. However, this is no more a criticism of how people choose to spend their holidays than complaining about traffic jams is a criticism of those who choose to drive to work rather than use public transportation. The point is that concern is not so much directed at individual consumers (who according to age and chance of birthplace, might well have been educated and socialised into the role of passive consumer) but rather towards the global web of advertising, reservations systems and buying power that empowers the multinationals in their 'rational' manoeuvring towards product standardisation and the 'rationality' of global markets (the reference to rational and rationality intended as irony). It is no coincidence that along with hyperinflation and unemployment, McDonald's franchises (termed McGulag Archipelago by Tim Luke in Ritzer, 1993:131) became the overpowering cultural and economic icon for what Reagan/Bush called the 'New World Order' (for a brief but important note on this phrase see MacCannell, 1992:309). Thus we see that the variables which influence choices for individual consumers (a phrase that is becoming increasingly meaningless in the age of 'Hypermall') are defined not only by what the producers (or more likely their corporate accountants) feel is more efficient to sell us, but also by the complex life-motivators that define postmodern living. Choices, then, are so bound up in consumerism and bound to the 'born to shop' mentality that perhaps psychoanalysis is a better tool than reprehension in coming to terms with (or analysing) global consumer trends.

The roots of this type of global consumerism is traced by Bayley (1991:52) to Prince Albert's Great Exhibition of 1851 which was: 'a primal media event, it suggested the entire world was available for consumption'. George Ritzer, in his *McDonaldization of Society* (1993:129) strikes a more sinister note by claiming that 'whole industries are now in the business of producing and marketing unreality. Indeed, much of the McDonaldized society is involved in the production of a wide range of unrealities.' While these remarks are made in relation to synthetic music and synthetic food we can see that *metatourism*, as we term it, and of which the modern package tour is a major component, is an example *par excellence*. Another driving force for global tourism is that of nostalgia of one sort or another, with Roland Robertson (1992:146) suggesting the idea of the 'nostalgic paradigm', and in the context of his concerns over global dynamics and global significance, warns us of the dangers of over-simplifying our analysis of nostalgia. However, as Urry (1990:106) reminds us, even this becomes part of the cash nexus. In discussing the privatisation of Britain's museum sector he notes that this: 'ha[s] inspired particularly new ways of representing history, as *commodifying the past* . . . There is little doubt that similar developments are taking place in many industrialised countries' (our italics). He continues by saying of the United States that 'the trappings of history now festoon the whole country'.

It can be seen from the foregoing that tourism is not so much about suntans as it is about being a major part of the globalisation of culture, and that while it provides income and enjoyment for millions, the pleasure and leisure aspects should not form a protective sheath over its dichotomies and paradoxes. Those who study tourism should not merely concern themselves only with that which is business or that which is easily quantifiable. While such an approach may provide a mask of respectability for tourism studies in a world dominated by quantitative method, neglect of the qualitative issues will inevitably lead to a poorer tourism product for both the hosts and guests.

CHAPTER 1

Supply and demand: the commoditisation of tourism

Introduction

There is a sense in which tourists, tourism professionals and tourism academics have developed a degree of cynicism about their subject. This manifests itself in a number of ways. For the world-weary tourist, this fatigue is epitomised by the Australian folksaying, 'been there, done that', and in the tawdry souvenir T-shirt decorated with the usual icons of tourism such as lazy palm trees and lurid sunset, all emblazoned with the logo 'Ho Hum, another shitty day in Paradise'. (Seen in Fiji's Cumming Street souvenir shops until 1988, but since banned by Rabuka's post-revolutionary Methodist government.) For the tourism professional, there is the endless round of 'familiarisations' and 'educationals' (sponsored visits to resorts and destinations to 'sample the product'), of 'promotionals', where special sales incentives are given to encourage travel agency staff to 'sell the destination'. For the academics it is the tendency to drift towards the negative 'unctuous moralizing . . . cheap populist rhetoric' as David Harrison (1993:13) has observed in one of the perennial disputes that occur in academic journals. Another academic, Brian Wheeller (1991:91) argues that with sheer volume of visitor traffic as the root cause of most of tourism's problems, fashionable solutions to do with 'responsible' or 'alternative' approaches are not only élitist and wrong but 'dangerously misleading'. Here Wheeler is attempting to prevent a middle-class gloss being painted over tourism's basic *problématique*; put simply: how can less tourism (for surely that is what is implicit in calls for 'alternative tourism') be the solution to too much tourism? Butler (1992:39) adds to the 'alternative tourism' argument by asking (in relation to another proposal – 'appropriate tourism') by asking 'appropriate to whom?'

The characteristics of contemporary tourism

In a sense, the debates outlined above illustrate the range of forces driving contemporary tourism. It is important to acknowledge that tourism is of course not the only subject of such debate. Robert Hughes (1980:383–5)

14

expresses concern over the commodification of the Arts – in particular, Modern Art. His seminal work *The Shock of the New* devotes much of its time to tracing the progress and process of commercialisation and commodification in the visual arts. In somewhat despondant mood, he asserts:

> . . . one of the inescapable facts of the 1970s, which nobody could have foreseen in 1920 or even in 1950, was the way in which the meaning of *all* vanguard art activity, polically oriented, socially aimed, or not, was being gutted by the market. Twenty-five years ago, one could spend time in a museum without even thinking about what the art might cost. The price was not relevant to the experience of the work. Price and value were completely distinct questions; the latter interesting, the former not. But in the middle sixties there was a stir of change, caused by dealers . . . who . . . started to take a more aggressive role in merchandising. First there was a trickle, then a stream, and finally a brown roaring flood of propaganda about art investment. The price of a work of art now became a part of its function. It redefined the work – whose new task was simply to sit on the wall and get more expensive. By the end of the 1970s, we were getting to the point where everything that could be regarded, however distantly, as a work of art was primarily esteemed not for its ability to communicate meaning, or its use as historical evidence, or its power to generate aesthetic pleasure, but for its convertability into cash.

While at first glance the parallel to be drawn from this somewhat (but necessarily) lengthy quote with tourism might be fuzzy, a moment's consideration is worth the effort. If we invert the theme and consider, not so much the expensiveness of holidays, but their cheapness (a consequence of downward pressure on package holiday prices), then the parallel becomes clear: where the function of art (as Hughes sees it) is not to engender aesthetic or cultural values, but to be a part of the global cash nexus that is the characteristic of the modern auction house, then the role of the cheap package holiday is to provide a moment of superficial pleasure to the holidaymaker (fulfilling the basic requirements of Sand, Sea, Sun and Sex), the point being that the cultural location is almost immaterial.

Another possible parallel between the Arts and tourism exists: that between mass media (and within that, mass culture) and mass tourism. Walker (1983:18) sees mass media as a term which denotes systems of communication which:

> 'mediate' between relatively small, specialised groups of cultural producers and very large numbers of cultural consumers . . . [that] millions of individuals are exposed daily to a spectrum of powerful mass media is a uniquely twentieth-century phenomenon.

15

Walker develops this by asserting that the main characteristic of mass culture is the technological means of reproduction and distribution. Cultural products become cheap to make, are plentiful and can be rapidly distributed. He continues: 'On the positive side, technology ... ha[s] brought about a tremendous democratization of culture. On the negative side, millions of people have become mere consumers of culture produced by others' (Walker, 1983:18). Here, the same technology that has created the ability for massive and instant communication has also created the conditions for homogenisation, blandness and undifferentiated products, including the ubiquitous package holiday of sun, sand and sea. In this light, the logic of applying Walker's next line of argument to mass tourism and metatourism is compelling:

> 'success' in the media is often measured in quantitative terms – consequently their cultural content is predominantly low-to-medium in character ... an item which appeals to millions [is thought to] represent the lowest common denominator of taste ... Power in the mass media is concentrated and centralized. (Walker, 1983:18)

However, the arguments for not applying them are almost as strong. For there is an underlying élitism in assuming that all that is 'mass' is necessarily bad, in

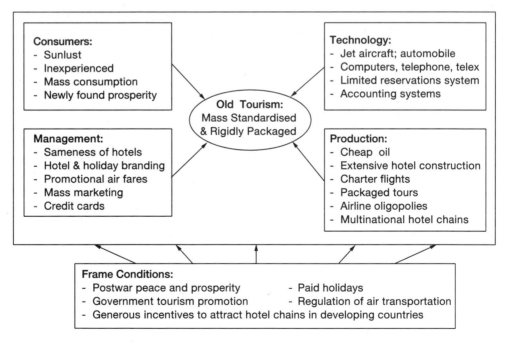

Figure 1.1 The characteristics of 'old' tourism.
Source: Poon (1993:34).

16

poor taste and trivial. 'Mass tourism' is not, in itself, inherently bad or fraught with negatives. As Butler (1990:40) notes

[the trend for rejecting mass tourism] ha[s] met two fairly significant problems: one the economic value of mass tourism ... and two, the fact that many people seem to enjoy being a mass tourist. They actually like not having to make their own travel arrangements, not having to find accommodation when they arrive at a destination, being able to obtain goods and services without learning a foreign language, being able to stay in reasonable, in some cases, considerable comfort, being

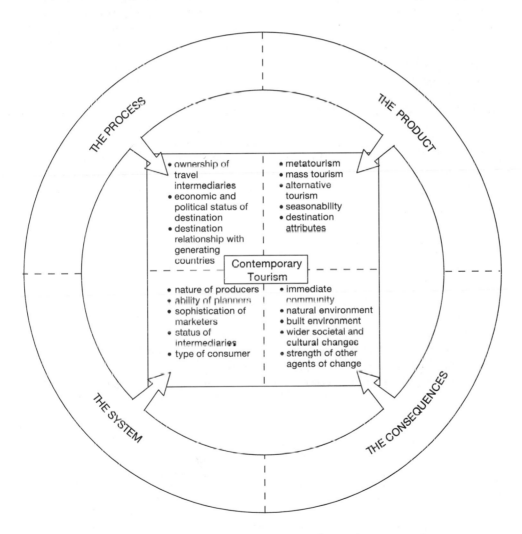

Figure 1.2 Contemporary tourism: an alternative perspective.

17

able to eat reasonably familiar food, and not having to spend vast amounts of money and time to achieve these goals.

Interestingly, and even with the trend in the 1990s towards individual and independent travel (see Figure 1.1), perhaps the generally negative reaction to contemporary tourism has become an integral part of it.

MacCannell (1992: 25–31, 66) reminds us of Dennis O'Rourke's anthropological documentary film, *Cannibal Tours* (1987), which depicts a group of probably wealthy international tourists taking a luxury motor yacht trip along the Sepik River (in Papua New Guinea) – a trip currently advertised as 'Impressive! Exotic! Extraordinary! . . . You'll find yourself running out of film because there is so much to photograph'. As the extraordinary story unfolds we become increasingly aware that each group, the tourists and the local peoples, hold distorted views of each other. While the motivation for the villagers in becoming part of the backdrop to the tour is evidently an economic one (the film makes it clear that the villagers feel there is nothing to be learnt from the tourists), the motivation of the tourist is more obscure. Is it simply to visit a unique culture, or is there a deeper meaning in that perhaps the rich tourists finds a sort of satisfying reassurance of their own perceived economic and cultural superiority as they gaze upon the half-clad 'primitives'? Apart from the obvious anthropological implications related to perception of 'other', the film also serves to illustrate that contemporary tourism can itself be seen as comprising four parts: the system, the process, the product and the consequences. Figure 1.2 shows at least three things: first, that the four parts are interrelated, second, that they all help shape and frame the characteristics of tourism at a particular destination and third, that all the elements will change over time from both internal and exogenous influences. Finally, the figure serves as a reminder that tourism must be thought about in its wider socioeconomic and political environment.

While in certain contexts, such as the discussion of impacts, it is useful to use the term 'tourism industry', it is not an industry in the generally accepted sense of the word. Although we might even think of airlines, or ferry services, hotels or restaurants, tour operators and travel agents as industries in themselves (Mill and Morrison, 1985:xvii) they are, with their less than concrete links, some of the components that come together to form what we call tourism.

Edgell (1990:104) presents a conceptual representation of the way in which we might begin to see tourism as a system. Edgell draws the links between planning, national objectives, and policies to socioeconomic systems and markets (see Figure 1.3). Even given the clarity of Edgell's ideas, they do not encourage us to view the tourism 'industry' as we would view the motor industry. This might lead us, wrongly, to infer economic, political and social boundaries that simply cannot exist for tourism (rightly termed by Mill and Morrison (1985) as an activity with all the accompanying definitions of tourism

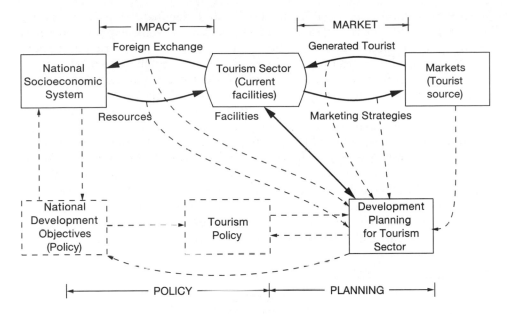

Figure 1.3 Conceptual representation of the system model of the tourism sector.
Source: Edgell (1990:104).

and tourists) in the way that it exists for a manufacturing industry or other service industries such as banking or insurance.

Mill and Morrison (1985:xix) describe tourism as a *system*, seen as comprising four parts: Market; Travel; Destination; (and) Marketing. While this acknowledges tourism's interconnectedness they also remind us that:

> . . . [for a variety of reasons] . . . businesses and organizations that have been . . . affected by tourism, often do not consider themselves part of tourism. Many people within the hotel industry or restaurant industry do not feel part of tourism. Their business begins when the customer walks in their front door. This myopic view has meant that those in the industry have ended up reacting to changes that have occurred outside their front door, rather than acting in anticipation of upcoming changes.

Gunn describes tourism as a 'functioning system' and stresses the importance of the relationship between supply and demand (1988:68); see Figure 1.4. Gunn takes the model further by describing the influences upon the system (Figure 1.5). In her description of the tourism system, Poon seems to place a little more emphasis on the industry side. The four components of tourism for Poon are: producers; distributors; facilitators; and consumers (Figure 1.6). Cooper *et al.* (1993: preface), in similar vein, explain tourism as having four elements: demand; the destinations; industry and government organisations; and marketing. However, underpinning their approach is the assumption that these elements 'have to be isolated for teaching and learning purposes'. This is interesting in that such a seemingly rational assumption precludes the holistic view that must be taken if the paradigms that arise from tourism's current structure are to be challenged with a view to addressing tourism's *problématique*. Should marketing be taught without teaching image formation (Uzzell, 1984); perception of 'Other' (Said, 1978) cultural trivialisation (Graburn, 1984; Wood, 1984) or 'Peter Panism'? (Selwyn, 1992). Is discussing the 'inevitability' of Doxey's (1976) Euphoria–Antagonism hierarchy going to move the body of knowledge forward without clear reference to the touristic structures that cause such attitudes to develop?(It might in any case be argued that Doxey's somewhat deterministic ideas have reached the

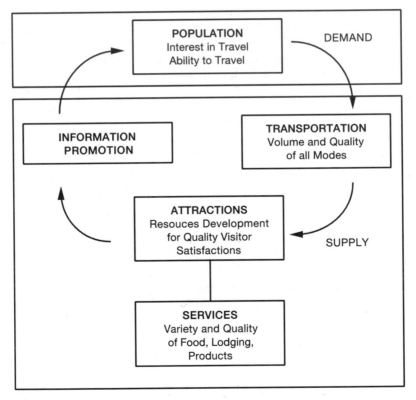

Figure 1.4   The functioning tourist system. A model of the key functional components that make up the dynamic and interrelated tourism system.
Source: Gunn (1988:68).

Supply and demand

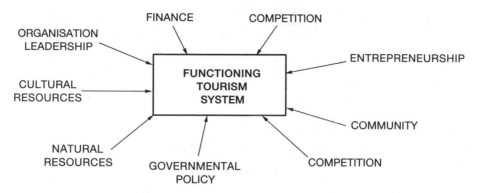

Figure 1.5 Influences on the functioning tourism system.
Source: Gunn (1988:73).

end of their lifecycle: in the (almost) 20 years from their inception the tourism
debate have become far more complex.)

Supply and demand

Whatever the approach to tourism or whatever type of tourism being looked
at, the power that drives the engine of touristic development is the market
dynamics that result from supply and demand factors. Poon has produced a
useful model of a 'tourism production system' (Figure 1.7).

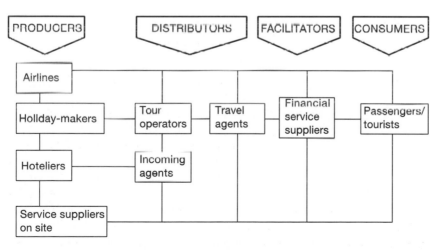

Figure 1.6 Conceptual representation of the system model of the tourism sector.
Source: Poon (1993:207).

21

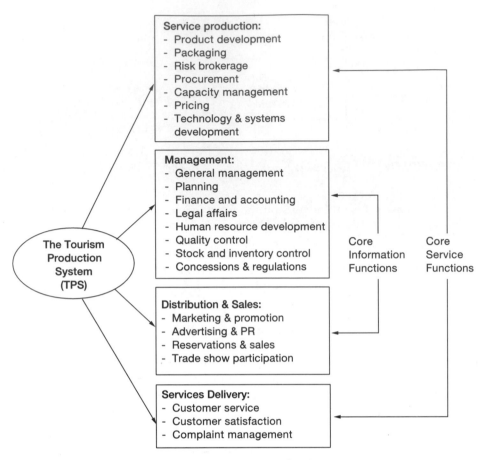

Figure 1.7   The tourism production system.
Source: Poon (1993:174).

Supply

Supply-side issues are normally seen to be concerned with the provision of communications, services, transport, accommodation (infrastructure and superstructure) and attractions (which might include cultural assets, shopping, mega-events or unique natural phenomena). However, for many destinations overshadowing this simple list of tourism supply components is the problem of seasonality. At the early stages of touristic development, this might not be perceived as the invidious problem that it is. While tourism is in its infancy, and peripheral to the local economy, involvement with it might be viewed as a short-term bonus. People and businesses can make a little extra cash from selling goods and services to the few tourists that they encounter. If, however, tourism increases in economic importance, perhaps becoming centre-stage in the local economic mix careful planning and marketing are required to ensure a steady flow of tourists. This is somewhat easier where weather patterns are relatively constant all year round (for example in the tropics), but for destinations in temperate climates, for example the United Kingdom, steps such as developing conference business must be taken so that the transition from mixed economy to tourist economy (if that is what is happening) is smooth. This means ensuring that the local workforce is given year-round opportunities for long-term career planning, and that local people are informed so as to be tolerant of the crowds and pressures that might arise from the multiple use of local facilities.

At about this stage, planners and tour operators might begin to talk about the 'tourist product'. However, once again we encounter a difficulty with an often-used phrase: to classify hotels, perhaps ancient artifacts, flora and fauna as being part of a product is one thing, but it is quite another when we consider that also included in this 'product' are unique lifestyles, cultural activities and, to put it clearly, the inhabitants of the destination; as Ascher (1985:13) reminds us, 'it is the nature and characteristics of these [third world] countries that are for sale . . . Driven by a variety of needs . . ., communities sell not only their labour but themselves . . . accepting what the tour operators offer in exchange'. It is here, perhaps, that the roots of discontent are planted.

The other characteristic of tourism supply which makes it unique (and differentiates it from manufacturing and other services) is the large extent to which supply is static; the number of rooms, the amount and characteristics of the supply-side elements cannot easily be jacked up or down or altered in other ways to meet short-term changes in demand. In this sense, and along with strategies for combating seasonality related problems, tourism planners and marketing managers have to set in place a framework for dynamic development.

Demand

Variety

In a simple sense (i.e. without drawing upon the psychological drive behind being a tourist), it is generally accepted that tourism is a discretionary purchase. However, when we do draw on these factors we encounter a difficulty in ascribing the purchase of a holiday with the characteristics of microeconomics: it is not simply the allocation of limited resources to a variety of commodities by rational consumers. Rather, the qualitative measure of ordinal utility (where consumers rank purchasing choices in bundles of 'commodities') is seen as the most appropriate framework for thinking about supply. Thus the purchase of a holiday is seen in its relative attractiveness within the normal constraints of price and income.

23

In the case of tourism there are several ways of thinking about the demand side of the supply–demand equation, some of them more complex than others. The three basic factors of demand are as follows.

Social, political, economic and technological

These may have long- or short-term effects on the level of demand, which may be economic problems in the generating country, poor image of the receiving country due to unacceptable political activity or changes in airline routes due to upgrading equipment.

Travel and movement patterns

Some of these will be rooted in colonial history or reflect past tourism trends; types of tourist activity. Typical of this is the traffic between the Indian subcontinent and the United Kingdom (consisting of a high percentage of family visits); the traffic between Sri Lanka and the Middle East (migrant contract workers); and the United Kingdom and the Spanish Costas (traditional mass holiday-making). Tourism planners must be aware of the different impacts these types of traveller will have on the destination.

Tourist motivation and decision-making process

Significantly, this will include the ability of the destination to market itself as an individual place: in some instances (such as with the Caribbean and the Pacific Island nations) tourists may be unable to differentiate between these long-haul 'Paradise' destinations. In some cases, for instance the generic sun, sand and sea destinations, the actual country is unimportant so long as the basic requirements that motivated the holiday instinct are met.

As established in the introduction, demand for tourism is rooted in developed world consumption patterns with all the concomitant economic and psychological factors. Cooper *et al.* (1993:15) see the framework for these factors consisting (in part) of:

- effective (actual) demand: the number of people who actually puchase travel and tourism;
- potential demand: those people who will travel when their circumstances allow it; and
- deferred demand: where supply elements such as transport or accommodation availability, actual or psychological climate have temporarily failed in some way.

We might add to that last point a lack of knowledge on the part of the tourist that the destination exists. Demand for travel can be measured by various tour operators and national tourist offices on a selected nation by nation basis to provide an overall picture of the likely demand for travel and tourism products as they affect their own 'product' or destination. For instance, research conducted in The Netherlands (Cleverdon, 1992) found a remarkably high propensity to travel, 70% of the population taking one holiday per year and 24% taking two holidays. For 1990 these percentages were quantified at 16.3 million holidays, of which 55% (9 million) were foreign holidays. Researchers for specific destinations or regions would then conduct a more detailed study to ascertain where the holidays were taken, or whether they were long- or short-haul. (As it happens, the long-haul figure for The Netherlands is about 500 000, 56% of total foreign travel.) The client would then want to know which destinations made up the long-haul market, in this case mainly meaning the United States with increasing interest in the Far East. Such market intelligence then feeds into the decision-making components of tourism's general process.

The process

Mill and Morrison (1985:xix) use the analogy of the tourism system as being 'like a spider's web – touch one part of it and the reverberations will be felt throughout'. Nash and Smith (1991:14) describe tourism as

> . . . a pan-human touristic process that originates with the generation of tourists in some society . . . , continues as these tourists travel to other places, where they encounter hosts, and ending as the give-and-take of this encounter affects the tourists, their hosts, and their home cultures.

This is clearly a development from Valene Smith's earlier, and less complicated, notion where she describes the foundations of tourism as resting on three key elements (1989:1):

- leisure time;
- discretionary income; and
- positive local sanctions.

When all three are in place and operative, then the process of tourism can take place. This process is, in a sense, governed by the actions of those who operate the component parts of the trade. These parts, or sectors, are:

- transport, with production carried out by the the carriers (air, sea, road and rail);
- accommodation, mainly serviced by the hotel sector (but with an increasing trend for private home stay in some destinations); and
- attractions, which consists of the cultural, built and natural environment.

These sectors are linked to their markets through a variety of business activities

25

that range from tour packaging to direct sales. A number of businesses will act as wholesalers, buying large quantities of tourism components (accommodation, transport and attractions) and selling them in smaller chunks to others, usually travel retailers.

Some producers will sell directly to the consumer, companies such as Euro-Camp operate their tour business on a mail-order basis, others such as Thomas Cook may sell through their own high-street retail shops.

Vertical integration

Vertical integration is the business phenomenon whereby firms seek to control various stages of production, delivery and marketing of their products. This has been something of an established practice within the production of mass tourism: airlines can own hotels, travel retailers and package tour companies. One of the key characteristics of contemporary tourism is not only the extent to which vertical integration takes place, but the increasing tendency for this integration to be global (Wyer and Towner, 1988:13–14). In the case of the United Kingdom, mid-1993 saw Airtours spending £9 million on a (failed) £260 million bid for its rival holiday firm Owners Abroad. This takeover would have strengthened the position of Pickfords Travel Service, the chain of high-street travel agents bought by Airtours in 1992. Airtours also spent £25 million on the leisure travel side of another major retailer, Hogg Robinson: all this, in addition to £20 million paid for Aspro Travel, the seventh biggest tour operator in Britain. Significantly, Airtours was making its first moves into hotel ownership, with the purchase of the Bouganville Park Hotel in Majorca. David Crossland, the chairman of Airtours, was reported in *The Times* (29 June 1993) as predicting that more hotel purchases would be made, 'mainly for hotels the company already featured in its brochures that had borrowed heavily and then suffered a downturn in custom'. The UK government's Office of Fair Trading was concerned enough about the increasing drift between public perception of travel agents as being independent retailers and the increasing fact of them being owned by package holiday operators, that they were contemplating launching a full-scale investigation into the extent and significance of the problem.

This linking of various parts of the tour operation may have advantages for the company (in relation to continuity of supply and economies of scale, with all the concomitant consequences for quality control and product merchandising), but for those on the periphery or serving large corporations this kind of integrated industry is very powerful, and has the potential to cause problems for consumers and destinations. Ascher (1985: preface) notes:

> International tourism is dominated by transnational corporations, which, in the context of the world economic crisis and of negotiations on a new international economic order, have embarked on a redeploy-

ment of forces about which there should be no misunderstanding . . .

The consumer might be affected through increased prices caused by lack of competition, and destinations, especially in the case of metatouristic destinations may, when faced with a transnational tourist corporation, lose some of their bargaining power. Paradoxically, the destination can also lose out when the 'product' (in the face of stiff competition) is sold too cheaply leaving little or no money for long-term investment and property maintenance.

Package holidays

Package holidays are the most obvious outcome or product of the holiday industry. However, the term itself carries connotations, along with the other pejorative term 'mass tourism'. This is what Turner and Ash (1975:11) have to say about this aspect of contemporary life:

> Names like Waikiki, Nice, Majorca, Acapulco, Bali and Marrakech roll across the page evoking images of sun, pleasure and escape. In a world dominated by bureaucracies and machines, we are offered these destinations as retreats to a childlike world in which the sun always shines, and we can gratify all our desires . . . Tourism is no trivial phenomenon. It is a visible result of the fourth of the great waves of technology which have changed social geography of the world since 1800. First the railways opened up the continents, carrying the food and materials which made possible the great nineteenth century industrial cities. Then came steamships which served as the sinews allowing the Empire builders to stretch across the globe to take what they wanted from their colonies. The car started to decentralize nations by sapping the vitality of the cities through the development of extended suburbs. Finally we have the aeroplane which, when linked with rising affluence, has led to a whole new tribe – the mass tourists. The barbarians of our Age of Leisure. The Golden Horde.

Turner and Ash are clearly polemic in their view of this phenomenon of postmodernism, but they recognise that such a tribe could not exist without the growth and power of the market makers such as Hilton, Avis, Thomas Cook, Neckermann: the extensive support network.

Turner and Ash (1975: 107–8) recognise that however you describe the tourism industry, what lies at the heart of it all is what they term 'people-processing' (a term that lies at the heart of metatourism):

> Just as the great meat-packing companies take live cattle into their slaughter houses and find a profitable use of every part of the resultant carcass – be it bones, hooves or meat – so do the great tourist

conglomerates try to control as many stages as possible as their clients are separated from their money in the course of a holiday. Thus the airlines want to own hotels; banks want to own tour operators as a way of increasing their hold on the traveller's cheque business; well integrated tour operators will try to bypass travel agents by selling direct to the public; others will charter airlines, cruise liners and their own hotels. Until the passenger leaves his hotel and ventures into the local restaurants, all his money may have been going into a single company. That is integration at its clearest.

While in one sense this is cynicism at best and sophism at worst, there is a message here for those who fail to acknowledge tourism's *problématique*: tourists are seeking an alternative to the worst excesses of the short-haul package market. Another writer who expresses considerable concern over the business of mass tourism and the package industry is Jorst Krippendorf (1989:xii):

> A restless activity has taken hold of the once so sedentary human society. Most people in the industrialized countries have been seized by a feverish desire to move. Every opportunity is used to get away from the workday routine as often as possible. Shorter trips during the week and on weekends, longer journeys during the holidays. The fondest wish for old age is a new place to which to retire. Anything to get away from home! Away from here at any cost!

Thus the paradox of package, mass and metatourism is that while on one hand people seek vacations as a sort of rejection of hectic and unsatisfactory city living such as the Northern Line (in the case of London's metro system), the aggressive drivers, welfare and education cuts – indeed, if you asked people if they wanted to go on holiday to experience noise and crowds, very few would answer yes! – the package tour industry gives us, in many cases, precisely what we seek to reject. Think of how airports can plunge into chaos at peak times, with flight delays during summer 1991–2 at London's Gatwick Airport reaching record levels.

Consider the regular traffic jams on the access road into London Heathrow Airport, the crowded concrete blocks of Torremolinos, Athens or Blackpool . . . we seem to drag with us all the problems of industrialised society and bring them, as Krippendorf notes, 'as presents for our hosts'.

Perhaps in reality what tourists are seeking is the familiar, and the package industry helps transform both tourists' perception of their destination through advertising, and the reality of the destination through creating the necessary hotels, services and amenities.

CHAPTER 2

Motivation, tourists' perspectives and marketing

Brief encounters – an introduction to tourism motivation

Introduction

This section discusses the importance of understanding tourism motivation in aiding the marketing and planning of tourism. It begins by adopting a historical perspective of tourism, proceeding to provide an outline of general motivational theory and its relevance to understanding the nature of tourism demand is discussed. Followed by reference to types of tourism and tourism typologies, the scene is set to examine, in the second part of the chapter, the role of image in attracting tourists towards destinations.

The use of tourist surveys

Our first glimpse of Miss Adela Quested, one of the film's two central female characters, reinforces the reality-effect of England as physically and psychologically drab, for she is swathed in brown, or 'neutral tones' as the creative directors of Ralph Lauren might say. She enters the Peninsula and Oriental Steam Navigation Company office to buy passage to India – a journey that she hopes will deliver her not only to a fiancé but to unknown and eagerly anticipated romantic adventures. While waiting for the clerk to write out her ticket, Adela is strangely drawn to the portraits of India hanging on the office walls . . . In dramatic contrast to the dark dampness of England, 'India' is brilliantly sunlit and 'naturally' elicits a strong response from Adela. The painting of the Marabar caves – represented as suggestively erotic dark holes leading into the recess of the Marabar Hills – particularly arrests Adela's gaze; indeed, she can manage only a strangled 'I see' in reply to the clerk's observation that these caves are located a mere twenty miles from her own destination. (Donaldson (1993:90), describing the opening scenes of the film *Passage to India.*)

Donaldson's passage identifies many of the reasons why we travel, in the belief that tourism will satisfy our desires. Many tourists could identify with the needs of Adela Quested: the desire to escape from the drabness of our surroundings, the anticipation of beautiful landscapes and culture (the image of the 'exotic other') and the excitement and need of romance and lust. However, when Adela Quested arrives in India she finds the climate and culture different than she imagined, difficult to adjust to and personally disorientating, ultimately culminating in an accusation of rape in the dreamy Marabar caves.

This literary example helps to explain why the marketing and planning of tourism requires an understanding of the motivations of tourists, if the visitor's experience is to be consistent with the tourist's expectation. Understanding is a key element in the promotion of destinations to the right market segments and planning development to minimise the negative impacts of tourism while maximising the positive. Although many tour operators, hotels and transport businesses have instigated post-experience questionnaires designed to measure the level of customer satisfaction, relatively little research has been conducted by the private sector to determine the motivations of tourists. Other surveys conducted by destination planning authorities into source markets are usually related to factors of the destination that either encourage or dissuade tourists to visit it, or to test the level of awareness of a destination.

Krippendorf (1989:24), referring to motivatory studies conducted by destination authorities, observes 'many things remain hidden in the subconsciousness and cannot be brought to light by simple questions . . . so much for the reliability of information obtained from studies of tourists' motives and behaviour'. Goodall (1991:60) elaborates the same theme, that expressed motivations are often extrinsic, being modified by social factors and pressure. He comments:

Such conditioned motivations are extrinsic, induced by social pressures, and there is a danger that the real, deep rooted, personal needs of the individual are neglected. The latter are the real inspirations for holiday-making although it is the former which are actively revealed by research.

Lundberg (1972) in Dann (1981:189) adds: 'What the traveller says are his motivations for travelling may only be reflections of deeper needs, needs which he himself does not understand or wish to articulate.' However, Krippendorf does continue to say that 'despite these reservations, their results are very instructive because they show the general direction of motives and provide pointers for judging the weight of each of the reasons given for travelling'.

Expanding the concept of motivation beyond adoption and interpretation within management strategies in the tourism industry, more profound questions can be addressed concerning the role of tourism and its significance within contemporary society. To comprehend fully the motivations of the tourist, it is necessary to have an understanding of motivational theories and be able to analyse the significance of tourism in meeting the needs of individuals, living in a contemporary society which has shifting social, ethical and political values.

The commodification of tourism

Fukuyama's (1992) polemic text *The End of History* offers a discourse, that the failure of alternative political systems to democracy, notably totalitarianism and authoritarianism, has meant that liberal democracies have and will continue to spread globally. The embracing of capitalist ideology and free market economics, by an increasingly large international community under the generic title of globalisation, will permit continuing opportunities for the development of tourism. The impacts of this process will be felt by the host regions who participate in the international tourism market, the transnational corporations who develop tourism for profits and the consumer, who will find an ever-widening choice of tourism destinations and holiday type to choose from. Money, in fact hundreds of millions of dollars annually, is being exchanged internationally in the name of tourism. Although less tangible than extracted or manufactured commodities and officially categorised as part of the service industries, tourism has economic, environmental and cultural effects on those regions where it develops. Unlike banking and insurance whose activities are predominantly unseen by large segments of the population, tourism has a much higher visual profile. The tourist has become a symbol, a form of postmodern 'commodity', which passes between countries, encouraging international money to flow in pursuit of it. The 'gaze' (to use Urry's (1990) expression) may be seen from two different views. The tourist may be seen as a 'commodity' by countries bringing economic benefits, while the tourist may 'gaze' upon the destination, as a form of commodity competing with other alternative purchases for his/her discretionary income. This 'tourism commodity' may be bought with 'freedom of choice' by workers in liberal democracies in preference to a wide range of other commodities for sale and competing for the individual's discretionary income. For destinations to compete in an expanding tourism market, pursuing tourism development in a sustainable way means that the understanding of motivations of tourists will be critical to providing the correct usage of resources. Unfortunately for the tourism industry, tourism motivation and behaviour are not understood. Pearce (1993:114) describes the complexity of tourism motivation in the following passage:

> Some of the novel features pertaining to tourism motivation are that the tourists select a time and a place for their behaviour often well in

31

advance of the event, that the behaviour is episodic across the life span, influenced by one's close relationships, that satisfaction may result in the behaviour being repeated or a new form of holiday attempted, and that there is a constantly evolving interplay between how well tourist motivation is understood and what is provided to satisfy this motivation. In summary, tourist motivation is discretionary, episodic, future orientated, dynamic, socially influenced and evolving.

'Our mission: to go where no man has gone before' – the expansion of the frontiers of tourism

Tourism is usually regarded as a recent phenomenon, certainly in its international (i.e. post-1950) mass form, with more than 400 million (and still growing) international recorded arrivals. As the boundaries of 'choice of tourism destinations' seems to expand annually, establishing the peripheries of a new Empire from a European and American core, the above expression seems to be the motto of a growing number of tour operators and tourists. Exoticism and virgin territories are, of course, very much a western perception of the world, but hasn't the 'Med' really become a bit 'naff'?

However, historical evidence about tourism activity seems to indicate a pattern of choice and movement that has some parallel with contemporary tourism. Wealthy Romans escaped the heat of the summer by heading to the coast of the Adriatic and the Mediterranean. It would seem that the main motive for this exodus was the physiological need to escape the heat of the cities. Actual demand, that is, the number of Romans who could participate in this seasonal migration, as opposed to the perceived demand, that is, the number of inhabitants of Rome who would have liked to have spent the summer at the seaside in a villa, was decided by determinants such as wealth and time. A servile class was needed to free wealthy Romans from the mundane tasks of everyday life. Wealth was needed to buy servants, the summer villa, to free oneself of the necessity to work, and to pay for transportation between the origin and destination. Determinatory factors were critical in Roman times for allowing participation in tourism, just as they are today.

The concept of a servile class is not of course unfamiliar to contemporary tourism. Without, for example, waiters, cleaners, attendants, hostesses and reception staff, much of what we expect as part of the tourist experience would not exist. Indeed for many tourists it is the fact of being served for two weeks that is a most appealing aspect of the holiday. As Buck (1978) in Dann (1981:192) states:

> To live a short time surrounded by gracious, deferring servants may have a powerful appeal among those seeking escape from 'egalitarian

affirmative action norms' as well as those middle class, do-it-yourself capitalists who are ready to pay for a week or two of being treated as visiting potentates. Sleeping in a castle or chateau and surrounded by a covey of fawning attendants are, for more than we may appreciate, a dream realised.

The concept of a servile class may be interpreted as overstating the relationship between the tourist and the employee. Unfortunately, many tourism employees may be faced with few other alternatives than serving tourists. There are ethical issues to address concerning such phenomena as the sex tourism industry and exploitation of women through tourism, and the role of multinational operators charging US$400 per night for a hotel room, while paying hotel waiters US$20 per week. However, it must be stressed that tourism in many countries may offer employment opportunities that are perceived as worthwhile, especially when the alternatives are considered.

The existence of surplus labour permits the employment of workers on low wages; to provide services for tourists, allowing commodification of the basic physiological needs of the tourist such as food, drink and shelter. Utilising a Marxist analysis, the large workforce in developing countries provides the right conditions for commodification of labour. Without this supply of surplus labour the mechanism of metatourism would not be as influential, as low labour costs support the profits of transnational corporations and encourage their expansion.

If the Romans were driven primarily by physiological need, what evidence is there in the history of tourism to suggest that we fulfil higher-level needs through participating in tourism? Pilgrimages to such places as Mecca and Lourdes were, and still are, an important tourist activity. To pilgrims this type of voyage provide a meaningful experience, allowing the opportunity for self-development and inner exploration.

Perhaps the most dramatic example of the use of travel to address higher-level needs was through the development of the Grand Tour. This tour, which became popular from the beginning of the 16th century, was brought to an end by the Napoleonic Wars across Europe. It lasted for three to four years, and was participated in predominantly by the wealthy young nobility of England. The aim of the tour was to provide a cultural, technological and philosophical learning experience for the young nobility to create a class of professional statesmen and ambassadors. Participation was, of course, limited to an extremely small minority – the aristocracy. According to Gill (1967) one of the most notable tutors was the philosopher and economist Adam Smith, who wrote *The Wealth of Nations*, ironically the first noted advocate of minimum government interference in the marketplace! (A precondition that is necessary to allow tourism globalisation.) Interestingly, he travelled as tutor to the young Duke of Buccleugh and met both Voltaire and Quesnay.

The fulcrum of change to transpose travel into the tourist system recognisable in contemporary times was the Industrial Revolution. This event had a dramatic effect upon, first, the culture of Britain, and slightly later that of Western Europe and the United States. The reason that it first took place in Britain was the availability of surplus labour resulting from the enforcing of the Enclosure Acts, which pushed people off their lands: not too dissimilar to what is happening throughout South East Asia today with families being cleared off their rice paddies, so that 'golf cities' may be built for Japanese and Western tourists. Significantly from the perspective of tourism, it changed the political, cultural and spacial interaction of society so greatly that the consumption of tourism in its modern form may be traced to changes that began during the last century.

Structurally, the population changed from a 20:80 rural to urban ratio in 1800 to a 40:60 rural to urban ratio by 1850, to a dominant urban population by 1900. People were forced to adapt from living in the countryside as part of a semi-natural ecosystem into a purpose-built urban system. The nature of factory work led to a change in work orientation, from task-related to time-related. This rural to urban shift changed society to allow the creation of the economic and social environment, which stimulates demand for tourism. Statistics show the demand for tourism is higher in urban areas than in rural areas. Although this may be partly accounted for by comparatively higher levels of disposable income and longer holidays, the need to escape the urban environment is strong. Dann (1981:191) refers to a state of anomie for many in society. He explains: 'Anomie refers to a situation of perceived normlessness and meaninglessness in the origin society.'

Clarke and Critcher (1985) identify how the urban area was progressively divided into separate spatial areas. Leisure was forced into specialised areas through legislation such as the 1835 Cruelty to Animals Act, which barred traditional land workers sports such as cock-fighting, dog-fighting, pugilism (interestingly not fox-hunting) and the 1835 Highways Act, forbidding the playing of games in the street. Increasing commercialisation of leisure meant that stadia were developed for football, cricket, rugby, etc. and the development of music halls and later the cinema. A 'spatial mental map' was implanted into the subconsciousness of the new urbanite, where work, home and leisure were interpreted as having separate spatial and time zones.

The spatial and time zoning of life dating from the Industrial Revolution has particular relevance to contemporary tourism. Krippendorf (1990) interprets much of mass tourism as being driven by the escape motivation from modern day urban life. However, how different it may prove to the normality of everyday life is questionable, as displayed in Photo 2.1. It is participated in within a different spatial area, often both geographically and geomorphologically, and conducted within a specified time zone of, usually, 14 days. This marked cultural change, combined with rapid technological advantages during the Industrial Revolution, permitted increased commodification of tourism. In 1841 Thomas

Photo 2.1 Tourists on their way to the beach of Calvi, Corsica.

Cook organised the first group tour, using the railway between Leicester and Loughborough for the purpose of a temperance group meeting.

A society that has progressively become more highly structured, both in terms of work and leisure, offers increased opportunities to commodify the recreational activities people choose to pursue in their leisure time. Tourism may be one of these activities. Increasing legislation, such as the Holidays with Pay Act (1938), increased disposable income; technological advancement, particularly the jet engine, improving knowledge of other countries through cinema and television, have all been major factors in increasing demand for travel. The industry responded to this demand through making the purchase of travel and associated services increasingly accessible to a widening social spectrum of western society. Certainly, since the late 1950s we have witnessed the *debourgoisement* of travel, and the accessibility of international travel to a wider social spectrum than ever before. Whether we will see a continuation of this trend, with the introduction of 'alternative' more expensive forms of tourism such as 'ecotourism', is uncertain.

Why do people need a holiday?

Motivational theory is the subject of numerous psychological texts. While motivational theory has predominantly been applied to management studies aimed at increasing the productivity of workers within the capitalist system, the emphasis in this section of the chapter will be to explore theories which give an understanding of, and allow the interpretation of the motivations of tourists.

Based on the premise that motivation derives from a real or perceived need, it is possible to analyse tourist choice of destination and, to an extent, behaviour, as a consequence of need deficiency. Brown (1964) notes that Freud's earlier psychodynamic analysis of motivation led him to believe that all human behaviour is driven by two basic instincts: a life instinct called Eros and a death instinct called Thanatos. Certainly, the more socially pleasant of the two instincts relates to behaviour influenced by the Eros instinct! This instinct leads to behaviour orientated to self preservation, the libido or human energy system finding release through sexual gratification. The Thanatos instinct channels behaviour into a drive towards death and a release from anxiety and striving, a return to the inorganic state. It is by nature a self-destructive instinct and therefore the aggression associated with this instinct may be channelled into other outlets, for example violence to other people, or combining with the libido in the form of sexual sadism or masochism. Freud adopted this pessimistic stance to explain the carnage of the First World War. Although this theory has been criticised and modified because of its European cultural bias, the notion of dynamic forces and of unconscious factors are widely accepted in psychoanalytical theory to understand motivation. Ethnologists accept that there is an innate aggression in animals including man which influences his needs and motivations.

Pearce(1993) draws attention to the other theories of psychology relevant to the analysis of motivation. Behaviouralist theories as developed by Hull and Skinner (see Atkinson *et al.*, 1990) focus on external influences and how this modifies and controls behaviour. Behaviour is conditioned by external stimuli such as reward and punishment systems for actions. Behaviourists and social learning theorists interpret aggression as a learned response to frustration. Other outlets take the form of behaviour such as dependency, achievement, withdrawal and resignation, psychosomatic symptoms, self-anaesthetisation with drugs and alcohol and constructive problem-solving (Atkinson *et al.*, 1990).

Using psychoanalytical theory to analyse marketing in the tourist industry, advertising directed at these two basic drives is evident. Covertly or overtly, tour operators' brochures not only offer the three Ss of Sun, Sea and Sand in your destination, but also a fourth S of Sex. 'Beautiful people in beautiful places', 'your chance to buy "paradise" for two weeks' are not unfamiliar slogans. Sometimes the relationship between the destination and sexual opportunity may be substantially more axiomatic. Stag tours to Bangkok are not aimed at fulfilling males' need for the understanding of Buddhist culture or providing a setting for philosophical reflection of life! Pattaya also strongly advocates the fourth S as shown in Photo 2.2.

Activity tourism, in particular sports and adventure tourism, perhaps offers channelled outlets for behaviour resulting from innate or learned aggression

PATTAYA

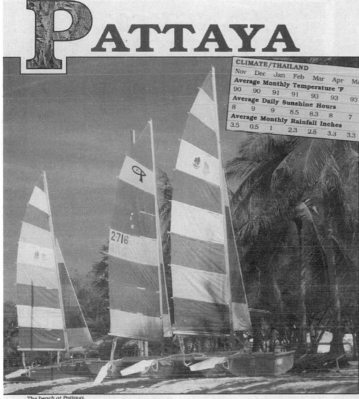

CLIMATE/THAILAND												
	Nov	Dec	Jan	Feb	Mar	Apr	May	Jun	Jul	Aug	Sep	Oct
Average Monthly Temperature °F	90	90	91	91	93	93	93	91	90	90	89	90
Average Daily Sunshine Hours	8	9	9	8.5	8.3	8	7	7	6.5	6	5.5	6
Average Monthly Rainfall Inches	3.5	0.5	1	2.3	2.5	3.3	3.3	4	3.8	8.8	11	3.5

The beach at Pattaya.

Wherever you've been, whatever you've seen, this famous beach resort some two hours drive from Bangkok will rock you back on your heels. Pattaya came into being as the principal R&R (rest & recuperation) resort for American soldiers serving in the Vietnam war. We'd guess

there's getting on for a thousand bars in Pattaya... and then there's the nightclubs, discos, and restaurants. If you could imagine global TV announcing the end of the world in 24 hrs time, then what goes on in Pattaya all the time, is what the approach to doomsday would probably be like.

If you can suck it, use it, eat it, feel it, taste it, abuse it or see it, then it's available in this resort that truly never sleeps. Pattaya is not for prudes, nor do you need to be out-going; five or so paces outside your accommodation and you will have received more lewd invites than you could imagine. Needless to say, this resort is ideal for singles of whatever age, for you won't remain on your own for long!

The beach is good sand formed on a long bay, and once again, whatever your desire is, you can buy it in Pattaya. Scuba diving, deep sea fishing, windsurfing, sailing, sea-scooters, motor-boats; there are even really big power boats available for hire (about £20 per hour) if you're up to it. If you'd rather sit back and let someone else do all the work, there are a myriad excursions available, both by sea and land.

Restaurants range from the very best serving lobster straight out of an aquarium, to frail Chinese gentlemen frying fresh chicken in huge woks by the roadside. Just thinking about Pattaya makes us exhausted all over again.

If you're looking for a quiet sojourn on a tropical beach, then this is no resort for you. Pattaya is for those souls seeking the sort of experiences they'd previously only read about, but never really believed.

Pattaya: you better believe it!

...and if you're too lazy to come off the beach, she'll bring lunch to you!

Photo 2.2

which may otherwise be exhibited in a more socially unacceptable form. Many sports and contemporary leisure activities such as 'Quasar Laser' and simulated war-paint games, act as a form of repressive tolerance, which allows an outlet for aggression in a socially acceptable and controlled form, through the application of rules. Clarke and Critcher (1991:62), commenting upon the growth of organised sport in the last century, observe

> Bourgeois leisure had been forced to become privatised; entertainment was home-based, centring on religion, reading and music, occasionally supplemented by annual holidays at the seaside. While this was held to be sufficient for the bourgeois woman and girl and while adult males could absorb themselves in their work and obtain illicit pleasures elsewhere, the problem of young bourgeois males proved more intractable. It was as an outlet for their pent up energies and as part of a more ordered socialisation that organised sport emerged ... The encouragement of organised sport was simultaneously a means of controlling the characteristically anarchic behaviour of public schoolboys and of redirecting the public school ethos toward a model of what would subsequently be defined as 'muscular Christianity'.

Sometimes tourism may appeal more openly to our aggressive instincts, as a recent newspaper article showed. The column, entitled 'Tourists rush for kill a seal pup holiday' (*Evening Standard*, London, 5 July 1993), describes the marketing of a 'sick' but commercially successful holiday. In return for paying $3000, thousands of Americans have the satisfaction of clubbing seal pups to death on the Newfoundland ice. 'People want to come out and kill and it's a good market for us', said Mike Kehoe, executive director of the Canadian Sealers Association, which is promoting the 'Kill a Seal Pup Vacations'. Does this sound like 'tourism the fun industry'? Or how can the visits to the 'Holocaust Theme Park' in Washington DC be explained? Gourevitch in the *Observer* Supplement (30 January 1994) observes how tourists upon entry to the 'Holocaust Memorial Museum' are issued with an identity card, matched to their age and gender, of an actual holocaust victim or survivor. They can then push their bar-coded card into computerised stations as they proceed through the exhibition to find out the fate of their phantom surrogates.

Less dramatically Johnston(1992), commenting on adventure holidays in the mountains of New Zealand, found risk, defined by using adjectives of challenge and danger, as an essential part of the adventure experience. For downhill skiers risk was identified by 35.6% of the sample as meaning 'challenge', 27.2% as 'danger', 22.4% as an 'uncertain outcome' and the rest a hybrid of the above three meanings. Hall (1992) writes

> The ability to meet a challenge is closely relate to the concept of 'flow'. Flow is a special feeling that occurs when the abilities of the individual meet the demands of an activity or situation. Flow has seven aspects: a

centring of attention; transitoriness; richer perception; forgetting oneself and being totally immersed in the requirements of the task at hand; disorientation with time and space; enjoyment; and momentary loss of anxiety and constraint.

Johnston (1992:8), citing Ewert (1989), notes 'the concept of risk taking is central to outdoor adventure activities as the absence of risk may result in a decrease in satisfaction as well as a decrease in the desire to participate'.

Another important cultural and behavioural instinct, subconsciously influencing westerners' motivations, is the Judaic and Christian doctrine purported by major Christian philosophers such as Kant. Gosling (1990) notes:

Kant believed nature to be a collection of irrational forces which needed to be subdued and kept in check by human effort. 'Man' was a rational and spiritual being whose holiness was associated with his moral personality, and part of his moral duty was to subdue nature. Thus the world of morality, with inherent possibility of holiness, was sharply distinguished from the world of nature.

From a behavioural viewpoint, it is possible to interpret elements of Kantian philosophy in the need to be challenged in the wild environments depicted by Johnston. The interpretation of this action could be of the individual trying to subdue nature and gain ascendancy over the natural environment. Conversely, it could be hypothesised that in fact the risk element represents a passage through which an individual may believe they must proceed to have a closer and more symbiotic relationship with the environment.

Owing to the complexity of modern life and our separation from our natural environment, the individual will be faced with a variety of perceived needs to establish a state of physical and mental wellbeing. The most significant and widely quoted pieces of work examining human motivation was by Maslow (1954). His theory, called 'the hierarchy of needs', organised the behaviour of the individual according to expressed and subconscious needs. The hierarchy of needs is shown in Figure 2.1

Physiological needs are identified as those needs for human survival such as food, water and shelter. Safety needs manifest themselves in a desire for a predictable and orderly world. This can be achieved through a regular schedule or rhythm in everyday life, very often structured around a regular occupation. Love and self-belonging are interpreted as a need for acceptance in a group, often the family. Esteem needs may be subdivided into two categories. The first is for self-esteem within which the individual develops a high evaluation of himself. The second, higher-level esteem need is social esteem, which is a desire for esteem from other people. This involves such factors as reputation, prestige, status and importance. Self-actualisation is a form of self-fulfilment which allows full development of one's potential in the area of your choice.

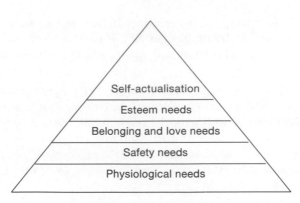

Figure 2.1   After Maslow's Hierarchy of Needs.

Critically, Maslow states that to progress to a higher level of need we do not have to satisfy completely the lower-level needs. He hypothesises that the 'average citizen' may be approximately satisfied at any one time 85% in his physiological needs, 70% in his safety needs, 50% in his love needs, 40% in his self-esteem needs, and 10% in high self-actualisation needs. This would imply that motivation to participate in a particular activity or perform a certain action will be driven by a combination of different needs, with different weightings attached to each, unique to the individual concerned. Any assessment of motivation will therefore need to incorporate a methodology which permits it to conduct a multivariate analysis, as opposed to a single-trait analysis of tourist motivation.

An important point made by Maslow is that the future action of the individual will be governed by the level of need. For example, the person who is extremely hungry will regard Utopia as a place where there is plenty of food. For the sun-starved British tourist Utopia may be a sun-drenched beach for two weeks. Our perception of Utopia will therefore be governed by the extent to which we have fulfilled the different levels of the hierarchy of needs.

The model developed by Maslow allows incorporation of biological elements, or physiological need, into the model. Ryan (1991) includes relaxation and sexual opportunity as two of the primary motivators for participation in tourism. Although Ryan identifies these two elements as psychological need, they may also be interpreted as a physiological need. Certainly holidays where the main aim is physical recuperation or explicit sexual motivation, for example stag tours to Bangkok, can be interpreted as serving a lower level of human need as identified by Maslow, compared to other types of holidays centred on culture and education.

Krippendorf (1989:24), in analysing tourism motivation, draws attention to the role of travel in physical recuperation. He questions whether the transition from industrial to service-based economies has reduced the need for physical recuperation from holidays. He notes

> Our civilisation has freed us from a large part of manual work, but in exchange we have had to buy such sedentary diseases as heart and circulation disorders. The so-called prosperity diseases have also become much more frequent: diabetes, high blood pressure, cancer of the respiratory tract as a result of cigarette smoking, alcoholism and many others. And what is especially striking: about half the diseases are not of a primarily organic nature but the consequence of nervous stress, another product of the modern age.

Mill (1990:42) identifies the physical need as the most important motivatory element of vacation tourism. However, he subsequently qualifies this against changing external influences, notably change in work patterns. He notes

> Today the escape may be more mental than physical. As the physical demands have been reduced for many people, the mental demands have increased. It is increasingly difficult for the white-collar manger to 'clock-out' mentally at the end of the day. It often takes several days in a vacation spot before the person seeking mental relaxation can tune off the office.

The work experience is a key cultural factor in modifying or creating need within the individual. For the majority of workers in developed economies, work has changed from being primarily task-orientated before the industrial revolution to being primarily time-orientated. Many workers experience lack of autonomy, lack of meaningfulness to their work and isolation. As the formative education system orientates people to the centrality and importance of work, the type of work experience or lack of it will be a critical element in determining our satisfaction of different levels of need as expressed by Maslow.

Parker (1983) produced a model identifying three basic relationships between work and leisure, of extension, opposition and neutrality. It is possible to adapt this model to help analyse the relationship between type of work and likely holiday choice and behaviour. Parker states that at the extreme end of people in the opposition category would be those people who hate work so much that the quality of the leisure experience is determined by how much unlike work it is. Workers who experience this opposition are likely to be in jobs which offer very little autonomy or self-determination. Consequently leisure choice maybe marked by a revolt against authority. In terms of tourism this alienation from the workplace and the seeking of opposition to the work experience may manifest itself in a complete rejection of the system, which is easier to achieve in a foreign country. The type of behaviour associated with the opposition syndrome could be hypothesised as being characterised by the 'lager lout'.

Parker identified 'extension' as work determining the choice of leisure activity in a positive way. People who fall into the extension category are likely to have occupations with a high amount of autonomy and probably socialise with people from work. Work is central to their life and will often extend into leisure time. It is difficult to categorise the type of holiday associated with the extension pattern. The authors remember a colleague in a tourism consultancy for whom they worked, who would visit regional offices during his holiday if he was in the area. This is extreme but the choice of destination may be closely influenced by work colleagues or an awareness of the destination gained through the workplace. Activities chosen in the holiday period are likely to be those that create a similar social environment to the dynamics of the work place, for example competitiveness, team exercises and individuality.

Parker observes that the largest number of people categorised by work–leisure relationships fall into the neutrality group. In this relationship the worker feels indifferent about his job and the choice of leisure activity will be determined neither positively nor negatively by occupation. Workers tend to be detached from their work and this often extends into leisure time, leading to a market segment that wants to be entertained and largely passive. This category represents a large market and would help to explain the success of man-made attractions such as leisure parks and theme parks.

The decision to visit a destination is therefore a complex amalgam of needs, motivating an individual to set and prioritise goals, in a belief that achieving these will satisfy the perceived needs. It must be reiterated that tourism is one choice out of a range of alternative activities, or other consumer goods, on which the consumer may decide to spend his or her money. Also, the needs of any individual are likely to be influenced to varying degrees by the environment they live in. In particular, tourist needs are likely to be influenced by the evaluation of past holiday experiences; hence Pearce's ... tourists have a tourist career similar to a work career, which will be modified by past experiences, level of education, peer groups, physical and cultural environment, occupation and lifestyle. There are then a range of 'push factors' (to use a geographical expression) which will encourage the tourist to leave home. These factors may lead to a range of possible destination choices, while the reality of actualising any of them will be modified by determinants such as levels of disposable income and vacation allowance, position in the lifecycle (e.g. choice of destination maybe limited by dependants such as children or infirmity in old age) and technological advancement (e.g. the development of the Channel Tunnel will make day trips to Paris and Brussels a reality).

As well as 'push' factors there are also 'pull' factors (usually the physical and cultural attributes of a destination) which will lead a consumer to decide that their needs can be met through the purchasing of this destination. However, unlike other products the consumer has no chance to sample the product before buying it. The product or destination is therefore largely sold on its image, as exemplified in Donaldson's quote concerning a *Passage to India*. The importance of image is expanded in the next section of the chapter.

The relationship between motivations, external influences and image, is shown in Figure 2.2 below. This figure incorporates the multitrait needs identified by Maslow, leading to the formation of goals, decided upon to satisfy these needs. Importantly, it recognises the external factors that will influence these needs and recognises that future choice of a tourism destination will be influenced by the type of visitor experiences a tourist has encountered. Tourism may therefore be seen as a form of progression for any individual, that will be modified by past experiences and external influences.

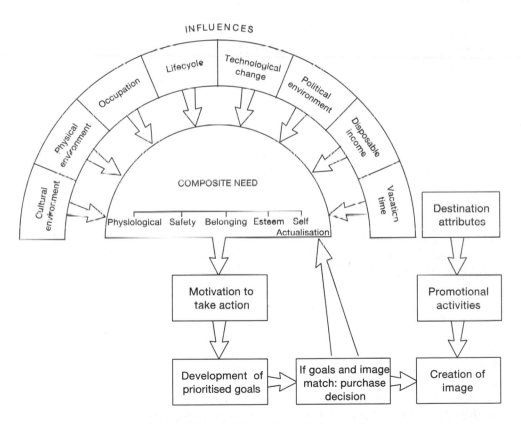

Figure 2.2 Model of demand for tourism.

Anything for anyone: a place for everyone

The growth in international tourism demand, post-1950, has been enormous. Projections from the World Tourism Organisation (WTO) are for over 600 million international arrivals by the year 2000. A tourism market has developed based upon a tour operating industry that continues to expand its range of products. There seems to be a tourism 'commodity' on offer to cover all possible interests and tastes.

A very broad classification of types of tourism may be expressed as follows:

- business;
- pleasure; and
- visiting friends and relatives.

Although business travel can be regarded as a necessity, it is often sold as a fringe benefit to a potential job candidate. As well as appearing exciting, though regular business travellers will vouch for how monotonous and demanding business travel often is, the image of travelling for business fulfils esteem needs. Esteem is gained from the commonly held perception that jobs that involve business travel, even cabin crew to an extent, are seen as high profile and prestigious jobs.

The business market (tourism by definition is not simply about holidays) is significant in economic terms to particular destinations and multinational hotel chains and transport carriers. The business market has special significance in city locations and in an increasing number of resort hotels who hold conference, seminar and training meetings as a means to increase revenue and extend the tourist season. It is the highest-spending market segment, particularly lucrative at its upper end. The battle for this market between the different airlines and international hotel chains is intensive. The advent of 'Club Class' in the 1980s has led to a concentration on quality service as a means of attracting the business traveller, with factors such as seat width, easy check-in and a high level of in-flight attendance all being examples of factors used to win this market share. Progressively, Virgin Atlantic targeted the business woman, while the majority of other quality airlines (e.g. Lufthansa and British Airways) seem to concentrate on the business man. Similarly, for any five-star hotel to compete in the business market it must be able to offer a high level of business service, including available secretarial support, even faxes and computer terminals in bedrooms. The business world deals with commodities and in turn is dealt with as a commodity by the tourism industry, with competition not being based primarily on price but on the quality of the service on offer.

The main reason, however, for most tourism activity is pleasure. Included in this could be visiting friends and relatives (VFR). As the world becomes more of a global village then propensity to travel to visit friends and relatives is likely to grow. This will have significance for destination planning authorities with strong historical and cultural links with other countries in terms of marketing opportunities and facility development.

What is pleasure travel? There is no simple answer to explain the large diversity of holidays on offer in the marketplace. A underlying premise of pleasure travel is that the individual participates in it out of free choice for an intrinsic reward. It is, of course, true that no choice is made completely freely, and that cultural and social factors in the home environment will influence our choice subconsciously if not directly, as explained. True freedom of choice would imply that we are all self-actualised individuals with the strength of character free to make such choices. Naturally, this is not true. Freedom of choice does not mean uninfluenced choice. Paradoxically many of the reasons that we choose to go holiday – for example, for physiological and psychological recuperation – may be overridden by the needs for safety and belonging. The 'wakes weeks' of the industrial north in England, where whole communities moved to the seaside, have left a legacy into the mass tourism of the Mediterranean age, where groups of friends travel together for the purpose of holiday-making.

Bull (1991) refers to a limited number of traits which seem to be especially important in determining tourist behaviour. These are as follows.

Venturesomeness: the degree of 'risk' tourists want.
Hedonism: the degree of comfort required on a trip.
Changeability: the extent to which tourists are impulsive or seeking something new.
Dogmatism: the extent to which a tourist cannot be persuaded to change ideas.
Intellectualism: the degree of 'culture' tourists want.

An important consideration is that the tourism market is not homogeneous. It is composed of individuals, who, as explained earlier in the chapter, will have a composite set of needs to be fulfilled through tourism. However, attempts have been made to group tourists together into broad typology groupings, which help further clarification and segmentation of the market. The importance of typology groupings to the tourism industry is demonstrated in the case study at the end of Chapter 2, which outlines a typology survey conducted by a leading travel organisation.

The earliest model, and still one that forms the basis of tourism typology theory, was established by Stanley Plog (1974). Using a sample comparison of flyers to non-flyers Plog identified definite personality traits identifiable to different groups of flyers. Using a sample of 4000 people Plog constructed a cognitive–normative model based upon psychographic type. At one end of the continuum are *psychocentric* tourists and at the other end *allocentric* tourists.

The allocentrics are explorers and very adventuresome and likely to choose remote and 'untouched' (by tourists) destinations. Mid-centric are

45

likely to display characteristics of limited adventure but wanting home comforts. It is this group that represents the mass of the tourism market. Psychocentrics dislike destinations that offer unfamiliarity and insecurity.

It is possible to hypothesise that these typology groupings relate to Maslow's 'hierarchy of needs' and to Parker's work–leisure model. It may be suggested that the psychocentric is dominated by safety needs and has an occupation that offers little autonomy or opportunity for self-development. Conversely, the allocentric may be portrayed as the self-actualised individual, having a highly prestigious occupation. However, these are perhaps too simplistic and naive cross linkages and much more research would be required to confirm or disprove these hypotheses.

Plog's model was later developed by Butler and Waldbrook (1991) to explain destination development and environmental impacts. Critically from a marketing aspect, Plog also established the mediums through which to have access to these psychographic groupings. He found that psychocentrics were heavy television watchers, while allocentrics were more print-orientated. He also established that there was no connection between income and trait, apart from the extremes of each side of the continuum where the highest rated allocentrics had the highest income and the lowest scoring psychocentrics has the lowest incomes. Indeed, Plog's initial research made no relation between group type and income.

One of the criticisms of the original model was that it was static and did not accommodate change in market taste. Plog (1987) adds a dynamic element by adding that allocentrics pick up new products and pass them through each of the groups. As the group below becomes more familiar with the product they lose their apprehension about it; this product would include holiday types and destinations.

Other typology models have concentrated on behavioural aspects and interaction of tourists at their destinations. The most important interactional models are those of Cohen (1974) and Smith (1977). Both models contain similar typologies, the work of Smith progressing that of Cohen, to establish more typology groupings. Both models offer a continuum in different terminologies between Cohen's Drifter (Smith's Explorer) and Smith's Charter (Cohen's Organised Mass Tourist). The drifters and explorers display traits of discovery and a search for the exotic and strange environment, while the trait of the mass-organised tourist is the search for relaxation but in a familiar and secure environment. The relationship between tourist typologies and destination choice is discussed in the second part of the chapter.

Based upon the evidence of increasing demand for tourism, it is certain that where the determinants of demand such as disposable income and holiday allowance allow, people will purchase the 'commodity of tourism'. In response to this phenomenon a global industry has developed, encompassing the principle of both 'mass' and 'metatourism'. There is both a globalisation and standardisation of tourism as international corporations aim to provide a globalised standard product, with associated universal quality, for travellers who want the minimum of inconvenience during their trip. Also there are increasing numbers of destinations who are willing to put themselves into the 'tourism commodity' marketplace in pursuit of the economic benefits of the industry. For all tourist tastes there is a product to buy, from murder weekends and transcendental experiences in the Greek Islands to jungle trekking in Indonesia and coral-reef diving in Belize.

Perspectives on the tourists' view of the world

Introduction

This section examines the importance of concept formation and destination image in influencing tourist choice. In aiming to examine and clarify the complexity of the 'tourism product' it asserts that adoption of marketing theory, established as successful in the commercial world, can, through the central paradoxes of tourism, have special, unplanned effects on tourist destinations: leading to places, people and cultures being treated as commodities for consumption. Central to this must be an understanding of tourist typologies (as explored in the preceding section of this chapter) and the ways in which they are based on behaviour patterns and interconnect with marketing.

Tourism, by its very nature, is driven by some kind of desire to travel, to go to another place. Whether the individual tourist is motivated by the journey itself (i.e. hitchhiking across Europe to India, East–West across the United States on a Harley-Davidson, or North–South by train from Boston to Patagonia) or whether it is the actual destination that inspires the travel (i.e. with a tourist taking the quickest and easiest route), an understanding of the creative processes that give us our perceptions of the world, including our view of other countries and other peoples, provides a useful insight into the major driving force behind the process of tourism. The actual growth in tourism demand, which is based on a variety of psychological, socioeconomic and cultural factors, has been well reported (especially in Poon, 1993; Cooper *et al.*, 1993). Mathieson and Wall describe four different types of tourist based on Cohen's 1972 work (Table 2.1). It should be recognised, however, that Cohen's early work was based on stereotypical categories. Philip Pearce describes a way of seeing traveller categories (largely self-explanatory) and certain behaviour patterns, albeit based quite heavily on a judgemental process (Table 2.2).

The decision to travel in itself can be, at one level, relatively easy to understand. Travel represents a well-established form of leisure and is an intrinsic part of postindustrial culture: 'Tourism, the ultimate freedom' as the

Table 2.1 Fourfold classification of tourist experiences and roles.

1. *The organised mass tourist.* This role is typified by the package tour in which itineraries are fixed, stops are planned and guided, and all major decisions are left to the organiser. Familiarity is at a maximum and novelty at a minimum.
2. *The individual mass tourist.* In this role, the tour is not entirely planned by others, and the tourist has some control over his itinerary and time allocations. However, all of the major arrangements are made through a travel intermediary. Like the organised mass tourist, the individual mass tourist remains largely within the 'environmental bubble' of home country ways and mixes little with members of the host community. Familiarity is still dominant.
3. *The explorer.* Explorers usually plan their own trips and try to avoid developed tourist attractions as much as possible. In spite of the desire to mix with members of the host community, the protection of the 'environmental bubble' is still sought. Novelty now dominates but the tourist does not become fully integrated with the host society.
4. *The drifter.* Drifters plan their trips alone, avoid tourist attractions and live with members of the host society. They are almost entirely immersed in the host culture, sharing its shelter, food and habits. Novelty is dominant and familiarity disappears.

Source: Mathieson and Wall (1982:19).

US Travel and Tourism Administration terms it. One leading commentator observed:

> Along with a handful of other things – television, the computer, recreational sex – the ability to travel the globe freely sets those who live in the late 20th century apart from all those who lived before it. (*Economist*, 23 March 1991)

These freedoms are, in some senses, framed not only by the determinants of demand such as disposable income and availability of leisure time, but also by cultural framing: the need for prestige, the need to take cognisance of (but not necessarily obey) the relevant taboos related to gender, sexuality, age and spending patterns: 'old people go on cruises but not skiing trips', 'nice girls don't go on singles holidays', or 'single men go to Thailand for only one reason', and so on. Douglas Pearce develops Plog's 1973 personality type analysis of traveller types (Table 2.3).

Given that some definitions of tourism motivations allow for purposes other than leisure, for instance health, business, pilgrimage or education, we can also recognise that under certain circumstances the decision may be taken out of the tourist's hands. For example, travel and choice of destination may in some sense be forced (for example, due to family pressure). The decision may be spontaneous, such as in the case of 'packing a weekend bag and driving to the coast' or it may be planned well in advance, perhaps in response to the heavy round of holiday promotions and advertisements screened on TV during

Table 2.2 The five major role-related behaviours for 15 traveller categories.

Traveller category	The five clearest role-related behaviours (in order of relative importance)
Tourist	Takes photos, buys souvenirs, goes to famous places, stays briefly in one place, does not understand the local people
Traveller	Stays briefly in one place, experiments with local food, goes to famous places, takes photos, explores places privately
Holidaymaker	Takes photos, goes to famous places, is alienated from society, buys souvenirs, contributes to the visited economy
Jet-setter	Lives a life of luxury, concerned with social status, seeks sensual pleasures, prefers interacting with people of his/her own kind, goes to famous places
Businessman	Concerned with social status, contributes to the economy, does not take photos, prefers interacting with people of his/her own kind, lives a life of luxury
Migrant	Has language problems, prefers interacting with people of his/her own kind, does not understand the local people, does not live a life of luxury, does not exploit the local people
Conservationist	Interested in the environment, does not buy souvenirs, does not exploit the local people, explores places privately, takes photos
Explorer	Explores places privately, interested in the environment, takes physical risks, does not buy souvenirs, keenly observes the visited society
Missionary	Does not buy souvenirs, searches for the meaning of life, does not live a life of luxury, does not seek sensual pleasures, keenly observes the visited society
Overseas student	Experiments with local food, does not exploit the local people, takes photos, keenly observes the visited society, takes physical risks
Anthropologist	Keenly observes the visited society, explores places privately, interested in the environment, does not buy souvenirs, takes photos
Hippie	Does not buy souvenirs, does not live a life of luxury, is not concerned with social status, does not take photos, does not contribute to the economy
International athlete	Is not alienated from own society, does not exploit the local people, does not understand the local people, explores places privately, searches for the meaning of life.
Overseas journalist	Takes photos, keenly observes the visited society, goes to famous places, takes physical risks, explores places privately
Religious pilgrim	Searches for the meaning of life, does not live a life of luxury, is not concerned with social status, does not exploit the local people, does not buy souvenirs

Source: Pearce (1982:32).

PLOG

Table 2.3 Travel characteristics of psychographic types.

Psychocentrics	Allocentrics
• Prefer the familiar in travel destinations	• Prefer non-touristy areas
• Like commonplace activities at travel destinations	• Enjoy sense of discovery and delight in new experiences, before others have visited the area
• Prefer sun 'n' fun spots, including considerable relaxation	• Prefer novel and different destinations
• Low activity level	• High activity level
• Prefer destinations they can drive to	• Prefer flying to destinations
• Prefer heavy tourist accommodations, such as heavy hotel development, family type restaurants and tourist shops	• Tour accommodations should include adequate-to-good hotels and food, not necessarily modern or chain-type hotels, and few 'tourist' type attractions
• Prefer familiar atmosphere (hamburger stands, familiar type entertainment, absence of foreign atmosphere)	• Enjoy meeting and dealing with people from a strange or foreign culture
• Complete tour packaging, appropriate with heavy scheduling of activities.	• Tour arrangements should include basics (transportation and hotels) and allow considerable freedom and flexibility

Source: Pearce (1987:15).

the Christmas period. It is here, perhaps, that the tourist's early misconditioning may start. The decision will often result from negotiations and research with family and friends, the process of choosing a holiday becomes part of the enjoyment. The decision to purchase a holiday has historically always been seen as a service purchase. In a sense this might be somewhat unfortunate, for while tourism is frequently described as an intangible product there are large parts of it, such as the size of the seat on the aircraft, the taste of the meals and warmth of the sea, that are clearly both measurable and thus thoroughly tangible. Many of the decision processes and motivations will be the same as when a 'tangible' product (such as an automobile) is bought.

This may be a general belief in the product: 'Volkswagen make reliable cars', 'Kuoni put together reliable holidays'; or related to ego-stroking, 'Golf GTIs are driven by successful people', 'only the rich and famous go to Mustique'. The analogy between purchasing an automobile and purchasing a holiday may not be as fanciful as it first seems. Both are likely to be key financial decisions, related to risk taking, choice based on research, research influenced by sophisticated advertising and media exposure. Both products are identifiable with important reference groups (role models perhaps) which gives some explanation as to why automobile manufacturers are involved in motor racing and why resorts which are first 'discovered' by the rich and famous soon become popular with 'ordinary' tourists.

A classic case of this is the French resort town of Nice, which began its life as a place to visit during the mid-18th century when it began to be frequented by a group of convalescent upper-class Englishmen who were seeking refuge from damp English winters. By the mid-1930s, the eve of the Second World War, it had evolved into 'the premier centre for a cosmopolitan winter society whose upper class culture transcended national identity'. The history is described in some detail by Nash (1979). In it, Nash observes three trends in the social origins of tourists:

- *democratisation:* inclusion of the lower classes, made possible by readily available transportation modes such as railways and cars, together with economic advances by an increasing middle class;
- *internationalisation:* the exclusively English haute bourgeoisie expanded to include French, Russian and eventually US and German élites; and
- *from sick to healthy:* curative devices such as spas and climate were taken for granted but increasingly the visitors included healthy people.

Nash also elaborated three trends in the aristocratic culture:

- the move from lodging at an auberge to staying at a Grande Hotel;
- the elaboration and sophistication of touristic activities; and
- the shift from simple to complex social arrangements (enabled by the availability of the Grande Hotels).

Nash's final point is that while any comprehensive review of tourism would include touristic metropoles, their satellites and the transactions between them, it is the leisure culture that tourists create (or have created for them) that is the key to entire touristic enterprise. The influence of Nice as a destination role model became clear during the mid-1990s when officials on the Balearic Island of Mallorca (Majorca) were moving towards upgrading the city of Santa Poucça 'to make it become like Nice' (Selwyn, forthcoming).

What is also interesting about Nice, as a case to study, is that it enables us to look at a complete cycle of development. We can still see the remnants of this desire for exclusivity in modern society. The desire to emulate the lifestyle of the 'idle rich', for instance, was found during the late 1980s in informal talk among a group of expatriate residents of Fiji, staying at a very upmarket resort (taking advantage of heavily discounted local rates following the military coup). The following revealing comment was elicited: 'Just being in this place makes you feel that you've arrived, it sort of legitimises you. Provided you wear the right labels, Calvin Klein, Gaultier and Comme des Garcons, the tourists think that we're as rich as they are ... we all end up wearing the same suntans!' This minor obsession with labels and 'designer' products is a manifestation of the functional symbolism that goods (including tourism) play in cultural identity.

So, the tourists in the symbolic surroundings of crystal clear swimming pools, hand brushed and picked beaches, thick towels and the instant service associated with (for example) a Sheraton Resort, feel enhanced by the functional symbolism of 'designer' items. This passion for symbolic success has also been illustrated by the cult of the suntan (a phenomenon decreasing less quickly than one would imagine, given contemporary knowledge about melanoma). Travel and purchase decisions are clearly linked to travel motivation, which in turn is a component of the general motivational nexus.

A central paradox of tourism is that it is at once a search for both the exotic and the simplistic. This 'pursuit of the exotic and cultivation of the simple' (Turner and Ash, 1975:19) is at least, in part, the product of a wide-ranging, long-established urban culture which has been, as Krippendorf (1987: xiv) describes, 'shaped by everyday life'. He continues:

> People go away because they no longer feel happy where they are . . .
> In order to be able to carry on, they urgently need a temporary refuge
> from the burdens imposed by the everyday work, home and leisure
> scene. Their work is increasingly automated and functionalised; it is
> also determined by other people. They feel the monotony of the daily
> routine, the cold rationality of factories, offices, apartment blocks and
> transport, shrinking human contact, the repression of feelings, the loss
> of nature and naturalness . . . life has been reduced to mere
> existence.

Here we have a clearly described rationale for getting away from it all; a recognition that 'away' will be temporary (as opposed to emigrating, living in an isolated cottage or desert island, or buying a villa in Provence (*à la* Peter Mayle), and that life at home is 'mere existence'. In discussing the links between life in the industrialised north and tourism motivation Krippendorf uses several key words and phrases that form almost the exact opposite of key words (or phrases) to be found in travel brochures (Table 2.4):

Turner and Ash also developed the theme of holiday-making being a result of alienation on the part of those in the industrialised countries of the North. They attack the inequalities of North–South tourism. They try to explain it in global economic/development terms: the 'poor South' being 'invaded' (to use their word) by holiday-makers from the 'rich North'. Turner and Ash assert that the pursuit and cultivation of 'sunlust' holiday destinations (i.e. those destinations developed to service the need for hot, beach, swimming and disco holidays for workers from the cold North) requires 'an imperialistic culture with a unified and dominant style that has been expanding aggressively –

Table 2.4 Keywords and phrases in travel brochures as palliative for the postmodern condition.

Krippendorf†	Tour brochure
Monotony	Reject all calls to conform to the norm*
Automated and functionalised	Break the mould*
Emptiness and boredom	Energy and excitement*
Cold rationality	Rainbow of romance
City centres . . . totally geared to work	Fantastic natural scenic backdrop*
Enslaved by the force of circumstances	Fast, free 'n' easy funtimes*
Living space is shrinking	Scenery unchanged by time**
Ever growing mountain of excrement	Islands of beauty and tranquility**
[apartments as] Grey structures resembling silos and bunkers	Sumptuous palaces**
Tragic development	Exotic holiday playground
A feeling of being boxed up	A million miles away**

* *The Club* (budget edn) Summer '92; ** *ASEAN Explorer* (Thai Adventures, 1992);
† Krippendorf (1989:xiii–xix, 9, 17, 83–5).

either absorbing or stamping out alien cultures'. This is an extreme view which found a certain level of favour with some development economists and early tourism anthropologists. It is now widely recognised that it is problematic to view tourism in entirely negative terms: for some countries, especially those with a limited resource base, whose only natural endowments might be described as warmth and geographic location, tourism offers a real chance of economic diversification.

Krippendorf phrases things more carefully, seeing the 'invasion' as 'ignoring or refuting the local environment'. Perhaps here is another paradox, in that this imperialistic cultural attitude is formed within a personal construct or 'perceptual bubble', where holiday experiences seem to draw together towards uniformity, a blurred manic consumerism where tourists 'can . . . enjoy total freedom and abandon themselves to the consumption of the package of concentrated experiences' (Krippendorf, 1987:5). Thus, the pessimists would have us believe, the search goes on, tour operating companies and tourists seeking new destinations only to consume them in a sort of global 'cannibalism' (with cannibalism acting as a metaphor for power, control and ultimately consumption). Yet this act, with its protective modes of air-conditioned transport and five-star accommodation, takes place within environmental and psychological bubbles – thus preventing the very fulfilment that our travellers think they are seeking. The curious thing is that many holiday-makers do not seem to mind.

Concept formation in the context of tourism: people and destination

Our concepts and perceptions, the way in which we try to make sense of the world, are formed by a huge variety of inputs. These will range from listening to our parents as children, having a physical disability, culture-specific attitudes and social fashion to the daily newspaper we read, the type of education we received and the amount of television we watch; it might be argued that the sheer magnitude of stimuli leads, as one observer of the Arts sees it, to a sort of information overload:

> Unlike our grandparents, we live in a world that we ourselves made. Until about fifty years ago, images of Nature [and the natural world] ... [dominated] almost every relationship ... If this sense has now become dimmed, it is partly because for most people Nature has been replaced by the culture of congestion: of cities and mass media. We are crammed like battery hens with stimuli, and what seems significant is not the quality or meaning of the messages, but their excess ... capitalism plus electronics have given us a new habitat, our forest of media. (Hughes, 1980:324)

In the stream of information that surrounds the holiday, there are occasions when images and words used in that powerful form of cultural production, the holiday brochure, could at best be described as patronising and at worst, racist. Given the sophistication of market segmentation and the care with which brochures are put together, one is forced to ask what motivates the copywriters? Are they deliberately reinforcing in the minds of their clients images or concepts of foreign destinations and peoples that match existing racially stereotyped images and feelings of white superiority? Visual evidence from the brochures seems to lead us to the reluctant conclusion that holiday brochures are essentially for white consumption: images of black faces interrupt images of silver beaches and waving palm fronds only to serve as one of the icons of paradise or 'exotic' sexual fantasy. (An exception to this was the now defunct 'Club 18–30' holiday brochure, which portrayed images of young black Britons enjoying themselves along with the other holiday-makers.)

In general, these images match a variety of psychological needs: holidays are defined in tourism textbooks as being 'needs satisfiers' (Middleton, 1988: 50, 52; Ryan, 1991: 25–9) ranging from the search for exotic (a key word in the selling of holidays) to satisfying a Robinson Crusoe fantasy – this is a curiously apt fantasy: one interpretation of Defoe's story is that it acts as a metaphor for cultural imperialism and taming the wilderness.

Bradley, in discussing international marketing, asserts that 'it is not the marketing environment itself that is important but the firm's ability to cope with it' (Bradley, 1991:7). For tourism firms, be they national, transnational or global, this 'coping' must focus on the customer. An understanding of how people form ideas, opinions and perhaps even how they generally gain knowledge about the world they live in is an essential part of this focus. This means not only understanding the psychology of 'selling' and 'buying' in order to sell more products to the customer (in order to sustain the viability of the firm), but also to understand that advertising, as a component of marketing, is a powerful tool. Wrong or misleading images portrayed about people and destinations can not only spoil a holiday by creating a false perception about the place, but can impact on residents by creating antagonism between visitor and visited, thus affecting the sustainability of the destination. As established earlier, traditional tourism products are framed by four well-recorded characteristics: intangibility, heterogeneity, perishability and inseparability. These idiosyncrasies mean that in marketing tourism there has to be a much higher demand for sensitivity towards the sociocultural environment. Underpinning this is the need to understand that the implications arising out of perceptions (or misconceptions) about place and race are more complex than perceptions about the relative merits of washing machines or automobiles.

Michael Hutt's paper *Looking for Shangri-la: from Hilton to Lamichhane* (Wiley, forthcoming) reminds us that many in the West have opinions about those that inhabit the poorer regions of the world. These opinions may have been formed by watching a Band Aid performance, or seeing TV news reports on Oxfam as they deal with countless tragedies around the world. Hutt's viewpoint is that mass media and popular literature create the most available images of distant and alien cultures. Hutt uses the example of James Hilton's 1933 novel *Lost Horizon,* claiming that the book has had a 'role in the shaping of western preconceptions [about] the Himalaya'. Hutt suggests that 'the phenomenon of one culture looking at another through the distorting lens of a myth which it has evolved for itself, is neither new nor confined to the West'. Lowenthal (quoted by Britton, 1979) termed this tendency to promote Third World holiday destinations as Paradise as 'the distorting lens of the picturesque'. Britton takes the argument further by examining the image of the Third World in tourism marketing, citing the (then) Premier of St Vincent James Mitchell's polemic speech 'To Hell With Paradise' which attacks the 'Eden' concept and expresses concern over the possibility of local people believing that advertised stereotypes are appropriate behavioural models. As Britton concludes:

> There is ample room for the creation and dissemination of promotional material that neither alienates the prospective visitor with oppressive visions of misery, nor pretends to depict an air conditioned Utopia, but shows uncontrived landscapes and the efforts and hopes of people at work on their economic and social development.

Jamaica Kincaid put it more succinctly: 'We are more than just a beach, we are a nation' (Kincaid, 1988:23).

The tourist brochure

Literature in its broadest interpretation is not the only input which makes up a person's concept of the Third World as tourist destination. We are, as Hughes (1980) suggested earlier, bombarded with stimuli, not least of which is the ubiquitous travel brochure. The brochures present images which are not always balanced with an appropriate measure of responsibility. The 1989/90 edition of *Go Places*, a UK holiday brochure, provides a useful illustration of stunning irresponsibility:

> PATTAYA ... *If you can suck it use it, abuse it or see it,* then it's available in this resort ... Pattaya is for those souls seeking the kind of experience they'd only read about, but never really believed. (p. 12, our italics) – as displayed in Photo 2.2 (p. 37).

If this invitation by an international (but foreign to Thailand) company to go and do whatever you want with the population of Pattaya were not enough, there is evidence of a higher degree of racist material:

> The people probably sleep with a smile on their faces ... to refuse a request or say no is not in their understanding; ... to come to terms with the Thai people, you must regard them all as Peter Pans. *Eternal children who have never grown up.* Then the silly jokes and 'the lights are on, but there's nobody at home' demeanor, will make more sense. (Our italics)

The brochure's information on The Gambia also provides an example of incipient racism and, of course, concept formation: 'There are no culture shocks in the Gambia. It's a friendly little country *where every smiling face looks like the bus conductor back home*' (p. 41, our italics). Perhaps nations subjected to this kind of cultural imperialism (defined somewhat polemically by Paul Harrison (1993:48) as 'conquer[ing] not just the bodies, but the souls of its victims, turning them into willing accomplices') need to question the value lost in terms of pride and dignity, perhaps monitor what is being said about their country. This would not prove a popular move, but then radicalism is not always popular.

Conclusion

We can see that one of the central dilemmas for tourism promoters is that while they seek to fulfil our search for the exotic there is also a hidden agenda in that many tourists also seek security. The nature of modern tourism is such that the tourist is interested in things, sights (and sites), customs and cultures different from their own, precisely because they are different. As Cohen expresses it:

> Gradually, a new value has evolved: the appreciation of the experience of strangeness and novelty. This experience now excites, titillates, and

gratifies, whereas before it only frightened. (cited in McIntosh and Goeldner, 1986:184)

However, even though such novelty and strangeness are essential elements in the tourist experience, tourists wants to feel that in the event of things becoming too strange they can fall back, for we are still:

> basically moulded by . . . native culture and bound through habit to its patterns of behaviour. Hence, complete abandonment of these customs and complete immersion in a new alien environment may be experienced as unpleasant and even threatening . . . they [want] to experience the novelty of the macro-environment of a strange place from the security of a familiar micro-environment. (Cohen, 1985)

Thus the tourist is transported not only in a conceptual bubble derived from an amalgam of stimuli, but in an environmental bubble comprising well-trodden paths equipped with familiar means of transportation, accommodation and food. The environments draw together to form, as noted previously, 'the distorting lens of the picturesque'.

The role of the tour guide in concept formation

A key actor in the cultural process of concept formation has been the tour guide. The modern role of tour guiding has its roots in the Grand Tour of the 17th and 18th centuries: 'The most satisfactory method of travelling was . . . under the direction and with the help of a *vetturino* . . . who acted as guide and courier' (Hibbert, 1987:107). They acted as intermediaries between traveller and innkeeper, and 'offered themselves to strangers of quality to serve as guides in surveying the curiosities of the place' (Hibbert, 1987:161). The role of the contemporary tourist guide is far more complex and these complexities are illustrated in Figure 2.3.

As Cohen (1985) asserts: 'For all its apparent simplicity, guiding is a complex concept'. Cohen then argues that the modern role of guide consists of social mediation and cultural brokerage, the principal components of which are:

- *The leadership sphere,* relating to his role as responsible for the 'smooth accomplishment of the tour as social enterprise', and 'leading the way'.
- *The mediatory sphere,* with the guide acting as middleman between his party and the local population, sites and institutions. (Cohen, 1985)

Within this second sphere lies the key to tour guide as concept-former. The role of mediator calls for information to be passed, and interpreting 'the strangeness of a foreign culture into a cultural idiom familiar to the visitors' (Cohen, 1985). The guide sets a framework for attitudes about place and people. This is done through the dissemination of information, facts and

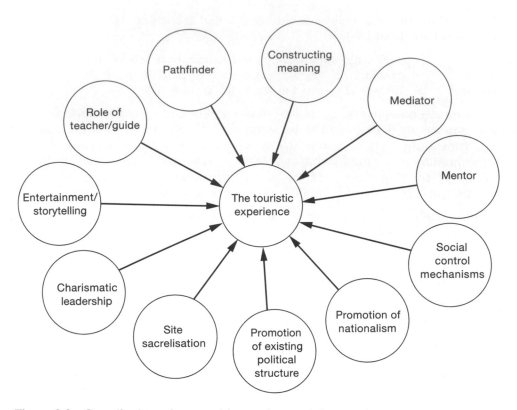

Figure 2.3 Contribution of tour guides to the touristic experience: seminar session with MA Social Anthropology of Tourism (1990) student cohort, Roehampton Institute.

figures. However, this information is rarely neutral; in some countries (especially politically sensitive ones) such information frequently reflects the policies of the establishment and is imparted to maintain a desired touristic image of the locale or to engender positive social and political impressions: 'What appears as information may thus be subtly transformed into an interpretation of the visited site intended to influence the tourists' impressions and attitudes' (Cohen, 1985). The guide thus mediates in the encounter between cultures, translating the unfamiliar, as McKean (1976, cited in Cohen) puts it: '[they] ... play a Janus-faced role ... as they look simultaneously towards their foreign clients and their ancestral tradition'.

In thinking about the role and power of the tour guide, it should not be assumed that the tourist arrives at the destination with a completely open mind about whatever strangeness he may encounter. The very act of choosing a tour means that a process of conditioning has commenced, preconceptions and expectations will have been formed as a result of a variety of media inputs (not least of which will have been the brochure). For the student of the broader aspects of tourism the interest lies in discovering who the actors are that control the processes of conditioning.

The key actors in this cultural process, be they college teacher, travel agent or the tour guide, have a potentially crucial part to play in redressing the information balance. In a sense they set the agenda, or at least they are in a position to manipulate the (total) learning experience of the tourist to avoid the promotion of Third World destinations as exotic needs – satisfiers using local population and culture as Disney-like characters on a canvas of simplistic images.

CASE STUDY: TOUR GUIDES IN SRI LANKA

The following case study details the way in which one particular country controls and monitors the licensing of tour guides where they are trained, examined and licensed by the Ceylon Tourist Board. The guides are self-employed and often combine guiding with other work, such as university teaching. The job of tour guide is generally held in high esteem by society at large (a factor which is probably a reflection of the positive way in which Sri Lankans regard education and 'knowledge'). They tend to make arrangements with a particular ground tour operator and acquire business referrals through the approved register of tour guides. There are four official grades of tour guide. Each of these grades perform a different type of function.

- *National Guide Lecturer:* the basic qualification for entry into training for this grade is GCE 'O' level. There is also a foreign language requirement. Candidates are then interviewed as to their suitability. Training lasts for about 120 hours spread over evenings and weekends. At present this is available only in Colombo (the capital city). Assessment is through a four-day practical tour covering general commentary, impromptu commentary, use of microphone, etc. There are also written theory examinations.
- *Chauffeur Guide Lecturer:* the basic qualifications for entry into training for this grade is GCE 'O' level or at least two years practical experience with a tour company. There is also a foreign language requirement. The training course lasts for 68 hours and performance is assessed through exams and a technical tour.
- *Area Guide:* the basic qualification for entry into training for this grade is GCE 'O' level or to have worked as a guide under licence from a local authority for at least two years. There is also a foreign language requirement.
- *Site Guide:* the basic qualification for entry into training for this

59

grade is GCE 'O' level or to have worked as a guide under licence from a local authority for at least one year. This, too, carries a foreign language requirement.

Candidates for all the above have to meet 'personal standards' (described in an interview with local officials as having evidence of proper 'moral' conduct); this includes formal police clearance.

There are a number of issues and challenges facing the training and organisation of tour guides. While the general framework for selecting, examining and licensing appears to be fully functional, any increase in tourism will generate a considerable demand for more guide lecturers and structures might distort the market.

Among other issues to be faced is the possibility of introducing a formal code of conduct for guides. Such a code would set out a clear set of guidelines for dealing with tourist clients and professional travel trade contacts and could be written in consultation with both tour operators and the guides' guild. Training for national tour guide lecturers is perceived to be resting on the shoulders of too few personnel. This leaves the training and examining of tour guides in a vulnerable position and has been a contributing factor to the shortage of guide lecturers. In addition, courses for National Tourist Guide Lecturers are conducted almost exclusively in Colombo. This is due to the limited number of examiners and course organisers. Also, there are no arrangements concerned with the long-term refreshing and updating of tour guide lectures once they have been issued with their licences. Finally, the tour guide training curriculum does not cover the vital areas of guest relations, meeting and greeting processes or emergency/first aid procedures.

TYPOLOGIES CASE STUDY

A leading travel company recently conducted a Global Travel Survey to establish a typology of the travelling public. Four nations were included in the survey: the United Kingdom, Japan, West Germany and the United States. 'Travellers' were defined as those who had spent at least one night away from home in paid lodging during the past year.

The company sponsored the research with the following objectives in mind:

- To provide a better understanding of the needs and attitudes of the travelling public, not just in the United States but in Europe and Asia as well.
- To determine travellers' satisfaction with various industry components and services.

- To analyse the outlook for leisure travel among the travelling public; and
- To identify barriers to travel among non-travellers.

The survey found that there are basically five types of leisure travellers. These groups experience travel in different ways even if they travel to the same place, and travel fits into their lives in different ways regardless of how often they travel. The five basic types of travellers are:

- Adventurers
- Worriers
- Dreamers
- Economisers
- Indulgers

The characteristics of each typology grouping are as follows:

Adventurers

- are motivated to seek new experiences;
- value diversity;
- seek new activities, cultures and people;
- are independent and in control;
- travel plays a central role in their lives, and
- don't need to be pampered.

They tend to agree with the following statements:

'I feel confident that I could find my way around a city that I have never visited before.'

'I really hate travelling with a group of people, even if they're people I know.'

They tend to disagree with statements such as:

'I only feel comfortable if all the details of my trip are set in advance.'

Worriers

- suffer considerable anxiety about travelling;
- travel is relatively unimportant to them; and
- are not particularly adventurous.

They tend to agree with the following statements.

'Most travelling is too stressful for me.'

61

'I worry a lot about home when I'm away.'

'I have a fear of flying.'

'I really don't have much interest in travel.'

'If I were going to another country, I'd want someone like a travel agent to help me make the important decisions.'

Dreamers

- are fascinated by travel;
- their own travel tends to be more mundane than might be expected given their travel ideas;
- their trips are orientated more toward relaxation than adventure;
- lack confidence in their ability to master the details of travelling; and
- are anxious about the stresses of travel.

They tend to agree with the following statements.

'I feel like I have to travel to enjoy life fully.'

'I can tell a lot about a person by knowing what kind of vacations they take.'

'I like to be able to impress people by telling them about the interesting places I've visited.'

'People trust me for advice about travelling.'

'I pay a lot of atention to news stories that affect travellers.'

'I really rely on maps and guidebooks when I travel to a new place.'

Economisers

- travel primarily because they need a break, i.e. travel is not a central activity for this group;
- seek value in their travel;
- their experience of travel does not add meaning to their lives; and
- their sense of adventure is low.

They agree with the statement:

'Travelling "first class" is a waste of money, even if you can afford it.'

Indulgers

- like to be pampered;
- their travel is not a central or important experience;
- are generally willing to pay for a higher level of service when they travel; and
- do not find travel intimidating or stressful.

They are most likely to agree with the following statements:

> 'I don't worry about how much things cost when I travel.'

> 'It's worth paying extra to get the special attention I want when I travel.'

They tend to disagree that:

> 'Travelling "first class" is a waste of money, even if you can afford it.'

Tourism marketing: an alternative perspective

Consuming destinations

As demonstrated in the previous section, the implications arising from some holiday and travel brochures is that the totality of a destination, including cultural and physical environments, are available for consumption if the tourist can pay enough. Not only do some tour companies play a role in this; governments, also, act to place destinations and indigenous lifestyles into the marketplace for tourist consumption. In the context of Malaysia's '2020 Vision' (the ambition to achieve developed country status by the year 2020) tourists are being invited to share the 'indigenous experience'; but this has led to some debate about the wider role of indigenous people in the new Malaysia (of their role apart from being a tourist attraction:

> 'Do they [tribal peoples] want to sit in their longhouses [tribal dwellings] for ever or join a more advanced society?' asks Malaysia's deputy Minister of Tourism, K.C. Chan. 'They are so used to their life in the jungle. If they can earn a better living from tourism, why not? It's part of the modernisation process, the 2020 vision. *We should not be proud of backward people.*' (our italics) (*Guardian*, 7 January 1994)

Tribal rights groups stand little chance in the face of such strong views. Comments such as those above from a government minister demonstrate the low priority given to community aspects in tourism marketing and planning (given that all three are inexorably connected). Academics have not always made the connection: Middleton (1988:217) makes what seems to be three perfectly reasonable points about the relationship between government policies and the marketing strategies of national tourism offices:

- generate increased tourism revenue;
- channel demand by season, and by area of the country; and
- protect consumers' interests and enhance the quality of the product.

However, while he writes of consumer protection, he appears not to acknowledge the need for residents' protection. It might be argued that residents' protection has no place in a marketing book, but whatever industrial process is being engaged in (the scale of metatourism/mass tourism allows us to think of them as industrial processes) residents have a right to protection. In some cases this protection means monitoring the local water supply for chemical run-off from agribusinesses or monitoring smoke from a factory; for tourism it might mean attempts at avoiding overcrowding (thus enabling the local population a chance of leading a 'normal' life) or somehow 'protecting' cultural assets from debasement. Maintaining these links (community, planning and marketing) is vital. Given that the main purpose of tourism marketing is to sell holidays, which in turn will secure the markets for development and economic improvement, these extra complexities (including the impact of consumption taking place at the place of production) must be taken into account.

Even so, for almost all countries the economic significance of tourism has been the driving force in encouraging its development. Thus many governments take on a role in tourism marketing (or national image building) so there is often a partnership between government and the private sector which will involve cost-sharing.

At whatever point on the continuum of alternative tourism to metatourism, destinations cannot simply remain themselves: accepted and accepting. For tourism to take place, attractions and facilities for visitors must be available. The relationship between supply and demand is illustrated by Figure 2.4. Here the holiday purchase is placed at the centre of the tourism market with the triple pressures of demand, supply and the marketplace each shaping the final decision to purchase. In turn, each of the three factors are themselves shaped by economic, cultural and political conditions that shape the external environment.

Managing access to, and the provision and planning of touristic amenities in response to the marketplace and the development of appropriate marketing initiatives requires a delicate balance, especially if the markets are calling for 'improved standards' or 'better provision'. Creating 'new' circumstances for the tourist without altering the essential character of the destination area is

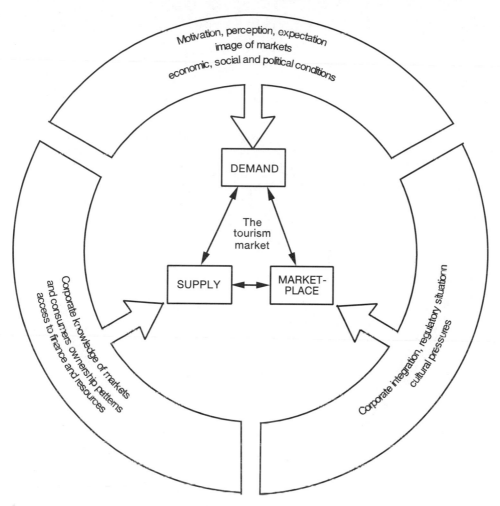

Figure 2.4 The tourism market.

probably not possible. Here we have yet another paradox of tourism demonstrated. The basis of the 'tourism product' from both a destination and tourist's perspective is its physical and cultural attributes. It is these 'raw materials' that make it attractive. However, by encouraging increasing numbers of visitors, a destination must increase its amount of accommodation, amenities and other facilities (Figure 2.5). Here we see that a broader and alternative perspective may be taken of the tourism 'product'. Three broad influences, fashion and culture, technology and global communications (and) destination attributes *each of which are subject to change and are themselves interlinked* shape the three immediate influences upon destination when seen

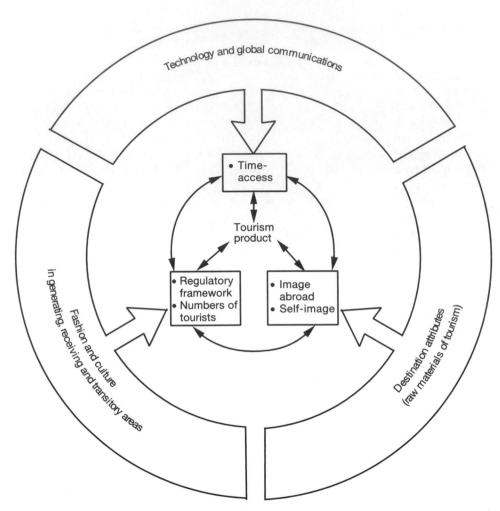

Figure 2.5 The tourism product: an alternative perspective.

as touristic product: image, regulatory framework and number of tourists, and the time/access factor.

The impacts of developments for tourists and the presence of the tourists themselves will lead to changes in the nature of the destination. The 'raw materials of tourism' can soon begin to be exhausted, especially where marketing and development strategies are aimed primarily at increasing numbers of tourists: a commentator describes it thus:

> In the developing world, [tourism] is blamed for polluting beaches, despoiling the countryside and contaminating the values of native people. In the industrial world, it is blamed for everything from the

haze of diesel fumes above London's Hyde Park Corner to the death of Venice. (*Economist*, 23 March 1991)

Paradoxically, then, a widely held perception seems to be that tourism can destroy tourism. This sort of 'get there before the tourist' idea is one motivatory factor in the tourists' search for wider horizons: further afield than the boundaries of Europe and the United States, a search for the 'unspoilt' and the 'natural'. This theme of search for the uncontaminated and exotic/ erotic foreigner, or 'Other', as Edward Said (1978) has described it, is developed by MacCannell (1989:3). His analysis of tourism uses the term 'the moderns'. He continues, 'For moderns, reality and authenticity are thought to be elsewhere: in other historical periods and other cultures, in purer, simpler lifestyles'. In postmodern and postindustrial society it is this search for the authentic, according to McCannell, that is a major driving force behind demand for tourism to developing countries, encompassing cultures perceived of as being 'unspoilt'. It is therefore in these countries' best interests for economic development to be cloaked in folksy underdevelopment . . . yet another paradox of tourism.

McCannell's theory helps to explain at least some aspects of the growing importance of long-haul holiday traffic to South East Asia and the South Pacific and other so-called 'exotic' destinations from the major tourism generating countries of the West. Such generating countries can be easily defined by measure of travel expenditure: more than 50% of total international travel expenditure is accounted for by nationals of just five countries: the United States; Germany; Japan; United Kingdom; and Italy. Table 2.5 illustrates the importance of these countries and their relationship to top tourism destinations and top tourism earners.

The use of this humanistic interpretation of tourism demand being influenced by the search for the 'unspoilt' and 'Other' has long been adopted directly or indirectly by tourism marketing. There is now an established literature in the field of tourism marketing based on established marketing techniques and methods from the business community. A key element of selling a destination in the marketplace, other than by price, is the development of a Unique Selling Proposition – the USP. Kotler (1991:273), the guru of marketing theory, explains the significance of the USP by reference to Crest toothpaste: 'Thus Crest . . . offered the benefit of "anti cavity protection" and became extremely successful. "Anti cavity protection" became its unique selling proposition.' While drawing similarities between the characteristics of toothpaste and destinations is tenuous, it does help to illustrate the point of the USP: *that it represents the critical factor for the consumer in terms of product discrimination, in a competitive market of similarly priced products.* The USP permits the consumer to perceive differences between what alternative products offer. From the point of view of the producer, it allows their product to be separated from competing products through a unique quality, a concept known as

Table 2.5 World's top spenders on travel abroad.

	1980	World share	1992	World share
Rank				
1	Germany		United States	
2	United States		Germany	
3	United Kingdom	48%	Japan	52%
4	France		United Kingdom	
5	Netherlands		Italy	
6	Japan		France	
7	Belgium		Canada	
8	Canada	16%	Netherlands	18%
9	Austria		Austria	
10	Switzerland		Sweden	
11	Italy		Switzerland	
12	Venezuela		Taiwan	
13	Argentina	9%	Belgium	10%
14	Australia		Spain	
15	Mexico		Australia	

Source: WTO.

product differentiation. Given the current state of the art of tourism marketing and promotion of long-haul (especially tropical) destinations, it is difficult for them to develop USPs from which to form the substance of their slogan or message. Promotional activities from the past mean that many potential consumers see 'all' tropical destinations as a collection of white beaches, green palms, blue skies and black servants. However, some destinations have managed to create a clear market image and 'product differentiation' (these include Singapore – but perhaps as a modern 'city-state' a unique example, and Indonesia – but increasingly the imaging of Indonesia and Malaysia is converging as far as the consumer is concerned). Thus, the USP for destinations in developing countries is likely to be increasingly associated with the uniqueness of unusual cultures as opposed to the physical environment, which may often be perceived as being similar by category of destinations, for example tropical islands, South East Asia, Africa, etc.

The nature of a destination, which Murphy (1991:166) likens to an ecosystem: 'where visitors interact with local living [hosts, services] and non-living [landscape, sunshine] parts to experience [consume] a tourism product', raises questions concerning the applicability traditional marketing theory to the 'destination product'. Middleton (1988:58) and Cooper *et al.* (1993:250) interpret the focus of marketing management decisions as being

PRODUCERS   CONSUMERS

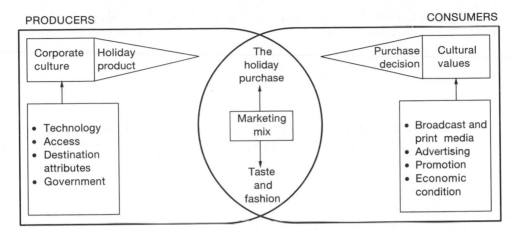

Figure 2.6   The links between producers, consumers and the marketing mix.

each of the four Ps: Product, Price, Promotion and Place. This is commonly referred to as the marketing mix. The links between corporate and governmental forces that influence the four Ps and consumers are shown in Figure 2.6. It can be seen that on the producer's side, corporate culture, technology, access and destination attractions all shape the holiday product. On the consumer side, purchasing decisions will be influenced by marketing, media and cultural mores.

   This mix has proved successful for tourism businesses but its applicability and suitability for destination marketing raises an interesting ethical dilemma about the extent to which marketing and promotional efforts can in themselves create wrong (unrealistic or salacious) perceptions of the destination. Given that it is a combination of the four Ps and the general external environment that will determine the image of destination in the marketplace, the market segments to which it will be sold, and the price it is sold for, those in a position to control the image and positioning of the destination, especially where such power brokers are foreign to the destination, have to take an ethical view.

   We have seen examples earlier in this chapter of how at least one tour operator chose to describe destinations and indigenous peoples. The image that the host community is simple, naive, and can be bought; that they are available for consumption either by the tourist as voyeur or through more direct involvement, as in the form of prostitution, is dangerous. Even so, responsibility for promoting indigenous peoples as some sort of product should not be laid entirely at the door of the tour operator. The overemphasis of tourism development for economic gain by national governments can also lead to overdevelopment which will ultimately destroy the natural and cultural resources that form the attractions base of that destination. The main influence in deciding the outcomes of any marketing strategy based around the four Ps will rest with those who retain the controlling influence over these four elements.

Product differences

The tourism 'product' has characteristics that make it different from other products. Medlik and Middleton (1973) use the following definition: 'As far as the tourist is concerned, the product covers the complete experience from the time he [sic] leaves home to the time he returns to it'. The tourist experience is one approach to a product definition, highlighting its intangibility. It is, of course, our experience as tourists that will decide how we evaluate and remember our holiday, what we say to our friends about the destination and the quality of the services such as the airline and hotel, and our decision whether to return to that destination again. This definition also demonstrates the magnitude of variables that can affect the tourist experience. Weather, pollution, hospitality, value for money, safety: many nouns have adjectives both positive and negative applied to them to describe experiences as tourists. The definition may also be extended in terms of the time duration of the experience. The experience could also include anticipation and excitement after having made the 'holiday purchase' (i.e. the booking), and should certainly include the reflective experience through memories and looking at photographs. This is another key difference between a manufactured product and the 'tourism product': unlike a car or a washing machine, all we have left after consuming the holiday product are our memories. So, as the tangible or nearly tangible component parts of this overall product comprise temporal, locational and services aspects (i.e. available time, a place to go and things to do) the tourism product may be interpreted as a consumption of services and experiences over a time continuum at a particular location.

From the point of view of businesses in tourism such as airlines and hotels, time and space are the major characteristics of the products they are marketing and selling. Airlines are selling (alongside their reputation for being a reliable and safe carrier) the space of a seat during the time span of a flight. Hotels are selling (alongside a good night's sleep and pleasant meal experience) the space of a hotel room for the duration of one night. These examples demonstrate another characteristic of the tourism product: it is highly perishable. If the hotel room is not sold that evening, if the airline seat is not sold on that flight, neither can ever be sold again and the possible revenue is lost for ever. Unlike manufactured goods (or even some services such as banking or insurance) it is impossible to store the holiday experience over time and space. The definition addresses the economic impacts of tourism in that given the diversity of the tourism experience the tourist will not only pay for direct services such as the airline or the hotel but also many indirect ones, such as shopping and entertainment.

Murphy (1991) adopts a destination perspective of the product: 'Resources and created facilities of a destination combine to produce an amalgam of activities and functions called a tourism product.' Importantly he refers to 'resources' which would include:

- the natural and cultural environment of the destination (and)
- place (location) and host community.

Destinations will be vastly different in their combination of, and reliance upon, physical and cultural attributes in forming the attractions base of that particular destination. In some cases, the extreme example being Euro-Disney, a destination may be totally man-made within less than a decade. Murphy's definition also demonstrates another key difference between a manufactured product and the destination product: the consumer has to travel to the destination in order to consume the product rather than sampling and purchasing it in a retail outlet and 'consuming' (which includes using) it home.

Middleton (1988:77–80) refers to a 'Total Tourism Product' consisting of 'destination attractions, destination facilities, accessibility of the destination, images of the destination and price to the consumer'. In this definition of tourist product the concepts of accessibility, image and price are introduced. Accessibility is a key issue in determining where tourists go. The propensity to travel is likely not to be influenced as much by distance as by accessibility, expressed in terms of time and price. Time is of utmost importance to the tourist and as long as the time and price elements balance into an acceptable equation, the tourist will be likely to purchase a trip to a chosen destination. The great technological leaps in the aviation industries post-Second World War, notably the continuing advancement of jet transport, to produce more powerful and fuel-efficient engines, means travelling times between destinations have been substantially reduced, closing the relevant distance between destinations and their generating markets. Technological advancement has also included the development of larger aircraft with resultant economies of scale and a reduction in unit cost of operation. The introduction of aircraft such as the Boeing 747–400 series, with their ability to fly further without the need for technical stopovers, and the Boeing 777, able to fly long-haul on two engines instead of four (thus reducing fuel and maintenance costs) and the generally greater capacity for passengers and cargo has ultimately meant better kilometre per seat cost-ratios. In some cases, these benefits have been passed on to passengers who, as consumers, represent a much broader social spectrum of the social population, and have the opportunity to travel further than ever before.

Middleton also includes image as being a part of the product and, as explained in the previous chapter, image is a key part in determining tourist choice. The inclusion of image in product definition introduces another key differential between the tourism product and other products: there is no

71

chance to sample the tourism product before you buy. The potential tourist does not enjoy the luxury of a 'test drive'. The closest the tourist may have come to sampling a particular 'product' before deciding to purchase it is by having visited the destination before. Unfortunately for the tourist, as already mentioned, defining the product by experience means that so many components are out of his/her control (for example, the weather and food). The chances of consistency of a similar quality of experience are therefore limited and certainly cannot be guaranteed. The purchase of the 'holiday of a lifetime' or 'the sort of holiday you can only do once' means an expensive outlay for the tourist, possibly running into thousands of pounds. Holiday loans offered by banks and building societies are now commonplace. There is likely to be a positive correlation between increased price, increased distance and perceived exoticism. The chance of the tourist having experienced the destination before is therefore substantially less than for short-haul tourism. It also less likely that members of their peer group will have experienced the destination. Their perception of the destination is likely to be based on the image presented by tour operators and the destination's marketing authorities. Paradoxically, it might well be that the further the tourist plans to travel (and the concomitant greater expenditure), the less likely they are to have had experience of the product. This places a great ethical responsibility on marketing agents to produce an accurate and honest portrayal of the destination. Tourists who are presented with idyllic images of Jamaica only to find that they cannot leave their hotels because of the threat of being harassed are likely to be less than satisfied; foreign visitors to the United Kingdom's capital city are likely to be astonished by the sight of beggars on the London Underground and the homeless sleeping rough in the doorways of the Strand. If the reality of negative environmental and social factors are chosen to be swept under the carpet, then negative impact upon the destination in terms of a drop in demand when these factors become public (especially if sensationalised in the popular press) is likely to be substantially worse than if the facts had been brought into the public arena more gradually.

The above demonstrates the complexity of trying to identify and characterise the tourism product, let alone to market it. There are many parts of the holiday experience that are out of control of the holiday producer. One bad experience from a customs official, coach driver, waiter or hotel receptionist can ruin a holiday. Importantly from the point of view of a producer this means quality control is very difficult to ensure. A hotel can aim to provide a high level of customer service and security in its environment but once the tourist leaves the hotel they are exposed to a wide variety of stimuli and experiences which will influence and determine the overall quality of their experience.

In summary, the 'tourist product' may be interpreted from the tourist viewpoint through an experience; from a business viewpoint through the selling of time and space; and from a destination view point incorporating characteristics of place and the host community as integral parts of the selling point of the destination. However, the use of the word 'product' (while an undeniably convenient term in the discourse of marketing management) is problematic and perhaps even dangerous in the sense that for tourism, the 'product' includes places and people that may not wish to be included. By using the term 'product' the association with consumption is axiomatic. From a business perspective this may be suitable and desirable. However, by putting destinations into the marketplace as products for consumption, the impacts that tourism brings to these destinations may be substantially more negative than positive, almost as though a framework is being established for the destination to pass into the decline stage of product lifecycle.

As well as applying the four Ps of marketing theory to destination marketing for continued growth, perhaps marketing strategy should encompass sustainable strategies that will address (instead of being framed by) the three Ps of negative impacts upon a destination: Pollution; Prejudice; and Prostitution.

CHAPTER 3

Globalisation, the North–South debate and tourism employment

Tourism in the context of globalisation

Introduction

It was probably the 'ozone' debates of the mid-1980s that first brought home to people that actions taken in one part of the world can have dramatic effects on other parts: 'global warming', with its attendant conferences and debates, illustrated that there was more to global theory than global products 'borne of a high-tech, fast-moving society, frequently allied with the motive to maximize profit' (Boniface and Fowler, 1993:3). The speed with which the American satellite news agency, CNN, reports events all around the globe are well documented, epitomised perhaps by the sight of a missile flying past the hotel room of the journalists reporting the Gulf War from Baghdad. Boniface and Fowler discuss this brilliantly, if cynically, in their book (1993:143–8).

Political action (or more accurately reaction) in the light of war, famine or other events is increasingly being defined in the West by TV news: 30 Californians killed in an earthquake of January 1994 received more attention than 20 000 peasants killed in India some months before . . . the news editor has video footage available, and thus decisions about lead stories are taken. Tourists shot and injured by Islamic fundamentalists in Egypt were deliberately targeted in the knowledge that attacks on tourists (be it in Tampa, London or Cairo – and for whatever reason) will be well reported. Tourism in Kashmir virtually stopped in 1992 following a series of kidnappings; in June 1994 the region was again in the news when, amid the daily tragedy that characterises India's impoverished millions, two British tourists were kidnapped by Kashmiri separatists. News coverage in the UK media of a virulent plague in India during September 1994 emphasised not so much the deaths and panic occurring in that country, but that aircraft coming in from the Subcontinent were being fumigated. This may well have been a rational move on the part of British officials, but there seemed a pervasive racism underpinning the reporting.

Tourism, then, is on the mainstream social and political agenda of most countries, and with it the resurgence of that modern myth: 'travel broadens the mind'. However, it could equally be claimed, with a somewhat jaundiced world-perspective, that under many conditions (for example, the self-contained package tour) far from broadening the mind, travel seems to confirm stereotypical images and increase prejudice. A report in *The Times Higher Educational Supplement* entitled 'Travel narrows the mind' (16 September 1994) stated that research covering some 3000 British students who had spent some of their study time at an overseas university experienced 'increase[d] xenophobia and reinforce[d] national stereotypes ... after residence abroad students look[ed] more favourably on Britain, but their regard for other countries drop[ped] dramatically'. Increased global communication seems not, in this case, to have increased international understanding. Conversely, anecdotal evidence (talking to tourists about their experiences) seems to indicate that the travel experience can truly touch hearts and minds. Pearce (1982:123–44) explores both positive and negative experiences in his chapter 'Inside the Tourists' Perspective'.

Globalisation theory

Given the increasing significance of globalisation, and the developing body of theory emerging, it is worth briefly examining the concept a little further. The term 'globalisation', first used in its contemporary sense in the mid-1980s, is rooted in the study of international relations and 'modernisation' (itself a contentious term in that some reject its predilection for concentrating on that which is measurable, such as employment, literacy, GDP, while neglecting 'quality of life' factors such as happiness). Its main themes explore the ways in which at one level (that is, at the level of trade and consumption) economic and political relations between nations and regions are increasingly framed by a sort of 'cultural convergence', where a set of values emerges across a range of countries with a tendency toward 'cultural homogeneity' (again we may refer to the influence of global marketing strategies of popular corporations such as Coca-Cola, Benetton, Marlboro, etc.). The paradox that globalisation theory tries to address is that in the face of this apparent cultural convergence there is increasing nationalism, fragmentation and polarisation. The extent to which the technological revolution in global communications has increased understanding between nations remains questionable. The underlying concern here, and one that is difficult to express because of its vagueness, relates to the 'pervasive spread of the values of consumerism, possessive individualism and status achievement' (Gill and Law, 1988:155).

75

The global economy then can be defined as 'the system generated by globalising production and global finance' (Cox, 1994:48). Cox reaches this definition after asserting that 'Finance has become decoupled from production to become an independent power, an autocrat over the real economy' (1994:48). The problem perceived by Cox in relation to globalisation is that of democracy. He sees those that idealise globalisation as being 'quick to identify democracy with the free market'. But he goes on to argue forcefully that 'Ideological mystification has obscured the fact that a stronger case can probably be made for the pairing of political authoritarianism with market economics' (1994:50). Certainly, the power accrued to global firms may be read as a threat to democracy: the case of powerful airlines making decisions that go against community consensus has been made (see Burns and Cleverdon (a) forthcoming).

Globalisation and tourism enterprises

By its very nature tourism is thought of as an international business (even though much of it takes the form of domestic tourism), but being international is not the same as being global. Bradley describes global industries as being characterised by the firm's competitive position in one country, being:

> significantly influenced by its position in other countries. In these industries firms do not operate with a collection of individual markets but a series of linked markets in which rivals compete against each other across these markets. (Bradley, 1991:100)

The general implication drawn from this by Bradley is that best advantage is gained by those firms that 'concentrate as many activities as possible in one country and serve markets from this base with a tightly coordinated marketing offering' (1991:100). While this has been so for both manufacturing and services, there have also been developments in decentralisation policies (allowing regions and individual operations greater response initiatives to the local condition) and a growth in customised products (for instance, far greater flexibility in customising package holidays). A particular problem that exists for some tourism firms following a global strategy, is that there exists something of a conflict between developing niche markets, which demands this customisation approach and globalisation which in some cases may imply homogenisation. The solution to the problem seems to lie with 'protecting' the customer from administrative elements that are best served through global policies (for a hotel chain this might be the standardised 'back of house' policies related to centralised inventory procedures, staff orientation policy and safety standards). Local management is then free to respond to the type of guest it receives. Thus, while the company operates on a global basis, in so far as the guest is concerned, they receive 'customised-customer care' at a specific location.

For tourism corporations, then, the motivation for globalisation is compelling. Their product relies on geographic diversity and unending search for the new 'paradise'. Technological advances in both transport and information systems have enabled these global service traders to think beyond traditional political–national boundaries. The 'pleasure periphery' is shrinking. In April 1994 Airtours (UK) announced a new round in the constant air-fares war that dominates certain sectors of European holiday travel. Fares from £499 were announced for the pre-Christmas season, with an entire 14-day package to Sydney including flight, accommodation and transfers available from £599. International competition has driven such corporations into thinking globally. By integrating corporate activities on a worldwide basis through referral systems, computerised reservation systems and vertical integration with other sectors, competitive advantage is gained by controlling the international distribution channel. Poon (1993:215) also describes how tourism firms are integrating diagonally: that is, not through buy-outs or takeovers, but through strategic alliances which bring together not only the travel and accommodation sectors but suppliers of insurance and financial services (travellers' cheques and credit cards). Poon terms these alliances 'information partnerships' (1993:224) which emphasises her central theme that information transfers through technology will come to dominate the marketing and management of the sector.

For transnational hospitality enterprises, Tse and West (1992: 124) identified four primary forces which underpin the motivation for international expansion:

- maturing hospitality industries with high levels of penetration in traditional markets find domestic growth problematic;
- increased travel to and from the Far East (leisure and business) has provided dramatic new market opportunities;
- increasing tendency for brand loyalty within the lodging industry means that a global presence is one rational response to this; and
- a global operation can provide opportunities to increase business in areas of economic upturn and hedge against economic downturns in other locations.

At one level, critical issues of globalisation are described by Tse and West as being generally the same as the challenges to be found in the domestic market (1992:121). However, they do note that 'perceptual maps of competitors and markets' need to be revised, with the best strategy for this being the establishment of an international headquarters which is able to take the global viewpoint. This head office macroview alluded to by Tse and West is seen by them as including the following:

- 'corporate intelligence and information gathering', including national sociopolitical environments and competitor activity; and
- 'assessing capabilities' concerning organisational and market strengths and weaknesses.

Tse and West (1992:124) have also identified four streams of thought for effective strategic management in a global context:

- effective global strategy as the successful practice of product standardisation;
- exploiting economies of scale through global volume, creating synergy through effective management communication and taking pre-emptive investment decisions;
- broad range of products sharing the same distribution channels, strategic cross subsidisation where necessary; and
- acknowledging the volatility of global markets through multiple sourcing, shifting production to gain maximum cost effectiveness and rigorous practice of arbitrage.

However, such strategies are not without their dangers. We have already referred to the paradoxes of niche operations in global markets, and of the standardisation versus customisation debate. In putting product standardisation forward as a strategic option for corporations the implications of this will have to be recognised.

Standardisation

One of the continuing themes for international corporations within the globalisation debate of is that of standardisation (see Figure 3.1). That is to say, standardising the 'product', which for our purposes may be taken to mean:

- the physical corporate product such as architecture, decor and promotional literature;
- the intellectual corporate product, meaning standard operating procedures and personnel practices; and
- the emotional product, meaning 'hospitality' and service attitudes from front line staff in dealing with guests.

As illustrated in Figure 3.1, all three are framed by changing consumer values which will include the motivation behind the final decision to purchase. We have seen that at one pole of the global strategic management continuum there is the simplistic argument that global markets require global non-differentiated products, and marketing. The problem for tourism enterprises (as opposed to, for instance, a manufacturing enterprise) is that part of the

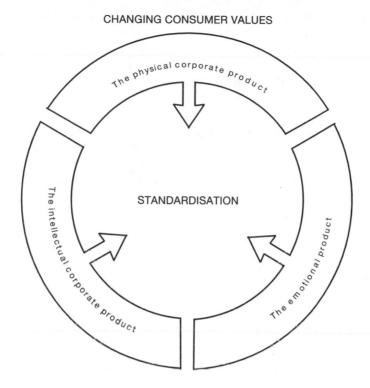

Figure 3.1 The pressures for standardisation.

product is the unique character of the destination attractions. These may well include culture and people. This invokes an intellectual argument (rehearsed elsewhere in this book) about whether culture and people should be enmeshed in corporate marketing strategies. The process of standardisation, an almost inevitable consequence of the vast chains of connectedness that comprise the major tourism groups, may dilute what is most precious about a destination: its individualism ... especially if it is being promoted to potential tourists in the industrialised and postindustrial world whose motivation for travel might well be a reaction to a lack of individuality. There are, however, certain aspects of standardisation that could be implemented as efficiency measures such as 'single sourcing'. For instance, Forte Hotels 'single source' all their international Information Technology provision from IBM (Jones, 1993:143). These issues will be dealt with at corporate level by the procurement division. Another argument for standardisation is that it assures consistency; this was (and remains to some extent) one of the founding tenets of the Holiday Inn empire and an idea which became something of an obsession in Holiday Inn's corporate thinking of the 1970s. Marketing and product were standard and global in spite of location or local conditions. In some instances this global strategy is clearly linked to financial success. The names McDonald's, Kentucky Fried Chicken and Coca-Cola conjure up a positive expectation of consistency in the products and confidence in the back of house operations (mostly to do with sanitation and safety issues).

While it is claimed that the drive for standardisation is becoming less of a priority in corporate strategic thinking (Olsen and Merna, 1993:95), the issue creates a paradox within the emerging work on creating customer-orientated organisations: a sort of cost–effectiveness continuum with 'reducing costs by standardisation' as one pole and increasing customer satisfaction through 'increased customisation' as the other. Bowen and Basch (1992:208) describe the greatest test for service-orientated organisations as being how non-routine enquiries or events are dealt with. Any moves away from standardisation are likely to be framed by the following three factors:

- greater understanding on the part of 'producers' that many of tourism's products are not 'naturally' homogeneous;
- customer reaction against 'industrialisation' of services (what Ritzer (1993) generally refers to as McDonaldisation of society); and
- realisation that the tourists themselves are not a particularly homogeneous group.

This has resulted in:

- greater decentralised decision-making (local managers taking responsibility and accountability);
- moves away from mechanistic (rigid and hierarchical) structures; linked to
- increased moves to organic (flexible interaction and lateral communication and knowledge sharing at all levels).

However, for some organisations, particularly those suited to an industrialised process such as fast food restaurants, there is no mistaking the underlying trend: not of postmodernism, postindustrialism or postFordism, but of *modernism*, that is corporate action firmly rooted in Taylorist 'scientific modern management'. The emphasis is on rationalism 'conveyor belt' work process (not only in an allegorical sense, but also literally in that in catering some ovens and grills literally work on the conveyor belt system). Thus we find a curious scheme of things where modernism prospers within postmodern society. In the final analysis, it is Ritzer (1993:157) who reminds us that so-called postindustrialism and the concomitant postmodern age is still defined by a capitalist mode of production which has been 'globally dominant for the past two centuries'.

Conclusion

Marketing, then, is an activity which has a particular poignancy when it takes place under the conditions of metatourism. The phenomenon of metatourism has not come about through any sort of 'natural' domestic economic or social process. Most Third World countries have little or no domestic leisure tourism upon which to build their international tourism. Demand for any significant form of tourism (other than individual travellers 'passing through') is not even likely to come from potential tourists. Rather, the process by which such countries become integrated into the global nexus that frames tourism is likely to be through the specific actions of development banks, international aid agencies, international tour and transport operators and foreign investors.

We can see that tourism is a global system in the social, political and economic sense of the word. What happens in one country, be it receiving or generating, has repercussions on other countries. The economic fortunes of countries that rely on tourism are inexorably linked to the social trends and wellbeing of the countries that generate the tourists. Robertson (1992:5) asserts that 'international politics is cultural, we are . . . in a period of globewide *cultural* politics . . . The "official" link between domestic and foreign affairs is rapidly crumbling'. We see this in the waiving of travel visa requirements and the easing of currency controls. Entry to and exit from the former Eastern bloc countries has never been easier. Access to travel and capital and the development of two-way tourism is creating global links through cultural political in countries as diverse as Japan (where outbound tourism was deliberately used by the government to increase Japanese awareness of the outside world) to Russia, where outbound tourism combined with business acts as a driving force for the new breed of entrepreneurs. Once again, it is Robertson who encapsulates the spirit of the moment:

> With the rapid growth of various supranational and transnational organisations, movements and institutions (such as global capitalism and global media system) the boundaries between societies have become more porous because they are much more subject to 'interference and constraint' from outside. (Robertson, 1992:5)

Tourism's place in the North–South debate

Destinations are attractive in the measure they are unspoiled. Yet the very act of going to them spoils them and despoils them. The westerner goes to find somewhere uncontaminated by westernisation. His visit, in itself, contaminates ... The western tourist is unable to escape his own shadow, and a protective wall of western comforts and debased imitations of local culture grow up around him. (Harrison, 1993:58)

Introduction

The purpose of this section is to provide a focus on the main characteristics of tourism and the Third World. A start was made in the opening chapter, which introduced the notion of metatourism as an analytical tool to help us understand the dynamics that shape the relationship between the so-called North and South. In relation to this pleasure industry, it is perhaps worth reminding ourselves that Third World governments do not enter into the garment industry to provide apparel for the fashion conscious, or develop cash crops in order to fill the plates of hungry Westerners. These are clearly and only economic activities, the intention of which is to bring in foreign exchange and create jobs. Given this axiom, it should also be quite clear that Third World governments do not enter the tourism business in order to provide holiday destinations in the sun where exhausted workers from the industrialised North can recharge their batteries by relaxing in the unhurried and friendly lifestyle of pre-industrialised conditions.

Concepts and dynamics of 'North–South' tourism

Most tourism actually occurs within and between the developed world (i.e. in Europe and North America); this is illustrated by Tables 3.1 and 3.2 (the top tourism destinations and the world's top tourism earners). However, much of the debate about tourism's effects are centred upon the Third World. This is easy to understand. Tourism between countries whose citizens enjoy relative equality of opportunity (social and economic), where there are distinct possibilities for reciprocal visits, are less problematic than between countries that have dramatic differences in living standards and far greater restrictions over travel aspirations and opportunity. The following two Tables (3.3 and 3.4) also demonstrate the differences in share of both arrivals and tourist dollar receipts between developed and developing countries.

In general terms, Fitzsimmons and Fitzsimmons (1994) provide us with an interactive (and thus holistic) model of an economy (Figure 3.2). This helps us to place trade and services in their economic relationship in relationship to consumer, infrastructure, manufacturing and, of course, the consumer. Tourism's place in this model, if we accept that tourism is a broad, generative and integrated sector, is difficult to place. It fits into seven of the eight categories put forward by Fitzsimmons and Fitzsimmons. In relation to the Third World, tourism was recognised as an 'industry' by international economists from about the 1960s, and this view became mainstream following the setting up, in 1967, of the World Bank's Tourism Projects Department. This organisation was given the brief to carry out feasibility studies and to make loans for suitable tourism projects. As an example of the scale of assistance, it lent £62 million to improve tourism infrastructure at Luxor in Egypt; the Bank stopped making such loans in 1980 (Gamble, 1989:31). Wyer and Towner (1988:20) capture the mood:

> [Tourism] appeared to capitalise on what might otherwise be con- sidered economic liabilities: under-developed scenic regions, unassimi- lated ethnic groups, non-industrial cities, small cottage industries and an exotic wildlife. It was a period when many former colonies were either emerging into the first years of independence or in their last years as colonial dependencies. The declining terms of trade for most exports during this period – 2.5% a year between 1971 and 1976 for underdeveloped countries . . . encouraged many to turn to tourism. It also appeared more attractive as import-substitution industries ran into difficulties.

Table 3.1   Top tourism destinations.

Rank	1980	World share	1992	World share
1	France		France	
2	Spain		United States	
3	United States	39%	Spain	40%
4	Italy		Italy	
5	Austria		Hungary	
6	Canada		Austria	
7	United Kingdom		United Kingdom	
8	Mexico	20%	Mexico	18%
9	Germany		Germany	
10	Hungary		Canada	
11	Switzerland		Switzerland	
12	Romania		China	
13	Yugoslavia*	12%	Portugal	11%
14	Poland		Czechoslovakia	
15	Bulgaria		Greece	

* Former Yugoslavia.
Source: WTO.

The way in which the international tourism industry and the Third World interacts presents a number of problems for social and political scientists (including Britton, 1982; Wyer and Towner, 1988; Ascher, 1985; Bryden, 1973). The concerns can be summarised as:

- the development of 'islands of affluence' in the midst of poverty;
- the use of scarce national resources for the enjoyment of wealthy foreigners;
- the 'demonstration effect' upon the local population of observing the mass consumption of indolence;
- economic multipliers, the main tool for 'measuring' the flow of touristic money through national economies, remain controversial and unreliable;
- the commercialisation of culture and lifestyles;
- the benefits are likely to accrue to foreign companies or local élites; and
- the reality of international tourism structures mean that control is likely to be external to the destination and defined by transnational tourism corporations.

Table 3.2 World's top tourism earners

Rank	1980	World share	1992	World share
1	United States		United States	
2	France		France	
3	Italy	40%	Spain	45%
4	Spain		Italy	
5	United Kingdom		Austria	
6	Germany		United Kingdom	
7	Austria		Germany	
8	Mexico	22%	Switzerland	16%
9	Switzerland		Singapore	
10	Canada		Canada	
11	Belgium		Hong Kong	
12	Brazil		Netherlands	
13	Greece	8%	Mexico	8%
14	Netherlands		Australia	
15	Singapore		Thailand	

Source: WTO.

84

Table 3.3 International tourism receipts: values, average annual growth rates and world shares by country groupings, 1980–1985–1992.

	Values (US$ Million)			Growth rates (Percentages)			World shares (Percentages)		
	1980	1985	1992	80–85	85–92	80–92	1980	1985	1992
World	103 535	115 070	297 853	2.3	14.4	9.2	100.0	100.0	100.0
Developed countries	72 788	80 386	215 483	2.0	15.1	9.5	70.3	69.3	72.3
Developing countries 1/	28 484	32 980	75 072	3.0	12.5	8.4	27.5	28.4	25.2
Others 2/	2 263	2 604	7 298	2.8	15.9	10.2	2.2	2.2	2.5
West Europe 3/	59 946	59 556	152 051	-0.1	14.3	8.1	57.9	51.4	51.0
Central and East Europe	1 708	625	3 270	-1.0	10.5	5.6	1.6	1.4	1.1
North America	17 735	23 766	65 537	6.0	15.6	11.5	17.1	20.5	22.0
Caribbean	3 483	4 978	9 574	7.4	9.8	8.8	3.4	4.3	3.2
Central and South America	4 285	4 396	8 441	0.5	9.8	5.8	4.1	3.8	2.8
East Asia and the Pacific	8 643	12 845	45 606	8.2	19.9	14.9	8.4	11.1	15.3
Africa	2 711	2 601	5 907	-0.8	12.4	6.7	2.6	2.2	2.0
Middle East	3 470	4 803	5 400	6.7	1.7	3.8	3.4	4.1	1.8
South Asia	1 549	1 400	2 037	-2.0	5.5	2.3	1.5	1.2	0.7
OECD	71 538	80 327	215 938	2.3	15.2	9.6	69.1	69.3	72.5
EEC	45 043	44 510	115 160	-0.2	14.5	8.1	43.5	38.5	38.7
EFTA	12 004	10 758	28 987	-2.2	15.2	7.6	11.6	9.3	9.7
ASEAN	3 140	5 014	16 239	9.8	18.3	14.7	3.0	4.3	5.5
Mediterranean countries	30 136	33 024	85 775	1.8	14.6	9.1	29.1	28.5	28.8

Source: WTO.

85

Table 3.4 International tourist arrivals: volume, average annual growth rates and world shares by country groupings, 1980–1985–1992.

	Volume (000 Arrivals)			Growth rates (Percentages)			World shares (Percentages)		
	1980	1985	1992	80–85	85–92	80–92	1980	1985	1992
World	287 787	329 616	481 563	2.8	5.6	4.4	100.0	100.0	100.0
Developed countries	180 234	214 087	298 901	3.5	4.9	4.3	62.6	65.0	62.1
Developing countries 1/	64 380	76 743	116 712	3.6	6.2	5.1	22.4	23.3	24.2
Others 2/	43 173	38 786	65 950	-2.1	7.9	3.6	15.0	11.8	13.7
West Europe 3/	150 357	182 828	241 101	4.0	4.0	4.0	52.2	55.5	50.1
Central and East Europe	39 473	31 436	49 118	-4.5	6.6	1.8	13.7	9.5	10.2
North America	47 321	50 477	76 659	1.3	6.2	4.1	16.4	15.3	15.9
Caribbean	6 750	7 968	11 655	3.4	5.6	4.7	2.3	2.4	2.4
Central and South America	7 316	8 032	12 823	1.9	6.9	4.8	2.5	2.4	2.7
East Asia and the Pacific	20 961	30 389	61 306	7.7	10.5	9.4	7.3	9.2	12.7
Africa	7 337	9 706	17 471	5.8	8.8	7.5	2.5	2.9	3.6
Middle East	5 992	6 240	7 921	0.8	3.5	2.4	2.1	1.9	1.6
South Asia	2 280	2 540	3 509	2.2	4.7	3.7	0.8	0.8	0.7
OECD	178 619	213 408	300 067	3.6	5.0	4.4	62.1	64.7	62.3
EEC	115 063	138 199	192 512	3.7	4.8	4.4	40.0	41.9	40.0
EFTA	25 110	30 585	35 928	4.0	2.3	3.0	8.7	9.3	7.5
ASEAN	8 300	10 011	21 205	3.8	11.3	8.1	2.9	3.0	4.4
Mediterranean countries	95 581	116 311	159 271	3.8	4.6	4.3	33.6	35.3	33.1

Low-income economies	**9 303**	**14 609**	**30 242**	**9.4**	**11.0**	**10.3**	**3.2**	**4.4**	**6.3**
China and India	4 694	8 392	18 380	12.3	11.9	12.0	1.6	2.5	3.8
Other low-income	4 609	6 217	11 862	6.2	9.7	8.2	1.6	1.9	2.5
Middle-income economies	**95 653**	**99 569**	**152 810**	**0.8**	**6.3**	**4.0**	**33.2**	**30.2**	**31.7**
Lower-middle-income	41 526	38 923	62 446	-1.3	7.0	3.5	14.4	11.8	13.0
Upper-middle-income	54 127	50 646	90 364	2.3	5.9	4.4	18.8	18.4	18.8
High-income economies	**180 656**	**213 040**	**297 175**	**3.4**	**4.9**	**4.2**	**62.8**	**64.6**	**51.7**
Exporters of manufactures	**112 349**	**120 900**	**167 874**	**1.5**	**4.8**	**3.4**	**39.0**	**36.7**	**34.9**
Low- and middle-income	44 082	40 155	72 040	-1.8	8.7	4.2	15.3	12.2	15.0
High-income	68 267	80 745	95 833	3.4	2.5	2.9	23.7	24.5	19.9
Exporters of nonfuel primary products	**5 951**	**6 986**	**12 153**	**3.3**	**8.2**	**6.1**	**2.1**	**2.1**	**2.5**
Low- and middle-income	5 420	6 219	10 954	2.8	8.4	6.0	1.9	1.9	2.3
High-income	531	767	1 199	7.6	6.6	7.0	0.2	0.2	0.2
Exporters of fuels (mainly oil)	**4 747**	**5 868**	**4 994**	**4.3**	**-2.3**	**0.4**	**1.6**	**1.8**	**1.0**
Low- and middle-income	4 075	4 950	3 953	4.0	-3.2	-0.3	1.4	1.5	0.8
High-income	672	908	1 041	6.2	2.0	3.7	0.2	0.3	0.2

Source: WTO.

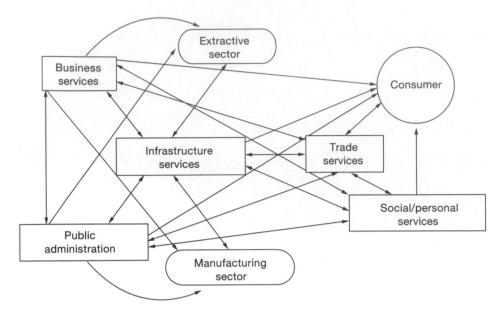

Figure 3.2 Interactive model of an economy.
Source: Fitzsimmons and Fitzsimmons (1994:4).

It is this last point, the likelihood of exogenous control of the industry and the reliance that has to be placed upon transnational airlines, hotel groups and service providers, that is the root of the problems. While tourism planners and tourism master plans increasingly address this particular *problématique*, it remains a continuing challenge for Third World destinations. Britton offers this illustrative analysis of the core–periphery nature of the political economy of tourism (Figure 3.3).

Here we see a definite hierarchical structure, with corporate head offices at the top. In Britton's model, these are seen dealing directly with the tourist industry and national tourist offices, which in turn (and down the line) deal with the resort enclaves. Metatourism takes this on a step by recognising that if the resort enclaves are owned and/or managed by transnational tourism corporations, communication lines might be such that large parts of the tourism sector and the national tourist office is effectively frozen out. Richter, in her analysis of the political nature of tourism, observes:

> Unfortunately, most how-to-do-it kits for tourism development have come in the form of advice from the World Tourism Organization or large travel industry firms interested in promoting this or that destination. As shown [throughout Richter's book] their advice is often at its best only concerned with large-scale, mass, or charter

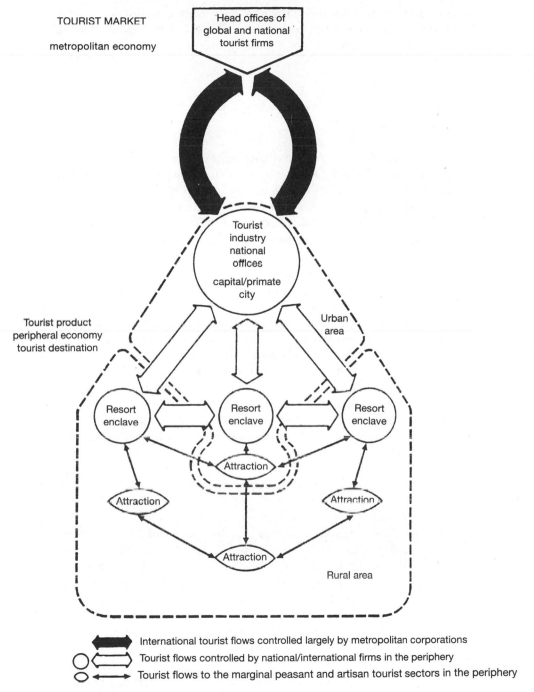

Figure 3.3 Enclave model of tourism in a peripheral economy.
Source: Lea (1988:15).

tourism and at its worst self-serving and misleading. In any event these organisations are concerned quite naturally with developing tourism and not with using tourism as a vehicle for development. (Richter, 1989:182)

DEVELOPMENT ASSISTANCE AND THE TURKS AND CAICOS ISLANDS

Linda Richter's provocative observations are encapsulated by the curious case of British Government tourism assistance to the Turks and Caicos islands in the West Indies. The group lies between Miami and Puerto Rico and are separated from the Bahamas by 30 miles of ocean. In many senses it is a classic 'micro-state' (Burns and Cleverdon, 1994) exhibiting all the characteristics such as limited human and physical resources; colonial ties; markets defined by exogenous influences and limited domestic investment capability. The group is made up of some 40 islands and cays which total 166 square miles, of which Providenciales accounts for 37.5 square miles. This was the island chosen for development by the Overseas Development Administration (ODA), the government department that develops policy and delivers Britain's official bilateral aid programme. The archipelago enjoys what most potential holiday-makers would describe as 'ideal' weather with temperatures ranging from 77–83°F. The population at the time was around 8000, of whom less than 1000 were on Providenciales. Like other microstates, it tried various forms of economic activity and has been particularly successful in establishing confidential offshore banking facilities.

Tourists first arrived on the island of Providenciales through the entrepreneurial activities of an American, Fritz Ludington, in the late 1960s. Club Med officials first visited the 70-acre site at Grace Bay in April 1980 after being approached by a firm of international estate agents in 1979. Club Med agreed that the site would meet their needs but insisted on infrastructure being in place, including an airport capable of long-haul traffic, 10 miles of paved roads and a minimum daily supply of 80 000 gallons of fresh water. Based on the advice of experts, and persuaded that a massive injection of assistance would enable the Turks and Caicos to cut its economic dependence on Britain, in the early 1980s the ODA agreed to provide the infrastructure to service the proposed tourism development at an eventual cost of some £6.11 million.

The rationale behind the aid package was that tourism would focus on a new 750-bed Club Mediteranée resort. A deal was struck between the British Government and Club Med: ODA would provide the airport and Club Med would construct the resort. The airport was completed on time; the resort, however, was another story.

Critics of the plans said that the scheme 'would provide an airport that was not necessary, paved roads for foreigners, and provide jobs where there was no unemployment' (Foreign Affairs Committee, 1983). The airport and roads were completed in 1982. Club Med in the meantime had not delivered its part of the deal, which was to complete the holiday village by December 1982; even as late as September 1982, work on the resort had not started. The (then) British Minister for Overseas Development, Timothy Raison, was driven to threatening legal action against the Club. Finally, in February 1983 Club Med signed a contract with a British firm (the same company that had built the airport) to construct a smaller 576-bed resort. This episode coloured the British government's view on assisting tourism for many years to come.

The dominance of tourism organisations from industrial countries in international tourism flows and the reliance upon foreign capital for destination development can be interpreted as a consequence of the colonial or other political systems that previously framed the relationship between developing and developed countries. Lea (1988:12) adopts a political economy approach to analyse tourism development as being a consequence of imperial domination of the Third World in the past and the pattern of trading links and spheres of influence established at this time. This reliance upon the developed world for capital investment and markets is the underpinning for what development economists and others have referred to as 'dependency theory'. Gamble provides two interesting figures (3.4 and 3.5) that illustrate the roads to either 'virtuous development' or 'vicious poverty'. Lea (1988:13) picks up the theme:

> Metropolitan companies, institutions, and governments in the post-colonial period have maintained special trading relationships with certain élite counterparts in Third World countries. These representatives of the ruling classes gain most benefit from the less-than-equal share of income and profits which remain inside a peripheral economy.

Burton, in her geographical analysis of tourism, provides a useful representation of the core–periphery regions of the world (Figure 3.6). As Richter (1989:17) succinctly puts it, 'Tourism development is a policy area only if political élites decide it to be.' In South East Asia, notably Thailand, Malaysia, Singapore and Indonesia, tourism has been developed with the aid of western capital: in this sense, tourism has acted as a catalyst to further economic development; such economies have developed quantifiably in the

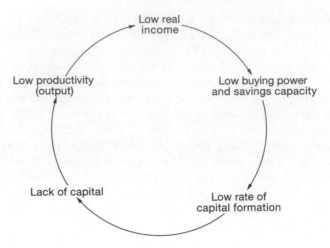

Figure 3.4 The vicious circle of poverty.
Source: Gamble (1989:9).

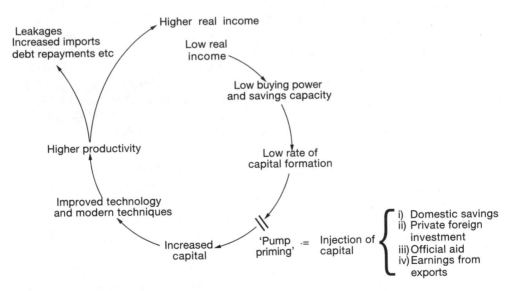

Figure 3.5 The virtuous circle of economic development.
Source: Gamble (1989:9).

last decade. This economic advancement is not, of course, due solely to tourism but where tourists enjoy countries as a destination, it may be

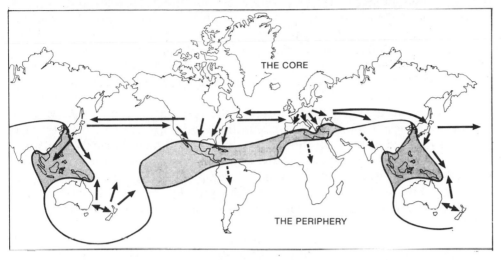

Figure 3.6   Core–periphery tourist regions of the world. □, Transitional zone of the economic periphery (tourist destination zone); →, major tourist flows; – – →, minor tourist flows.
Source: Burton (1991:85).

influential in creating the right sort of political image to attract capital investment. Richter (1989:6) states: 'The existence of tourism affirms the nation's legitimacy and a faith in its internal security.' Countries that are not privy to this political bonhomie, such as Vietnam, Burma, Cambodia and North Korea, have neither been able to develop their tourism sectors easily nor enjoyed the concomitant economic benefits. The case of tourism development being used to demonstrate political success was nowhere clearer than in the Philippines. Richter gives a fascinating account of how tourism was used for political advantage by the Marcos regime. Of special significance was the decision to hold the International Monetary Fund–World Bank Conference in Manila in 1976. Richter (1989:56) comments:

> The tantalizing prospect of hosting 5000 VIPs, even for just a week, led to a rush to complete 12 luxury hotels within 18 months, though the tourism master plan had not expected such accommodation needs for at least a decade . . . From a development stand-point, the expenditure of hotel financing alone is between 30 and 40 times the amount the government has spent on public housing.

The slogan promoted by Marcos to promote Philippine tourism, 'Where Asia wears a smile', hid the political agenda and lack of investment in the majority of the poor Philippines people. However, the conference was hailed a great success by the bankers, who were impressed by the tremendous

93

redevelopment of Manila Harbour where the new hotels were located, and the strong law and order situation that seemed to have been established under the Marcos regime. Yet, accompanying the development – indeed, driving development as Bello and Rosenfeld (1992) would have it – has been a series of conflicts such as the Korean War, the Vietnam War, Cambodia, the political position of Hong Kong and the perceived threat of North Korea illustrating the volatile political nature of this region. It is perhaps no surprise then that favoured countries who have enjoyed the political support of western countries, especially the United States, in this region for strategic reasons have largely prospered in terms of their economic development. For example, after the Vietnam War Thailand was positively encouraged by the United Nations to develop tourism as part of its economic development programme building on the links developed between the US military R&R (Rest and Recuperation) programme and Thailand as a pleasure playground during the Vietnam War (BBC '40 Minutes' documentary). Today Thailand remains one of the main tourism destinations in South East Asia and along with Malaysia, Indonesia and Singapore has one of the fastest growing economies. Evidence of American, European and Japanese investment in tourism can be seen in politically favoured countries by walking the streets of the central areas of the large cities of this region, such as Jakarta, Bangkok, Kuala Lumpur and Singapore. Hilton International, Inter-Continental, Sheraton, Ramada, etc. are evident along with the names of other major multinational corporations, including McDonald's and Pizza Land. In these cities you will also find the offices of all the major western airlines including American Airlines, British Airways, Air France and Lufthansa. The presence of multinational companies represent the icons of a modernised state and are symbolic of economic advancement and political success. Tourism can be used to achieve and demonstrate political success through exposing a country in the international market to the mass consumerism of the West. The presence of multinationals may legitimate a repressive political regime to the outside world. It may also offer internal political security; as Richter (1989:6) says: 'Tourists also help to support cultural facilities that soften the political realities and which could not normally be supported by domestic clientele.'

Destination attributes and resources as commodities?

Many developing countries have a natural resource base of both physical (coral reefs and long palm-fringed sandy beaches) and cultural attractions (including – with a sense of irony – smiling, colourful, simple peoples) that are perceived as 'exotic' by those in the generating countries (predominantly the West, but increasingly Taiwan, Singapore and other NICs which have a burgeoning and travelling middle class). This sense of the exotic is a clear 'push' factor in so far as tourist motivation is concerned, creating in some a desire to see or visit the exotic 'Other', as Said (1978) might term it. This broad range of supply factors, combined with encouragement from western banks and international lending agencies, such as the United Nations and European Union, reinforced with the rhetoric of tourism being the world's major growth sector, has led many countries to adopt a tourism development policy. Richter (1989:5) puts forward Young's observation which highlights the economic benefits of tourism as portrayed through quantification:

> A painstaking analysis by Soviet statisticians has revealed that the average profit, if that is the right word, from one tourist is equal to the export of nine tons of coal, fifteen tons of oil or two tons of grain. Further if Lake Baikal were exploited as a tourist centre, it would earn twice as much hard currency as the total export of oil from the USSR – without depleting its stock of raw materials.

While environmentalists may be a little more than concerned over the implication that the development of tourism is resource-free, the quantification of economic impacts and use of statistical analysis has produced a very convincing argument for national governments to develop tourism. When national governments of developing countries are also faced with large debts and a demographic structure where an increasing percentage of the population are children, and commodity prices have plummeted (see Susan George's radical book on the Third World debt crisis, *A Fate Worse Than Debt*, for a high quality and informed analysis of this problem) tourism becomes even more of an attractive alternative development option, or even a necessity. Gunn (1988) asserts

> Worldwide, tourism is looked upon as a smokeless industry with strong and stable economic impacts on host areas . . . Tourism is viewed as the new wave of economic opportunity and is promoted heavily for this reason alone.

Among many of the cited economic benefits are foreign exchange, contribution to Gross National Product, employment creation and income generation. Therefore for many lesser developed countries tourism offers an attractive and relatively quick development route to earn hard currencies, provide employment and to help repay foreign debts. In an increasing number of countries tourism has surpassed more traditional primary industries as the largest earner of foreign exchange.

Sinclair (1991) emphasises this point, commenting that in 1988 Kenya's travel receipts contributed 20% of the total export earnings and exceeded the receipts that were gained from the sale of tea and commodity crops. The position of many developing countries means that tourism is increasingly looked on as a development option. For some countries with limited physical size and resource base, *not to have tourism is not an option*. Timberlake and Thomas (1990) discuss the need of all developing countries to diversify their economies to help repay large debts. The virtual collapse of the world primary commodity market (see Susan George (1993) and Paul Harrison (1993)) meant that in 1986 prices plummeted to their lowest levels this century. Unfortunately this coincided with a time when many developing nations had taken large loans from western banks and governments against the security of high commodity prices achieved in the late 1970s and early 1980s. This left many developing countries with an urgent need to repay foreign debts but without the hard currencies to do so. Within this setting tourism development in the 1980s became an important consideration for many countries. In effect, this has meant that many governments interpret tourism as a commodity in terms of achieving similar economic and social objectives to more traditional commodities.

Not all economists would agree with the analogy of tourism as primary production of cash crops such as tea and cotton. However, this analogy can serve as a useful reminder as to the purpose and consuming nature of 'producing' tourism – especially if we re-examine the definition of a commodity: 'convenience: profit, expediency, advantage, privilege: an article of traffic: goods, produce' (Chambers Dictionary, 1972). Although economists and caring tour operators may be upset to read of tourists as articles of traffic, for tourist businesses from airlines to attractions which rely upon the tourist trade, it is the profit that can be made from this movement of tourists between countries that is the reason for their existence. Considering the major generating markets of Europe and the United States it is appropriate to apply the terms 'advantage' and 'privilege' to those tourists who can afford to visit developing countries. For developing countries it is expedient to develop tourism in hope of attaining the economic benefits already outlined.

Many governments of lesser developed countries encouraged by the quantification of tourism displaying rapid growth in tourism demand set against a background of a collapse in the commodity markets, interpret tourism as a complementary or substitute foreign exchange earner for traditional commodities. The way the tourism industry has been established in developing countries displays many similarities in its pattern of development and reliance on western markets to that of primary crop production.

These points illustrate the reliance of Third World nations upon the industrialised countries (generally the 'North' including Japan) for tourism development. This leads to an unequal power relationship between investing, generating and receiving countries: Third World receiving countries, in effect, have only limited control over how tourism is developed. Any private investor or major lending institution will have a range of criteria to decide where they will invest money for tourism development. Political stability and friendliness to the West is one of these. It is reasonable to speculate that Vietnam would have had a more substantially developed tourism industry than at present were it not for the trade embargo that had been placed against it until 1994 by the United States.

The *Guardian* newspaper (7 May 1991) highlighted the almost total reliance of Sierra Leone on western aid and western markets for the development of its tourism sector with the inevitable resultant metatourism. One of the world's poorest nations, the country has a pressing need for economic development. However, in 1989 tourism made a contribution of only 2% to the Gross National Product. Sierra Leone has just 8 hotels and most of the 25 000 tourists came from France, North America and the United Kingdom. In 1991 the government passed a Tourism Development Bill which offers incentives for foreign investment in tourism. Meanwhile, with funding received from the European Community the government hopes to improve the infrastructure of the country. It is clearly the case that without overseas investment, tourism development (with all the potential it offers) cannot take place. Equally clear is that tourism development alone is not sufficient to attract tourists; reliable infrastructure has to be in place. Thus we see a classic case of metatourism at its early stages, with supply being tailored by exogenous forces that will no doubt have negative effects on leakage and long-term sustainability.

Research conducted in Kenya into ownership of the tourism plant found that in 1988 there was direct foreign investment in approximately 78% of the major hotels in the coastal areas, 67% of hotels in Nairobi and 66% in the lodges in the national parks and reserves. Developing countries have the natural and cultural resources and assets to attract western tourists – who are important not only in the micro sense of providing direct economic benefits to various locations but also, in a macropolitical sense, in helping confirm a politically acceptable image to attract further overseas investment in other sectors of the economy. The icons of development will be an important factor in giving an outward message of development and an acceptance of capitalist values (which is usually perceived as being somehow 'democratic'). These are important conditions for the development of metatourism which can act as a substitute or complement economic benefits previously provided by primary commodities. Consequently the emphasis for development has been both political and economic. Historically, the role of western intermediaries has been (and continues to be) critical in establishing the growth of metatourism. The result of this has been that the full potential of economic and social benefits has not been realised.

The standardisation of many destinations as indistinguishable commodities by tour operators has not helped destinations control tourism development. Thus to paraphrase Ascher (1985) we find that standardisation increases the substitutability of one sunlust destination with another, enmeshing the destination even further into the metatourism system.

Conclusions

There are parallels to be drawn between the trade of tourism and primary commodity production between developing and developed countries which feeds into the metatourism model.

- A heavy reliance upon the sale of the destination ('commodity') in the developed world.
- Need for overseas and foreign investment to develop the infrastructure and superstructure required for tourism development.
- Reliance on foreign intermediaries such as airlines and tour operators to supply the tourists and market the destination.
- Extreme vulnerability in terms of demand to economic and political factors such as world recession, increased oil prices, terrorism, changing market tastes in tourism generating countries and competition from other destination countries.

In a more general sense, Jenkins (1991) sets out three areas which he sees as problematic in the research on tourism and the Third World:

- Too many studies lack a comparative dimension, not only between countries but often between tourism and other sectors in an economy. This limits their usefulness for policy formulation.
- Too many studies are based on a single discipline, usually economics, occasionally sociology. As a wide-ranging activity, tourism must be approached through multi-disciplinary analytical studies.
- The neglect of the social and anthropological aspects of tourism in developing countries should be rectified. (Jenkins, 1991:276)

In addition to this is the overriding problem acknowledged by Lea (1988:21) that there exists:

> differences in approach ... between a political economy model of international tourism, which seeks to explain present conditions in terms of evolving global relationships between rich and poor countries; and the functional view which aims to describe and classify separate elements to the tourism process ... political economy approaches are generally negative about tourism's overall contribution to Third World development [while] ... functionalists ... [imply] that tourism is generally desirable and that problems can be resolved by adopting appropriate practices.

Britton (1982) warns us against separating the discourse surrounding tourism from the wider political and historical debate (again, this is where metatourism allows a clearer focus), and while there is no doubt about tourism's ability to generate wealth, create jobs, act as an economic catalyst and create a favourable image for the destination country, underpinning tourism's *problématique* is its failure to acknowledge that changes are needed in the global economic structures that allow the developed countries to continue consuming global resources and accumulating global capital. Perhaps tourism operators could start to follow the lead set by Oxfam and its 'Fair Trade' (source: Oxfam brochure) movement which aims to ensure that small scale producers are paid a decent price for their products. The thrust of the movement is to try to ensure payment both directly and with forms of guarantee that reflect the producers' labour. Oxfam asks what constitutes a fair price and comes up with the following criteria:

- can the producers afford to buy enough food, medicine and other basic needs for their families?
- Can they afford to send their children to school?
- Are health and safety regulations in place at work to prevent accidents?
- Are producers given secure contracts and allowed to organise?

Using the example of Fair Trade goods (such as Café Direct, a brand of coffee produced under the criteria) going into major UK supermarkets, perhaps consumers should start to look at the relationship between Third World producers and First World buyers of tourism and see how comfortable they feel with the existing situation. As late as October 1994, no known examples of a holiday or tourism product receiving the Fairtrade Mark (© Oxfam) were known.

The *problématique* of tourism's employment

Introduction

Earlier in this book, we concluded that Jafar Jafari's definition of tourism (1977) was the most helpful in focusing on the human aspect of tourism. His is also a definition that takes account of tourism's *problématique* in terms of human and environmental issues. With this in mind, the next problem to be addressed is that of defining what is meant by 'tourism employment'. While this chapter will describe some of the characteristics relating to employment in tourism, it is clear that different sectors have very different forms of employment. These range from the clearcut national and international divisions of labour found in the agents of metatourism such as the airline sector; the clearly defined contracts and conditions of service by international corporations such as Ramada Renaissance and ITT Sheraton; the minimum wage, short contract, insecure conditions that characterise much of catering work in the UK; to the prostitutes working bars in any one of a number of tourist traps around the world (Burns, 1994:6). However, it is generally understood that almost any discussion about tourism and employment will be

99

dominated by hotel and catering; after all, it constitutes the largest component of the sector. So, while our working definition here of 'tourism employment' is not a complex one (let it simply be all direct employment created by the tourists' spending power) the issues are, in themselves, very complex. While most of the examples drawn upon will be from the hotels sector, the issues raised will be underpinned by reference to the wider net of employment through tourism, including the marginal and informal.

The characteristics of tourism employment

Tourism employment has certain characteristics that may be generalised to some extent. The first is that while there is an obvious relationship between tourism expenditure and employment generation, increasing tourism revenues does not necessarily increase the number of jobs: several factors enter the equation, such as productivity gains through technology, using high prices as a factor in creating or maintaining exclusivity or isolation, and the relative increase of dependency on imported goods as the tourist sector moves upmarket. Secondly, the particular nature of tourism in a given locale (including levels of service, extent of luxury or simplicity, labour costs) will determine the level and type of employment. Patterns of employment and the nature of that employment will inevitably change as the destination goes through changes resulting from fashion or marketing strategies. Thirdly, local availability or shortages of skills has an effect on employment characteristics: a high level of general education and training means less reliance on expatriate management and technical skills. This will apply to both developed and Third World countries: if tourism is proposed in undeveloped regions within industrialised countries, similar labour force structural characteristics will apply.

A fourth generalisation is that tourism employment may challenge or even distort traditional/conventional work patterns. It may take people away from other productive sectors of the economy, particularly agriculture (Bryden, 1973:18, 35) This newly created employment, perhaps carried out within the context of leisured and hedonistic lifestyles of the tourist, may well be fundamentally different from what has gone before. Other changes in patterns of employment might occur. Resort complexes operate on a 24-hour basis. This creates the necessity for shift and perhaps part-time work. Some of these part-time positions may be filled by people already in employment, or by people leaving one sector of the economy to join the tourism economy, thus making a further contribution to labour shortages elsewhere.

A further generalisation is that tourism employment patterns may be in conflict with traditional cultural patterns. For instance, staff may be required to work when they would normally be at church, temple or mosque. Shift work and night duty may cause jealousy between partners. This jealousy can be further exacerbated in a society traditionally dominated by males if women are promoted into positions of power and responsibility. A final generalisation is that where much of the employment in tourism is seasonal, it could be argued that it encourages those who only seek a part-time or seasonal commitment to work (Mathieson and Wall, 1982:81).

Hudson and Townsend (1992:56) ask whether such employment characteristics are 'an unavoidable corollary of reliance upon tourism?' They develop their question:

> While some undesirable aspects can be improved (for instance, by developing complementary summer and winter activities to avoid the problems of seasonality), others pose more intractable problems, as job characteristics are closely tied to the organization and character of the tourism industries. Indeed, given the intensely competitive character of these highly labour-intensive industries, there are very powerful pressures to increase competitiveness by cutting labour costs.

However, as Hudson and Townsend go on to observe, cutting labour costs may have an effect on competitiveness regarding quality of service. This dichotomy between cutting labour costs to improve productivity and the risk of losing competitive edge through losses in quality is debated well by Riley and Jones (1992:300):

> Quality speaks of skill, of continuity, of a stable workforce, the very opposite of the economic and technological cost-cutting pressures. Here then is the dilemma for the strategist. If the economics are at odds with the qualitative needs for skill development and continuity, how is skill to be maintained and how stable should the organization be?

For industries that rely on high quality guest contact, the answer is clear. Personnel officers and those who recruit for the tourism industry frequently refer to 'the correct attitude' as being the prime qualification in the 'people' industry. A paper presented in Phuket, Thailand at a UN/ILO-sponsored seminar on hotel and catering management (November 1986) referred to this attitude as comprising 'helpfulness, politeness, friendliness, cooperation, cost consciousness, sales mind and even pride in personal appearance etc.' The paper went on to suggest that building such attitudes would:

> take a long time and . . . a lot of sacrifice of the staff's convenience, habits and their routine . . . a manager or supervisor has to identify what desirable attitudes we like to develop in our staff or which improper attitudes we wish to change . . . and then go about building them or changing them through a systematic process . . .

101

While this may sound patronising or even draconian, we have to sympathise with managers working in a competitive environment in which personnel are a (perhaps the) key component in achieving and sustaining a successful hospitality enterprise. In a service business, it is right to offer training and assistance to their staff that enhances the product on offer. The problem comes about when trying to get the balance right between the maxim that 'the customer is always right' and the freedom of the individual employee to work with dignity. This can be achieved through developing clearly defined performance and service standards, a flexible and rapidly responsive reward system (including managers developing an ability to say 'thank you, well done' to their staff) and open and honest management. For the most part regular training can help achieve corporate goals including the development of a 'correct attitude'. Indications from at least one major international hotel corporation indicated that regular training

- enabled employees to feel more confident on the job;
- helped them to understand better the concerns of the hotel;
- demonstrated that the management valued their work;
- showed that the management was concerned with their wellbeing, and
- built a sense of partnership and responsibility towards achieving hotel goals.

Patterns of employment

In considering the ability of tourism to generate employment, we must also examine the nature of these jobs. In quantitative terms, the highest requirement is for semi- or unskilled jobs (the validity of this simplistic statement will be discussed later in the chapter). There is also the factor of seasonality, and the effect this has on jobs. Seasonality often means the development of part-time employment with consequential opportunity cost in career or self development for employees. In many countries, even those with a strong record of trade unionism, tourism workers (especially those in the hotel sector) are non-unionised. This can be seen as a direct consequence of another phenomenon related to tourism employment in the hotel sector: that of core and periphery workers. This means that, while many jobs might be designated semi- or unskilled, some key jobs, such as head waiters, chefs, accountants and engineers, have readily acknowledged specialisation. These workers tend to have different employment patterns than most of the workforce. They form a 'core' of year-round employees. Hudson and Townsend (1992) note that these core employees will usually be male. This is an example of the ways in which male and female employees not only have clearly differentiated roles, but are treated differently. Riley and Jones (1992) term the notion of core–periphery workers as 'the two workforces ... with some people having very strong tenure and others having very loose job tenure'. Many jobs traditionally associated with females, such as room maid or receptionist, can be seen to reflect what (probably male) managers interpret as a motherly, caring role. Enloe (1989:34–5) brings a feminist perspective to the notion of 'low skill':

> Since the eighteenth century, employers have tried to minimize the cost of employing workers in labour-intensive industries by defining most jobs as 'unskilled' or 'low-skilled' – jobs in other words, that workers naturally know how to do. Women in most societies are presumed to be naturally capable at cleaning, washing, cooking, serving. Since tourism companies need precisely those jobs done, they can keep their labor costs low if they can define these jobs as women's work. In the Caribbean in the early 1980s, 75 per cent of tourism workers were women.

(A notion which of course breaks down when certain male-dominated societies wish to inhibit the contact between female local employees and foreign male guests. This leads to a situation where so called 'room boys' are employed as the unskilled operatives in the housekeeping department.)

Unlike employment in the manufacturing sector, labour in the tourism industry is part of a service 'produce'. If that part of the ambience in a hotel or restaurant that relies on the mood of the staff is not right, then the product is not right (Urry, 1990:79). This places added responsibility on the management that has not only to reach financial targets expected by owners, but who also have to create formal (and informal) compensation measures to counteract: 'poorly paid service workers [enhancing] the almost sacred quality of the visitors' gaze upon some longed for and remarkable tourist site' (Urry, 1990:67). These measures may range from elaborate uniforms and job titles, unofficial free meals on duty, to turning a blind eye to petty pilfering (Gabriel, 1988:3). A reliance on the smiling and being 'good' to the customers creates something of a paradox, for while on one hand employees are treated as 'unskilled', on the other hand the employing organisation gains benefit from the value added to the product by 'service skills' (Bull, 1991:146). These 'soft-skills' are not formally recognised by employers. Reward comes through tips, or pleasant interaction with the customers. It could be argued that the ability to interact with guests is such an essential part of the service product, and that they can be improved with experience and training, that the hospitality industry should stop demeaning its workforce by dismissing such abilities as unskilled.

Conclusion

It could be argued that there are parallels to be drawn between the debates on defining tourism and defining what constitutes tourism employment. In the same way, we see the pattern of solutions mirroring the 'solutions' put forward for the *problématique* of tourism. That is to say, in looking for answers about the consequences of tourism we must examine the ways in which it is developing, the extent to which touristic developments match the host country's cultural environment. Equally, it is clear that while there are different employment practices in different countries, many of the characteristics of tourism employment could be considered global. The involvement of the consumer in the place and country of production (i.e. the tourist in the resort or hotel) means that this is much more so than, for example, for mining (child labour being used in Colombia) or for the garment industry (where harsh, sweatshop employment conditions in Sri Lanka are causing grave social concern). In addressing the *problématique* of tourism's employment, if it is to provide a quality work experience, which in turn will positively affect the tourists' holiday, we should be looking for culturally appropriate solutions which can be sustained through profound changes in recruitment, employment, training and staff retention patterns. This is especially so where the characteristics of metatourism are evident. In the same way that providing 'solutions' for tourism has concentrated on the symptom, not the cause (how can we more effectively move more tourists, accommodate them, etc. rather than developing a view about appropriateness of different types of tourism, the structure of tourism, and carrying capacity), the 'answers' to human resource problems are sought in divisive individual reward (or sanctions) systems rather than in the underlying causes of a demotivated and ineffective workforce where the ability to interact with guests (almost a prerequisite for successful employment in the service sector) remains undervalued and described as 'unskilled'.

CHAPTER 4

Commodities, culture and the division of labour

Commodification of destinations

Introduction

The aim of this section is to develop an understanding about the extent to which tourism can be interpreted as a sort of mass-produced commodity of international trade between the First and the Third Worlds. It considers the economic and political pressures for development, the reliance upon Western countries for tourism development and to supply the source markets for tourism. The end result is that destinations themselves may be 'traded' in the same way as a commodity.

Mass production: a question of demand and supply?

Bayley (1991:47) relates the history of the word 'consumer' to the development of the Western economy. He describes how the change from 'buyer' to 'consumer' came about:

> Mass production and all that it entails – investment, long lead-times, low unit costs and ready availability – replaced a system where simple makers could articulate and satisfy needs; the new distant customers alienated from the production process became consumers.

One of the most universal terms applied to the phenomenon of contemporary tourism is the expression 'mass'. The movement of peoples across international boundaries has facilitated the development of an industry serving a wide cross-section of the public and meeting the needs of the postmodern consumer.

For tourism development to fulfil the needs of mass consumerism, many of the characteristics needed for mass consumption referred to by Bayley must be fulfilled. These will include:

- mass production and transglobal repetition of services to meet the needs of hundreds of millions of people moving annually around the globe;
- investment from governments to provide the necessary infrastructure and financial incentives essential to attract corporate investment from global organisations viewed as necessary to provide the facilities for tourism;
- long lead-times by governments who wish to have tourism master plans drawn up and transnational corporations involved in strategic planning;
- low unit costs achieved through economies of scale as a result of horizontal, vertical and diagonal integration as demonstrated in Table 4.1 (Poon, 1993:223) and increasing employee productivity partly through the use of increasingly sophisticated information technology providing a global system of information and reservations for ready access;
- the standardisation of products such as package holidays which may be purchased from the travel agent or by telephone or computer with the minimum of inconvenience.

Thus the characteristics of contemporary international tourism are framed by mass consumption on the part of nationals from the most developed countries benefiting from low production costs. For example, salaries and wage costs in food and beverage departments as a ratio to total revenue in Australia are 32.4% compared to 12.4% in China (PKF, 1993:48). Up to 80% of all international travel (measured by volume) is made by nationals of just 20 countries (WTO, 1994a). As noted in Chapter 2, more than 50% of total international travel expenditure is accounted for by nationals of just five countries.

These tourists are also travelling greater distances as economies of scale and technology have pushed the peripheries of travel further outwards from the major source areas of Europe. With the continued advancement of new technology and improvements in the determinatory conditions of workers such as increased holiday leave and disposable income, the demand for long-haul travel has increased substantially. A powerful industry, in terms of its influence on the economies of developing countries, has developed to propitiate the phenomenon and serve the needs of the postmodern tourist. An international system has developed, based around supply and demand factors, as shown in Figure 4.1.

Of particular significance is the role of the travel intermediaries (loosely defined as the travel trade) in providing the link between the demand and supply functions. It is the intermederiaries who will have a major influence in the development of a destination, influencing speed of growth, type of

Table 4.1 Diagonal integration compared with other forms of integration.

Characteristics	Vertical integration	Horizontal integration	Diversification	Diagonal integration
Forms of integration				
Production focus	Many stages of production	Same stage of production	Many unrelated activities	Many tightly related services
Objectives of integration	Control over stages of production	Monopoly power/ concentration	Spread risks	Get close to the consumer/Lower costs of production
Integration mechanism	Acquisition/start new business	Acquisition/collusion	Acquisition/start new activities	Information partnerships Strategic alliances Strategic acquisitions
Operationalisation	Integrated production and management	Operate as one entity	'Arm's length'	Synergistic production/shared networks
Orientation of production	Production-orientated	Supply-orientated	Investment orientated	Consumer-orientated
Production concept	Economies of scale	Economies of scale	Production unrelated to markets	Economies of scale Economies of scope Synergies/systems gains
Examples	Ford (old days)	American Airlines	British American Tobacco (BAT)	American Express Midland Bank

Source: Poon (1993:223).

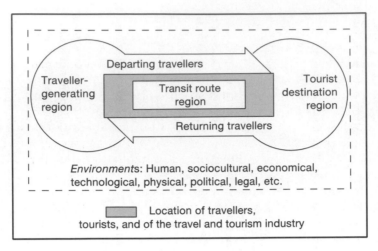

Figure 4.1 Basic tourist system.
Source: Leiper (1990, in Cooper *et al.*, 1993:3).

development and the markets it will serve. As Cooper *et al.* (1993: 189) have said:

> The principal role of intermediaries is to bring buyers and sellers together, either to create markets where they previously did not exist, or to make existing markets work more effectively and thereby to expand market size . . . In all industries the task of intermediaries is to transform goods and services which consumers do not want, to a product that they do want.

The most apparent intermediary is the tour operator who usually puts together, at a most fundamental level, the accommodation, transport and ancillary services into a package which may be bought by the consumer. As tourism has developed and its spatial boundaries expanded, increasing language, cultural and communication difficulties have reduced the ability and opportunity for the tourist to buy directly from the producer. The tourist has thus become increasingly dependent upon the tour operator. The role of the tour operator has not been limited to merely offering a conveniently purchased product. They have played a major role in reducing unit costs and offering lower prices to the consumer. This has meant that travel has become accessible to a much wider social spectrum and the phenomenon of mass tourism has been established. Ascher (1985: 57) describes how this has come about:

> [tour operators] were able to do this because of 'collective' pre-paration [economies of scale secured by mass production], because of their bargaining power with hoteliers and carriers, which is superior to

that of individuals, and because of the permanent or seasonal surplus capacity on airlines and in hotels.

Ascher continues this theme in relation to Europe, especially the Balearic Islands, 'Tour operators have thus developed operations on a truly industrial scale' (1985:58). The tour operator may thus act as an important catalyst to resort development and greatly influence the demand:supply ratio.

The fact that tour operators have the means to bring increased numbers of tourists to destinations (though sometimes a lower spending tourist than the independent tourist that may have previously visited) encourages entrepreneurial activity and an increasing supply of accommodation. As the supply of accommodation increases (often reaching over-capacity, such as on the Romanian Black Sea) the more opportunity there is for the tour operator to play hotels off against each other and reduce the prices they pay. The increase in supply of accommodation offers the opportunity to the tour operators to expand the numbers of tourists they take to a destination and reduce the prices to the consumer, which will also mean less revenue for the hotel owner, sometimes to the extent that wages are depressed and essential maintenance neglected.

Competition for the icons of development: the symbols of success

The dominant trend in international tourism (for the decade up to the mid-1990s) is for the growth of long-haul travel to 'exotic locations', particularly to the countries of South East Asia and Africa. Destinations such as Malaysia, The Gambia, Bangkok, Bali, Singapore and Hong Kong are all familiar names in contemporary travel advertisements. The regions of East Asia/Pacific and Africa have seen their markets grow throughout the last decade and it is predicted that they will continue to grow in importance in international terms. The World Tourism Organisation predict 5.4% average growth rate in international tourist arrivals for the Africa region, reaching some 7.06 million long-haul arrivals by 2010 (WTO, 1994c) and in the East Asia/Pacific region 7.2% growth is predicted – almost 43 million long-haul arrivals (WTO, 1994b).

However, the early development of a tourism industry in Europe, historically the dominant tourism region, helped protection of established markets through advanced marketing techniques. The early development of tourism administration organisations and systems gave direction to continued product development and international competitiveness. This meant that European countries have an established administrative and organisational advantage over developing countries trying to increase their market share of international tourist arrivals. Paradoxically, Europe's dominant position has also enabled it to determine, along with the United States, where tourism investment and development takes place in the rest

Table 4.2 Reasons for the dominance of Europe in international travel market.

- Early Industrial Revolution
- Developed infrastructure
- Small geographical areas of the countries and their close proximity to one another – higher propensity for travel
- Climatic and cultural diversity within a relatively small geographical area
- Development of national marketing and promotion organisations
- Development of a structured tour operating industry
- Ease of travel in member states for EC nationals

of the globe (a role increasingly being taken over by Japan) (see Table 4.2). Also the early development of state airlines and tour operators meant that these countries were in a strong position to control the international pattern of contemporary mass travel. Ascher (1985:23) summarises the position of developing countries hoping to establish themselves as competitors to airlines from industrialised countries:

> The Chairman of Kenya Airways recently drew attention to these inequalities: not only do the companies of developing countries have little direct access to the tourist-generating markets, but their operating costs are 30 per cent higher (fuel, servicing, maintenance and training being purchased at high prices from companies in industrialised countries); they have small fleets and networks and domestic networks are often virtually non-existent.

Nor have the airlines been content with controlling airline routes between the source and destination countries. They have integrated vertically particularly into the hotel market; Figure 4.2 shows the general principle of integration as it pertains to travel and tourism. Bull (1991:186) describes how this integration has a long history with PanAm establishing Inter-Continental Hotels as a subsidiary in 1946. Bull explains that the reason for this diversification into hotels of airlines was a wish to expand their operations at a destination, or control the supply of accommodation services in pursuit of a trading advantage in carrying passengers to their destination. Multiple airline/hotel affiliations have become normal, with sometimes two or more airlines involved in one hotel chain – a polygamous relationship. Examples of airline–hotel links include: American Airlines and Americana Hotels; Air France and Hotels Meridien; Japan Airlines and Nikko Hotels; KLM and Golden Tulip Hotels.

Implications of 'destination as commodity'

A trawl through the mass tour operators' brochures will highlight an undeniable observation: the destinations are presented through the brochure

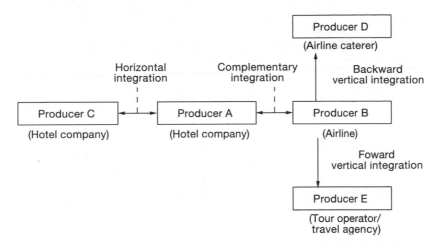

Figure 4.2 Main types of integration in travel and tourism.
Source: Bull (1991:72).

illustrations as looking virtually the same. This homogenisation of destinations is particularly characterised through the transformation of local architectural culture. Coastlines have been transformed into a bland vista reminiscent of a postindustrial city: from London to New York, Singapore to Tokyo. Krippendorf (1989:89–92) seems to hint at this idea of the tour operator treating the destination as commodity. Clearly the operator aims to reaffirm to the consumer through sophisticated brochure imagery that the holiday on offer can address the perceived needs of the tourist. Of course, the only way to achieve this commodity purchase is through monetary exchange.

The impact of individual tourist 'purchases' of a destination has a cumulative effect economically, socially and environmentally. These effects are accentuated toward the negative by the nature of the tour operators' business in the mass market (and especially so within the phenomenon of meta-tourism). The key to this is that competition in much of the industry (especially for UK tourists) is based upon price rather than the quality of the product. Changes in exchange rates for the dollar, the Spanish peseta or Greek drachma have immediate and sometimes dramatic effects on take-up of holidays. The vast supply of tourism destinations able to supply the four Ss of Sun, Sea, Sand and Sex has meant that there has been a concomitant supply of alternatives holiday-making places. Low prices built the sunlust holiday market: and in a sense, the large tour operators have trained their consumers to expect and respond to low prices: the acceptance of 'allocation on arrival' holidays (i.e. where the tourist books a cheap holiday and is not allocated the actual resort and/or hotel until s/he arrives at the destination) seems to indicate a lack of discrimination on the part of the tourist.

Social and cultural issues of tourism

Introduction

There is a brief but curious scene in Denis O'Rourke's documentary film, *Cannibal Tours* (which observes the contact between a party of relatively rich tourists on a luxury cruise boat on the Sepik River and a group of 'ex-primitives'). One of the tourists is posing some anxious-looking village children and young woman for a photo she wants to take. With a curve of her hand and quick demonstration the tourist asks them to smile. Either they don't want to or don't understand her request. In any event the smiles do not appear. Finally, in exasperation, she exclaims, 'Don't you people smile around here?' Clearly, only smiling natives will appear in her holiday snaps. In the context of O'Rourke's whole film, the incident is probably no more significant than other details surrounding the contact; no more significant than the early morning conversation in which the Sepik villagers were described by an Italian tourist as 'Not really living, more existing'.

We should of course understand that this type of contact, that is between tourists and what MacCannell (1992:18) would describe as recent 'ex-primitives' is both dramatic and unusual: dramatic in that the contrasts are so visually evident; the villagers look as though they have stepped off the pages of an early edition of National Geographic, while the tourists are festooned in protective headgear and expensive photographic equipment. The encounter is unusual in that such obvious culture-clashes, even within the controlled environment of a package tour, are rare. The incident not only demonstrates the effect that tourism can have on societies (and the effect that societies might have on tourists) but also illustrates the catalystic role that tourism plays in social interaction. It would be difficult to imagine that such a close encounter with ex-primitives could leave the sophisticated (yet paradoxically naive) tourists unchanged, and equally difficult to imagine that the sudden influx of outsiders with their cash and alien ways will leave the village culture unchanged.

Culture and tourism

Investigating the social impacts of tourism focuses on three areas: the tourist; the host and the tourist–host relationship. This takes account of the two-way social and cultural implications arising from visiting and being visited.

In the context of tourism, an understanding of cultural processes is important in two ways. First, culture (especially unique or unusual culture) is seen by tourism producers as a commercial resource, an attraction. Secondly, such comprehension might help deflect or ameliorate unwanted change to a host culture occurring through the act of receiving tourists.

The interaction between tourism and the inhabitants of Brisbane in Australia; Orlando (site of Disney World) in Florida; London, England; Paris, France and so on is perhaps a little short of dramatic, but important none the less. Tourism affects the lives of people by the way in which it shapes employment patterns, transport systems, national image, and even skylines and cityscapes. The effect is especially forceful if the receiving society is not economically advanced. Wolf (1977) termed the notion of sociocultural influence of tourism 'people impacts'. Such impacts are hard to measure. It is especially difficult to sort out the general impact on people of the process of so-called modernisation from the specific impact of tourism and tourists upon culture. Given the widespread growth of global broadcast media, it could be argued that the social effect of tourism is becoming more difficult to disaggregate.

Defining culture

> The idea of culture embraces a range of topics, processes, differences and even paradoxes such that only a confident and wise person would begin to pontificate about it and perhaps only a fool would attempt to write . . . about it. (Jenks, 1993:1)

For some, 'culture' may mean high art such as to be found in the great galleries of the world. A person who is familiar with art and music is said to be 'cultured'. While this is a particular use of the word it does not, however, define what culture is. A business studies student recently described culture as 'all the things that you learn and all the attitudes that you share with your own people'. Others will use the word to explain how a particular society functions. Sir Edward Burnett Tylor (1832–1917), an early anthropologist, introduced his book *Primitive Culture* (1871) by stating.

> Culture or civilization . . . is that complex whole which includes knowledge, belief, art, moral law, custom, and any other capabilities and habits acquired by man [sic] as a member of society.

Culture, then, is about the interaction of people as observed through social relations and material artifacts. It consists of behavioural patterns, knowledge and values which have been acquired and transmitted through generations. The essence of culture is contained in the value attached to traditional ideas. Professor Ron Crocombe, in discussing changes to Pacific Island culture by the introduction of (among other things) non-indigenous peoples, notes that 'Too much identification with one culture can lead to racism, religious persecution, or other negative and destructive feelings, but not enough can lead to insecurity and anomie' (1989:26). In emphasising the complexity of culture, Crocombe is implying that descriptions of culture are necessarily static snapshots at a given moment. Culture should be seen as dynamic: a society that does not take on board new ideas, or adapt to changing global conditions is in danger of cultural retrocession. To underline the complexity of thinking about these matters, we should bear in mind the warning that:

> To speak unproblematically of 'traditional' culture is not permissible. All cultures continually change. What is traditional in a culture is largely a matter of internal polemic as groups within a society struggle for hegemony. (Greenwood, 1989:183)

Greenwood's warning also reminds us of the dangers of the hypocrisy and paradoxes that surround attempts at 'cultural preservation'.

Culture as tourist product

> Logically, anything that is for sale must have been produced by combining the factors of production (land, labor, or capital). This offers no problem when the subject is razor blades, transistor radios, or hotel accommodations. It is not so clear when the buyers are attracted to a place by some feature of local culture, such as ... an exotic festival. (Greenwood, 1989:172)

In a sense here lies the key to the cultural *problématique* encountered by those who study tourism. Culture cannot be separated from the natural environment where it develops. If culture includes place, space and people, then further study becomes essential so that we can begin to address Greenwood's central concern. Proponents of tourism would probably see it from a supply-side point of view – as being based around the notion of attractions. These attractions may vary, but will almost certainly include cultural elements. Ritchie and Zins (1978:257) developed a list of twelve elements of culture that could be seen as attractive to tourists:

1. Handcrafts
2. Language
3. Traditions
4. Gastronomy
5. Art and music, including concerts, paintings and sculpture
6. The history of the region, including its visual reminders
7. The types of work engaged in by residents and the technology that is used
8. Architecture giving the area a distinctive appearance

9. Religion, including its visible manifestations
10. Educational systems
11. Dress
12. Leisure activities

The extent to which these components of culture are adapted by the local population and offered to tourists for consumption is likely to be framed by at least two factors. First, the relative difference and thus the relative novelty between cultural components of the visitors and the visited, and secondly, by the type and number of visitors. This theme is illustrated by Smith (1989). (Figure 4.4). While Smith's ideas about types of contact are useful, they seem to imply a certain homogeneity among tourist types. For instance, the 'rarely seen' 'explorer' might, at a superficial level, 'accept fully' the local condition, and will not demand 'Western amenities'; however, the personality, obsessions and motivations of an individual tourist (in this micro scenario) might have a dramatic effect – disrupting norms and causing tensions and jealousies within a village setting.

The government of Papua New Guinea certainly recognise the darker side of tourism and has tried to put into place a number of guidelines and legislative factors that are intended to minimise disruption.

CASE STUDY: PAPUA NEW GUINEA

Papua New Guinea is a South Pacific country that has possibly some of the most fascinating cultural assets in the world. Much of it remained unknown to the outside world until the mid-1930s; it has more than 700 languages and a modern democratic government that is firmly committed to preserving cultural heritage in the face of modernity. Its efforts to place *tradition* into the context of modern society with modern needs for finance and trade with the rest of the world are reflected both in a formal five-year culture plan and the National Constitution, which recognises that the people of Papua New Guinea must:

- Pay homage to the memory of [their] ancestors – the source of . . . strength and origin of our combined heritage.
- Acknowledge the worthy customs and traditional wisdoms of [their] people – which have come down . . . from generation to generation.
- Pledge [themselves] to guard and pass on to those who come after . . . [the] noble traditions and Christian principles that are [theirs].

This is an enormous responsibility for the people and their government; chapter one of the Cultural Development Plan places culture in its historical context, and is worth quoting at length in that it comes not from western academics, but from officials in a government who are facing the realities of coping with change:

> . . . it is true that . . . traditional lifestyle cannot be placed in a jar because, all societies evolve through time. Prior to the first contact with foreigners, the original inhabitants of this land already had well-developed and balanced traditions in their various villages or communities. There was then, already in existence richness and diversity of culture forms and political institutions.

> . . . The ways of life and belief systems were in harmony and produced an incredible variety of art forms. The songs, dances and artifacts of the nation amazed the outside world when they first came to light. These traditional cultures, which were strong and vital with their own integrity and honesty were to be changed with the coming of foreigners, pressures for change came in many forms, and for many reasons, but fortunately many customs survived the onslaught, and the constitution recognises the right for traditional beliefs to coexist with the adopted beliefs.

The chapter concludes with this firm warning: '. . . the people should be warned that large scale development bring with them certain destructive social habits. These habits confuse the members of old and new generations alike and lead to social disharmony in family units which are important bases of unity in a community and the society at large . . . Furthermore, they should be warned that large scale development will seriously affect the Cultural Heritage of the indigenous population.'

Turner and Ash (1975) acknowledge that there are occasions when tourism can serve a conservationist or even revivalist role for culture. They give the example of how tourist demand in the late 1950s led to a revival of Hawaiian handcrafts, when the art of grass skirt and mat weaving was on the verge of dying out. However, they also note that when a local artist or craftsman comes to value his/her work in terms of whether it will sell to tourists, then ancient artistic formulae lose their meaning and vitality. Turner and Ash mention New Guinea mask carvers, who make masks only for western art dealers and tourists, and that the masks, although still skilfully performed, are quite meaningless in terms of traditional ritual and symbol.

Hosts and guests: demarcating the encounter

> The anthropological view of culture is far different from the economists' and the planners' views of culture as a 'come-on,' a 'natural resource,' or as a 'service.' The anthropological perspective enables us to understand why the commoditization of local culture in the tourism industry is so fundamentally destructive and why the sale of 'culture by the pound,' as it were, needs to be examined by everyone involved in tourism. (Greenwood, 1989:174)

While descriptions and references to encounters between unequals may be poignant (as evidenced in O'Rourke's *Cannibal Tours*) and such meetings may carry severe consequences for the receiving population (as noted elsewhere in this chapter) the vast bulk of the world's tourism takes place between relative equals, that is as domestic travel, between European countries with broadly similar GNPs or, for instance, between the United States and Europe. This means that the biggest social problem to do with tourism in terms of scale is that of congestion and overcrowding. In many cases this is an accepted and expected part of the holiday experience. No one would dream of going to Coney Island, Disneyland or Paris in August without a willingness to accept crowds and queues at the attractions, museums and fast food outlets . . . in a sense, the crowds enhance the feeling of fun and enjoyment.

HOSTS AND GUESTS: A WORD ON USING THE WORDS

Having introduced the words 'hosts' and 'guests' it would be useful to spend a little time in examining some problems that accompany them: 'unpack the baggage', to use a travel metaphor. Valene Smith (1989) used these words in the title of her powerful and influential volume *Hosts and Guests: the anthropology of tourism*, which was first published in 1977. At first glance the meaning is clear; after all, they are not long, academic or unusual words, nor are they being used in an unusual context. And yet with the dictionary definitions of host being 'one who entertains a guest' and guest as 'a person receiving hospitality from another' we see implicit in these ideas the notion of willing participation and even an assumption of equality in the different roles – especially when we see that the definition for hospitality is 'a friendly welcome and entertainment given to guests'. When the two sides of the host–guest equation are unequal in status, relative wealth and education, we can perhaps perceive a danger in the unthinking use of such terms in relation to what is essentially a financial transaction.

A similar set of philological arguments can be presented about many other words that are used in connection with tourism, such as 'impacts' (does the use of the word imply an inevitability? If not, are there dangers in using terminology that might cause us to think there are no solutions?). Among the list of other words used liberally without due consideration to their roots and thus emotive power are 'exotic' and 'paradise'. (These last two words are implicit in the discussion of tourist brochures of South East Asia by Tom Selwyn, 1992.) Even the word 'tourist' carries with it a pejorative connotation. Many people who travel abroad and engage in sightseeing or eating in restaurants would be offended at being called tourists. They would prefer the word 'adventurer' or 'traveller'. There are two other words/phrases used in this book that seem to be losing currency or credibility: 'Third World' and 'Developing Country'. Development economists and anthropologists in particular feel uncomfortable with them; to date, an acceptable alternative which would not be redundant (as in the case of a First World, Second World and Third World order) or patronising as in the case of the West is developed, the rest of the world is not. The phrase 'North–South' has gained a certain level of acceptance as an alternative as we enter the end of the 1990s. It has been used in this book where the setting has been appropriate.

In a sense, both the 'host' and 'guest' will develop coping behaviours. Residents might simply take their own vacations at the height of the season and be somewhere else (perhaps even letting their own house out to tourists). Others might change their shopping habits and times so as to avoid the tourist crowds. Others might indulge in a sort of self-imposed hibernation. Other residents might engage in some petty entrepreneurship, such as selling home-grown flowers and fruit from outside their door to letting one of their rooms as a bed and breakfast facility. The tourists cope with the crowds by simply enjoying the atmosphere or by buying snacks and souvenirs, all in the knowledge that they will be going home by the end of the day, week, or whenever their holiday ends. However, the impact on most of the cities and places mentioned above is diluted because they are already economically, socially and culturally diverse. They have an established history of change stretching back, in some cases, over generations. They have large, diverse populations and so are much better able to cope with change than a society that has had limited contact with outsiders,

There is a fundamental difference between contacts that occur between cultures of comparable strength and generally equal wealth and those between developed and Third World countries. The difference comes about through the issue of power and control. While changes are made in all tourist-receiving areas, it would be reasonable to assume that much of the pressure for change at tourist spots within developed countries is politically intracultural, that is initiated by entrepreneurs or locally elected politicians in response to community pressure, planned and implemented by professional officers (architects, town planners, etc.) and received by the tourists as better hospitality, signage or parking facilities, etc. While this scenario can be played out in the case of developing countries, pressure will often be from central government responding to the business needs of transnational tour companies (who in return are assembling a product to sell in the holiday marketplace). The powers that shape the receiving country's economic structures and that shape its tourism industry and define and demarcate the pattern of arrivals are not only extracultural but located (or headquartered) in another country. These ideas are explored in considerable detail by François Ascher in his UNESCO sponsored book *Tourism Transnational Corporations and Cultural Identity* (1985) and by Steve Britton in his influential article 'The Political Economy of Tourism in the Third World' (1982).

The nature of the contact

Human consequences are an integral part of tourism; it is important to emphasise what an individual tourist or host may think, and this will no doubt provide a rich source of research for social anthropologists. The late Theron Nuñez noted that 'Tourists and more often their hosts are always *on stage* when they meet in face-to-face encounters'. He explains that tourists will have prepared themselves for their role by reading the literature and buying the appropriate costume. The host will 'rehearse a friendly smile' and 'assess the mood of the audience'. MacCannell, too, in his analysis of tourism and 'modern society' as he calls it (*The Tourist* 2nd edn, 1989: ix) refers to 'The current structural development of society [as being] marked by the appearance everywhere of touristic space. This space can be called a *stage set*, a *tourist setting*, or simply a *set*' (1976:100). Biddlecomb (1981:23) quotes a polemic from Jean-Luc Maurer: 'Everything about the behaviour of the Western tourist in the Third World is entirely artificial ... no more than an object whose functions are manipulated and controlled.' This is not true. There may be aspects that are manipulated (especially if we include broader arguments about pervasive advertising and image formation) but there is much that is true: such as a general feeling of wellbeing and of having learnt something that might be apparent in the tourist after completing a holiday.

In general terms, host–guest relations are framed by the following pressures:

- social relations between people who would not normally meet;
- the confrontational aspects of meetings between different cultures, ethnic groups, lifestyles, language, levels of prosperity;

- the behaviour of holiday-makers who may feel released from many of their normal economic and social codes constraints; and
- the behaviour of the residents as they reconcile economic gains against the cost of sharing their lives with strangers.

The level of cultural clash or social conflict which may or may not occur depends on:

- the similarities of living standards between host and guest;
- the number (social pressure) of tourists staying at any given time;
- the extent to which visitors can adapt to local norms; and
- the strength of local norms against the strength of acculturation processes.

The most familiar theoretical perspective on how 'hosts' and 'guests' interact is probably Doxey's Irridex 'irritation index' illustrated, along with an adaptation of it, in Ryan's work on the social science perspective of recreational tourism (reproduced here as Table 4.3).

While it is not entirely clear whether Doxey perceived the process as deterministic the description of how, over time and touristic pressure, attitudes in a given locale change towards tourists might be considered useful. Doxey takes as his starting point a situation of virtually no touristic activity, thus there is a sense of curiosity and interest in the rare passing tourist. This proceeds through a sort of neutral view and finally on to a situation where tourists are seen in a totally negative light (paradoxically underpinned by a realisation of the economic dependency upon tourism ... though this is not explicit in Doxey's work).

At this final stage tourists and tourism become the scapegoats for all that is wrong with society. The danger for tourists is that they cease to be perceived by residents as individuals on holiday who might be talked to or who might be interesting or interested. Instead, they become an unidentifiable component of mass tourists. In a sense, they are dehumanised. As such they can be cheated, ridiculed, or even robbed (after all, their presence is transient, and the acts can be repeated as rich pickings). Tensions can be heightened when there are visible differences between visitor and visited, for example skin colour, icons of wealth, or even a hire car with a distinctive licence plate.

This theme, in the broader context of the relationship between tourism, culture and the external environment, is illustrated in Figure 4.3. Here we see that the influences can be broadly set into four categories:

- the wider society at the destination;
- the immediate community living at a given locale;
- the number and type of tourist; and
- the natural and built environment.

120

Table 4.3 Doxey's Irridex and Milligan's Modification.

Doxey's Irridex		Milligan's 'modified version'	
Euphoria ↓	– visitors are welcome and there is little planning	Curiosity ↓	– that people should accept jobs that the hosts consider beneath them in status, pay and career prospects
Apathy ↓	– visitors are taken for granted and contact becomes more formal	Acceptance ↓	– of immigrants on the island, tourism is no longer a concern of the local people
Annoyance ↓	– saturation is approached and the local people have misgivings. Planners attempt to control via increasing infrastructure rather than limiting growth	Annoyance ↓	– coupled with an annoyance with tourists is an antipathy towards immigrant workers who are seen as contributing to deteriorating standards
Antagonism	– open expression of irritation and planning is remedial yet promotion is increased to offset the deteriorating reputation of the resort	Antagonism	– both sides are aware of resentment, and the situation amongst young people is volatile. Immigrant workers are blamed for all that tourists cannot be held directly responsible for

Source: Ryan (1991:137).

Categorising the influences in this way acknowledges a very broad definition of culture (culture as 'everything') rather than a narrow definition framed only by tourism and touristic activity (production and consumption). Wider societal influences will include the influence of religious leaders and movements (such as fundamentalism), regulatory frameworks which may well be shaped by international pressure from entities such as GATT or from head office decisions by global corporations. Changes brought about to the

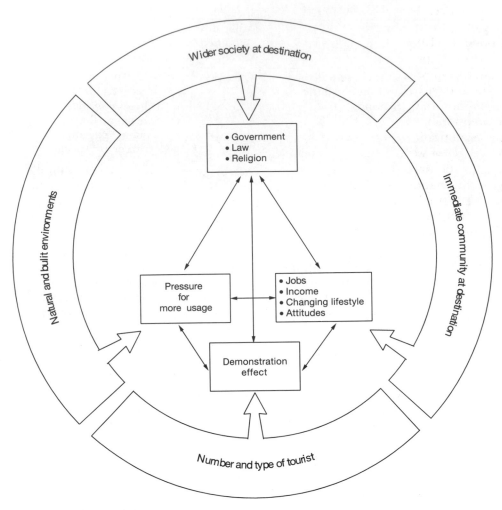

Figure 4.3 Influences on a culture broadly attributed to tourism.

immediate community from the general process of 'life moving on' (not the most elegant of phrases but one which has an immediate Gestaltist attraction) which would include patterns of employment, agriculture and lifestyle. Physical changes to the local (and perhaps national) natural and built environment will both have an affect on and be affected by changes in culture. The most obvious perhaps are changes in land use – either unproductive land being brought into use for leisure and tourism or productive agricultural land being transformed into (for example) golf courses. The number and type/mix of tourists will also affect culture in a number of ways, particularly through the consequences precipitated by the 'demonstration effect' (which will vary according to type and number of tourists).

Smith (1989:15) explores these issues in her representation of the 'Touristic impact upon a culture' (Figure 4.4). Here Smith indicates that different types of tourist will have different impacts upon the local culture. While the sexual metaphors of triangle (love triangle ... Pubis?) and penetration (a word used in the explanatory text by Smith, p. 14) are probably unintentional, they are useful in reminding us that sexual encounter is a strong motivational factor in tourism (either with other tourists, as evidenced by the use of words and images in brochures aimed at the singles market, or with 'exotic natives' as implied by the prurient subtext in the advertising of many international airlines (especially those of South East Asia). The full and tragic effect of this is discussed by O'Grady (1981) and Minerbi (1992), with Lea (1988) providing a useful introduction. As Smith (1989) explains, the response to tourism differs with the different type of tourist encountered. The proto- or incipient tourist, being few in number, and in a locale unused to tourism (virgin territory) will require very little from the 'host' population. Consequently, it is claimed that such tourists will have little impact on culture. In a simple sense, this is clearly true. However, account must be taken of the effect these trailblasing tourists will have over time. They will probably recount tales of their experiences to friends and other potential travellers, and the

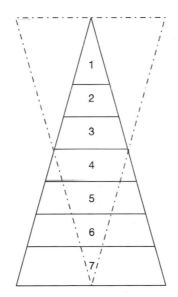

Figure 4.4 Touristic impact on a culture (Δ) and local perceptions of visitors (∇) expressed in types of tourism. 1, Explorer. 2, Elite. 3, Off-beat. 4, Unusual. 5, Incipient mass. 6, Mass. 7, Charter.
Source: Smith (1989:15).

appetite for tourism in the receiving area will have been whetted. The phrase 'see the place before the tourists get there' is a familiar one to readers of journalistic travel pages. The danger in this is that it allows the explorer to deny responsibility or any role in any development that may follow. For some cultures (perhaps especially the English) there is also the element of snobbery, in that carefully constructed conversations about holiday styles and destinations can also define social status – as demonstrated by a curious article in the *Independent* newspaper (31 January 1993) which, in an article titled 'Having a fine time: glad you're not here', came up with a (spoof) way of 'calculating the snob value of your holiday'.

Plus factors:

you need a visa	+1
visa only from Madrid embassy	+3
no UK tourist office	+1
can't get local currency in UK banks	+2
no direct flights from London	+2
no phrase book available	+1
adaptor won't fit local sockets	+2
there are no sockets	+4
civil war just ended	+3
Foreign Office says don't go	+3
your plane takes anti-missile precautions before landing	+4

Minus factors:

flights from Gatwick and Stanstead	−2
for each Holiday Inn and McDonald's	−1
it's in the 'on $10 a day guide'	−2
Thomas Cook can do you a package	−3
'Wish You Were Here' has been there	−2
'Travelog' has been there	−3
non-smoking rooms available	−3
direct calls to the UK possible	−3
credit cards accepted	−5
Vegemite sold in local store (or other signs of backpacking Australians)	−5

Source: *Independent*, 31 January 1993

The conclusions were: if you scored twenty points or more Mick Jagger follows you around the world; ten to twenty points and you remember when Inter-Railing was adventurous; nought to ten points and you still think Inter-Railing adventurous, less than nought and you think Everest is just a double-glazing company.

While at one level this exercise is simply a gentle way of poking fun at the snobbery that can surround travel and tourism, at a deeper level the ideas demonstrate, as the article states, 'The problem is that exotic hard-to-enter destinations can quickly find their way into the mass-market package holiday brochures. For example, in this year's programme of three million holidays, Thomson features former snob places such as Cuba, China, Prague and even the Arctic Circle.' Thus we see destinations consumed to feed a particular aspect of the industrialised world's cultural values.

As implied throughout this chapter, some academic writers have shown concern about the way in which tourism and culture interact; the way in which cultural shows are put on for tourists. However, some would argue (Stanton, 1989:247–62) that in a way, this is a good thing, in as much as while tourists gaze upon staged authenticity their attention is diverted from the real everyday life of the local people. In the same way, while tourism can be accused of cultural arrogance in the way that it manipulates local traditions and cultures into convenient time slots and places, others would argue that it is still a sharing process, so what if a tourist sees, even pays to see a half-hour excerpt from a ceremony that might take hours or even days to perform in traditional circumstances? This very act of the tourist involvement can help preserve the true culture, keeping the private culture from the pressure of tourists. In this sense, in somewhat conciliatory mood, Turner and Ash (1975) hold out some hope for tourism:

> it still has the potential to educate, since, in its highest form, it seeks to view and understand the origins and developments of cultures . . . there are . . . tourists who experience new feelings, who come to some new realisation of their relation to history when visiting cultures other than their own . . . . Observing the monuments of past or foreign cultures may . . . turn the tourists' thoughts back to the complexities of their own culture.

De Kadt (1979), too, sees the positive and has this to say on the subject:

> the frequent charge that tourism contributes to a degeneration [of culture] appears to be an exaggeration. Even though curio production, airport art and performances of fake folklore are of course stimulated by tourist demand . . . frequently arts, crafts and local culture have been revitalised as a direct result of tourism. To be authentic, arts and crafts must be rooted both in historical tradition

125

and in present day life; true authenticity cannot be achieved by conservation alone.

The implications

The social effect of tourist development could be represented by the polarities of a social-interaction continuum. At one extreme tourism-induced social change can lead to development, representing increased socioeconomic benefits. At the other, change can lead to dependency and reinforcement of social discrepancies based on an economy structured to suit the needs of a local élite and transnational tourism corporations. The position within the continuum that a destination may find itself depends on two major factors: the historic events that frame its current touristic condition, and the extent to which its political economy is dominated by exogenous forces.

The introduction of outside ideologies and foreign ways of life into societies that have been relatively closed or isolated can lead, as de Kadt (1976) identifies, to 'changes in attitudes, values, or behaviour which can result from merely observing tourists'. This demonstration effect is almost unavoidable when tourists possess greater financial and leisure-time affluence than local residents, and when their vacation behaviours are rooted in what might appear to the local population as conspicuous consumption and gazing upon others' lifestyles.

The corollary of explorer-type tourists having the least impact on culture and lifestyle in the receiving area is that mass tourists have the most impact. Linked to this is the different psychological framework associated with those that prefer to travel in clearly defined groups to well-known and well-developed destinations that characterise the mass tourism product (as illustrated earlier in this chapter by Valene Smith's linking of tourist types and their adaptation to local norms). As Graburn explains (1988:35),

> In sharp contrast [to 'spirit quest' or drifter-tourism with its accompanying self-imposed poverty] is the tourism of the timid – often parents of the youthful travelers – who have money and don't mind spending it, as long as they can carry the home-grown 'bubble' of their lifestyle around with them . . . Though undoubtedly enchanted by the view of God's handiwork [here, Graburn is exploring the theme of tourism as sacred journey] through the pane of the air-conditioned bus or the porthole, they worship 'plumbing that works' and 'safe' water and food . . . These tourists are likely to have the greatest impact on the culture and the environment of the host peoples both by virtue of their greater numbers and by their demands for extensions of their home environments for which they are willing to pay handsomely.

Conclusion

Cultural change comes about by things which are both internal and external to that culture. What concerns us then is the speed and type of change. In a sense, this is where Turner and Ash (1975), in stating that 'The tourists' superior economic wealth rapidly erodes the sensuous and aesthetic wealth of cultures that have developed in isolation from the western world . . . Tourism . . . has already begun obliterating cultures', are taking their polemic too far. It is safe to say that culture would change in the absence of tourism. Tourism then is simply one component (albeit a powerful one) of an emerging 'global culture' (as discussed in an earlier chapter) characterised by brand images and personalities such as Pepsico, McDonald's, Benetton, Ford, Marlboro, Madonna and Michael Jackson which dominate headlines, skylines and media. This tendency towards what might be termed 'global homogeneity' is assisted by global satellite TV such as CNN and MTV. Even within countries the requirements of a modern nation state are diluting ethnic and regional differences (Robertson, 1992:153); there is a tendency towards a homogeneous national culture. Greenwood (1989:184) describes '[cultural] dilution of all that is local and idiosyncratic'. Tourism has had a role to play in both assisting this cultural convergence (through bland hotel chains and standardised, rational holiday products) and, paradoxically, preventing it through revitalising interest in traditions and ethnicity. The whole notion of national culture, its commodification and heritage industry is discussed in a volume edited by Corner and Harvey (1991) entitled *Enterprise and Heritage: cross-currents of national culture.*

If the negative social consequences (if they can, in fact, be clearly established to the satisfaction of all members of a given society) are to be avoided, planners of all sorts, from architects through to social welfare agencies, must address the potential problems by careful planning activities that include early and frequent consultation: this is a fundamental rule in the management of any type of change. It is important to realise that the question of societal and cultural change is immensely complex. Issues concerning pornography, prostitution, the place of women in the tourism workforce, the notion of quality and permanency of jobs and the demonstration effect are just some of the concerns that social and tourism planners have to think about.

It is more difficult to redress the sociocultural balance between hosts and guests when it is done in circumstances of antagonism. This rancour may be caused as a result of rapid and uncontrolled growth, or perhaps where a local politician has used community ignorance of tourism for political gain. Under conditions of metatourism, the tourist is only one of a number of 'oppressors' – a list which might include local bureauocrats; indigenous élite; university professors; investors; and expatriate planters. The real object of hostility, for which the tourist is an admirable surrogate, is the new élite, old expatriate families and influential mercantile companies (which instruct and manipulate rather than engage in equal exchange) (Farrell, 1979).

CASE STUDY: TOURISM AND SOLOMON ISLANDS CULTURE

This case study comprises an extract from an article by a Solomon Islander reflecting on tourism and the process of change (Rajotte, 1980). It is followed by some questions that can be answered individually or in groups.

1. Tourism is a growing industry in Solomon Islands, although compared to other Pacific island countries it is still on a very small scale. However, this does not mean that it will not have any consequences or impact on the island culture. Acculturation – the process of cultural change brought about by contact with foreign cultures – began with Europeans in the 18th century, and tourism is a kind of social catalyst contributing to this acculturation process.

2. The impact of tourism has both advantages and disadvantages; with regard to creativity and excellence, tourism may help the islanders take pride in their art forms and culture. Tourism stimulates the preservation of traditional art, and thus helps to preserve the identity of the people of the Solomon Islands. The art forms, traditional songs and dances, etc. were nearly eradicated in the early stages of acculturation by the Europeans determined to Christianise and civilise the natives. In doing so they prohibited many activities that are now being revived by tourism. At that time, the natives were considered primitive and inferior in almost everything. However, as interaction progressed and the views of Europeans underwent change, there was a return of customary dances and songs as well as art. Tourism is helping in this revival.

3. There is a danger, however, of the art forms, dance and songs becoming devoid of their true meaning. This could come about if these traditionally valued practices were performed just for the sake of entertaining tourists and obtaining money for the perform-ances. Also, overdoing something could lead to the loss of its true value. If tourists were to ask some of the dancers or carvers to explain some of their items, many would not be able to give the correct explanations. This is because they are no longer conscious of the original meaning, but only of the money and other benefits that result from the production. In contrast to this, art forms and dance prior to European contact had an authentic meaning. They

were performed only at ceremonies and served to distinguish one occasion from another. Very often the older generations looks back and – because they are aware of this transition – they accuse tourism of having made a mockery out of their ancient traditions, condemning not only tourism but the westernisation process as a whole.

4. Tourism contributes to the intellectual development of the Solomon Islanders today because tourists are looked upon as successful people: they have to be in order to acquire money and be able to travel. In this way tourism acts as an incentive for Solomon Island youth to strive towards a high education level. They hope that this will enable them to secure good jobs or careers so that they will one day be like tourists and have plenty of money. When these expectations are not met, however, there is disappointment. When parents criticise and scold children, they may leave home and go to town. If they can find jobs at all they are lucky, otherwise they become hobos. The increasing number of vagrants in town has led to an increase in crime. Tourism, then, can act as a stimulant for the young to obtain a good education, but alternatively its effects can lead to frustration and crime.

5. Tourism is merely one aspect of modern change. It acts as a catalyst that is responsible for quickening some of the impacts of westernisation, and can lead to the deterioration of traditional values.

Discussion

This article raises some interesting issues for discussion. Check the following points against the article and discuss them in relation to changes that could be attributed to tourism and those that have resulted from the process of global communications.

Paragraph 1. The word 'acculturation' is used; what does this mean? Are there examples from other cultures?

Paragraph 2. How does tourism stimulate the preservation of traditional art helping to preserve the identity of the Solomon Islands?

Paragraph 3. Why did early European visitors consider natives as inferior? Do modern Europeans (tourists) have similar views, or has time changed their prejudices?

Paragraph 4. The phrases 'true meaning', 'true value', 'original meaning' and 'authentic meaning' are used in this passage. Can you define such terms? If the art forms are then being sold to tourists, can they be considered as commodities like a can of beans or carton of beer? Could we then use the phrase 'commoditisation of art'? What use is this phrase to us in coming to an understanding of the souvenir business? Could you guess at what someone might mean if they talked about 'airport art'?

Paragraph 5. This passage suggests that tourists can act as a role model for success. It further suggests that Solomon Island youth hope that they will one day be like tourists, and have plenty of money. Is this a helpful ambition? Could some youths hope, perhaps that one day they will be successful in other ways, and not like tourists? With their wealth and power, tourists demonstrate certain behaviours, material goods (camera, expensive watches, etc.) and lifestyles to groups of people who cannot realistically be expected to achieve this lifestyle. This is known as the demonstration effect. Is it only tourists who demonstrate this almost unachievable lifestyle? Do local people ever do this, or does this not count? Can television programmes give a demonstration effect, or is this fiction and so does not count?

Paragraph 6. It is stated that tourism is merely one aspect of modern change. Is this the case, or does the impact of tourism go deeper than other processes of modernisation?

Tourism, expatriates and the international division of labour?

Introduction

In general, when broadly-based political coalitions in favour of controlling transnational activities exist, the ability of labour to achieve its ends is at its greatest. However, in so far as a bloc of forces is able to achieve some success in developing countries, there is an increasing likelihood that transnational firms will shift production to developing countries, notably those with repressive policies with regard to organised and other labour. Such relocation of production has been occurring in the 1970s and 1980s, and is bound up with the 'new international division of labour'. (Gill and Law, 1988:218)

At first reading it might be thought that tourism, with its central theme of 'place' and geographic location, could escape this phenomenon. However, given the convergence of style of many resorts and holiday destinations (Sandals resorts, for instance, make positive virtue of the similarity between their properties) operators can, in fact, 'shift production' to locations that offer lower staff costs (always an important cost factor with 'the high-touch' service element of tourism production). Operators in industrialised countries also utilise the cheap labour of illegal or recent immigrants: an article in the *Observer* (4 October 1992) quoted Chris Pond of the Low Pay Unit as saying 'Many employers are prepared to use the vulnerability of illegal workers. They commit a criminal offence by employing illegal workers but the authorities are colluding in this.' The article specifically mentioned the restaurant and catering sector. The difficulty arises, when trying to make sense of all this, is that what a UK national might think of as low pay is worth a considerable amount when transferred into Polish zlotys, Russian roubles or Romanian lei.

For many regions of the world, migration and employment are key components in tourism. This could be either intranational migration in the form of moving from one area to another within a country to take up employment opportunities offered through tourism or extranational migration, that is moving from one country to another.

Tourism and the international division of labour?

Even given the above, there remains a sense that tourism as an industry is protected from the increasing tendency for this global division of labour (that is, the tendency for jobs in the global village to be shifted to where the cheapest available labour force exists) – the phrase 'social dumping' has been used in this context to describe such activities within the European Union. We have already established the special circumstance framing the purchase of a touristic product: consumption takes place at the place of production; we have also made the case that it is possible (but less easy) to shift demand from one touristic 'product' to another (which in effect means from one destination to another).

This international division of labour does happen, to a certain extent, through the use of Third World carriers such as Garuda (Indonesia), Air Lanka (Sri Lanka), Tarom (Romania: not Third World, but demonstrating all the key characteristics of such carriers) and the numerous national airlines that are arising out of the former Soviet Union. These offer fares (especially long-haul) considerably lower than, for instance, Air France, British Airways, Japan Airlines and Qantas. One part of that ability to offer heavily discounted fares is the comparative cost advantage of being headquartered in Paris, London, Tokyo or Sydney as opposed to Jakarta, Colombo or Bucharest and the relative lower pay scales. (This contradicts claims made in an earlier chapter about costs for Third World airlines being more expensive due to the dependence on carriers from the industrialised world: no matter, it is simply another conundrum.)

In another sense, there is a kind of global shifting of importance of tourism destinations, not only as they rise and fall in popularity and fashion, but also as labour costs rise (thus bringing the benefits to a local population promised through tourism) so profit margins for local owner and international tour operator are squeezed. Consumer sensitivity towards price within the travel marketplace (especially in mass markets) can lead to the holiday purchase decisions on the part of the tourist being changed: thus as labour costs in Indonesia rise, so the holiday-maker will go to Malaysia.

The position of expatriates

In 1977 Raoul Salmon, speaking of his home, Tahiti, noted that:

> Labour is unskilled [and] poorly motivated . . . To work in a hotel is considered uninteresting and being underpaid . . . Hotels cannot keep their staff very long . . . The same turnover is true of training for hotel jobs . . . Half the people starting do not finish. (See Farrell, 1977:16.)

Interviews by the authors with hotel operators in the United Kingdom and overseas some 10 years later revealed a similar pattern. By relying on a young, often female and deskilled workforce (Enloe, 1989; Bagguley, 1987) the opportunity for enhancing the tourist 'product' through the value added resulting from a stable workforce is lost. The past decades of phenomenal tourism growth in all receiving areas has allowed operators to rely on a constant turnover of tourists: the one-time visitor, in a sense mirroring the turnover of tourism employees that characterises tourism employment in many countries.

Under the pressure of day to day business operations, this message is not always acknowledged by operators. Governments for their part must show a commitment to educating and training the workforce at all levels. This commitment is not met with the establishment of the type of hotel schools that only serve to provide international companies and expatriate managers with a compliant, service-orientated workforce, but tourism education centres that not only teach vocational skills, but educate workers into dealing with the complex issues arising from being involved in an economic sector that (in the case of metatourism) earns its bread from hedonism and the cashing in on stark differences between rich and poor.

Fieldwork in Sri Lanka and the Cook Islands revealed dramatic differences in the position and importance of expatriates in the tourism workforce. In the case of Sri Lanka, expatriates are virtually non-existent. Nearly all senior positions in the sector are filled by nationals. Evidence suggested three reasons for this: first, the sheer amount of education and training taking place; secondly, the importance attached to training is a reflection of a culture that clearly views education as important in its own right and thirdly, there is the

increasing flow of nationals who have gained senior management experience
as expatriates themselves (notably in the Gulf), and are now returning to fill
senior positions. The case of the Cook Islands, however, matches the position
in very many other countries at a similar stage of development. Expatriates
hold virtually every position of importance, from general manager of a resort
to assistant pastry cook. Ankomah (1991:435) discusses in detail the reliance
on management contracts for hotels (72% in Sub-Saharan Africa, 47% in Latin
America, 60% in Asia compared to 2% in Europe). There exists, then,
something of a dependency culture in which countries are persuaded that the
industry cannot function without expatriates. Fiji provides a clear illustration
of this. Tourism has been an important economic sector since the mid-1960s;
a hotel school was established in the late-1960s charged with the responsibility
of training the workforce. Its management was under constant yet subtle
pressure from industry lobbyists (up until the mid- to late 1980s exclusively
white) to concentrate on training low level operatives (chambermaids,
assistant waiters, etc.). This has had the effect of stifling the development of
local talent for topmost jobs. The industry, unlike the situation in Sri Lanka,
still relies on a core of about 80–100 expatriates, taking most of the
management and top technical jobs. This expatriate élite does what it can to
perpetuate itself. Discussions about replacing foreigners with nationals, while
on the agenda at government level, seem to be diluted at a more practical
level. Immigration officers with responsibility for work permits seem convinced
of calamity if the operators do not get their Swiss pastry chef or Australian
general manager. Expatriates form a powerful lobby backed up by a strong
support network from the local power élites. It is this then that sets the
framework for failure of many countries to train their nationals adequately for
the very topmost positions.

Perhaps this failure can, to some extent, be attributed to a failure in
communication between expatriate management and the indigenous workforce. Inadequacies in work performance indicate the non-technical background of the workers, but at the same time evidences the inadequate training
and induction of workers to the tasks and operations of the establishment. In
other words, it reveals the inadequacies of expatriate personnel to handle
intercultural situations for which they in turn have had little preparation or
guidance.

Cultural clash

Many managers take the simplistic view that technological development is a
task of transferring knowledge and skills, without realising its cultural and
social implications. Managers put the blame for work performance failure on
the receiving end (workers) for its (their) incapacity to receive what is given,
rather than stopping to ask where the inadequacy of the 'donor' performance

133

lies. Perhaps expatriate workers in the private sector should receive induction courses with attention being given to both the economy and culture of the nation. Courses should ensure that all expatriates are motivated to carry out knowledge and skills sharing. Expatriate managers with responsibilities for training have had as little preparation as those on the receiving end. In other words, workers cannot be expected to manage culturally alien demands made on them any better than the expatriate personnel can be expected to manage in what is, for them, a similarly alien environment. Riley and Jones (1992:310) acknowledge that the culture of transnational hotels is Western European so that:

> training takes on the additional burden of culture transfer as well as teaching skills and knowledge . . . [this must be] a part of any training strategy because the easy route of imposing, without thought, American–European management style and definitions of skill and quality will lead to frustration.

This situation can be exacerbated when the dominant culture also defines the motivation and reward system. Pacific Islanders, for instance, who find personal motivation through family, church and sharing, may be puzzled when exhorted to work harder for the benefit of a foreign hotel or in order to gain some individual reward. While the social structure outside the world of work cannot be replicated, the 'family-feeling' phenomenon sometimes manifested in an integrated resort hotel could be used, along with ethnographic knowledge, to formulate culturally appropriate motivation. An excellent example of this is to be found at Habarana Lodge Hotel in Sri Lanka where, in 1992, General Manager Mahendra Hulangamuwa saw his role as going far beyond that of ensuring bottom line results for his owners. He developed strategies to ensure year-round employment, made overt efforts to purchase produce locally, and clearly saw staff as essential human resources (rather than units of cost!). It almost goes without saying that both he and the owners, Keells Hotels, are Sri Lankan. Other culturally appropriate motivations could be in the form of individual bonuses being accumulated for distribution to a whole village (especially in Polynesian and Melanesian tourism destinations where village–resort ties tend to be both formal and strong), or for support to village or resort sports teams or churches. Macauley and Hall (1992) report the Ka'anapali Beach Hotel as introducing a whole range of social and cultural strategies that eventually reduced labour turnover by 58.9% to an annual rate of 15%, the lowest on the island of Maui (the next lowest is 40%, with many other properties reporting turnover in excess of 100% per year), sick leave abuse reduced by 58% and donations to two major charities concerned with preserving the cultural traditions of the Hawaiian people increased by more than 100%. In a Western European context, the notion of developing a positive culture at the workplace is discussed at length by Lockwood *et al.* in Teare and Olsen (1992:312–38).

There are at least three factors that will eventually mitigate against the continued use of expatriates. First, there is the sociopolitical rationale for diminishing their influence, that is, as overt colonial (neo or past) attitudes and actions fade, so the automatic 'call for a white man' ceases. Secondly, as education in Third World countries improves and is better able to produce and encourage local talent, the need will lessen, and thirdly a double pressure on remuneration is likely to occur, with (a) labour costs for management converging between developed and underdeveloped countries and (b) the total cost of employing expatriates (including housing, family allowances and passages) increases dramatically.

CHAPTER 5

Economic impacts of tourism

Introduction

This chapter discusses the economic impacts of tourism focusing on the rationale behind tourism development, examining factors that determine the success of economic outcomes related to development policy.

The overall aim of any government choosing to pursue a tourism development strategy is economic advantage. In any national tourism 'development plan' the economic objectives are paramount and clear. The objectives for Greenland's tourism development plan for 1991–2005 states that: 'Tourism shall be developed as one of the principal industries of the country'. The supporting documents refer to an income of about $\frac{1}{2}$ billion DKK, corresponding to 33 000 tourists spending an average of 15 000 DKK each in Greenland (Greenland Tourism Development Plan, 1991:1). The plan, which in comparison to many tourism masterplans is enlightened by the high profile given to environmental and social objectives, also stresses the need for local participation and involvement of the community in the decision-making process. As is clearly demonstrated, the underlying aim (and thus catalyst to development) of any tourism plan is the creation of opportunities for economic improvement. Similarly, under the Finnish 'Travel 2000' scheme, economic emphasis is paramount:

> The Finnish economy is in dire need of foreign exchange revenues to narrow and eventually stabilise the yawning current account deficit. This can only be achieved through a successful economic policy and broadly based, competitive trade in exports. The tourist industry can and must do its share towards this end. (Finnish Tourist Board, 1993:4)

The three key goals to be achieved from the development of Finnish tourism are:

- an increase in FM1 billion in foreign exchange revenues (in real income) by the end of the 1996, and a further increase of FM3 billion by the year 2000;

- an annual growth rate of 3% in the consumption of domestic travel services; and
- improving the profitability of the travel industry; profitability ensures the healthy development of the trade and its scope for creating jobs.

Again, we have a government not only seeing the potential for tourism, but setting specific targets for it and then developing and implementing plans to achieve those ends.

Cyprus was reported as having tourism as 'the driving force [behind] spectacular growth' (*Guardian*, 25 May 1990). The article, quoting government sources in Nicosia, went on with the following assertion: 'Spectacular growth in tourism is fuelling rapid economic expansion in Cyprus. With growth rates of 17 per cent in 1988, 23 per cent in 1989 and a projected 15 per cent [for 1990] ... About 1.5 m tourists visit the south of the island a year, leaving some Cyp£475 million (about £600 million) in 1989, more than 35 per cent of the island's foreign exchange earnings.' The link between economic impact and tourism development was also demonstrated in an advertising supplement for Nigeria in the *Observer* (27 March 1994). The importance of tourism to the national economies of many countries was emphasised by Gokie M. Ibru, chairman of the Ikeja Hotel Group: 'I believe that we have not scratched the surface of the tourism industry in Nigeria'. The article continued:

> Tourism is the fifth source of foreign revenue earning, $55 million in 1991, and the government is anxious to develop the industry. At the end of last year the Nigerian Tourism Development Corporation was established to boost both domestic and international tourism. Nigeria offers a tropical climate, wildlife parks, rain forests, beach resorts, exotic tribal festivals where the art, music and religious rites of some of the country's 250 ethnic groups are displayed.

Gokie Ibru's quote clearly sets an economic value on both environment and indigenous culture in the tourism marketplace. It demonstrates (especially for Nigeria which in recent history set economic faith in oil production) a relatively recent realisation that 'traditional culture' is a resource with a capacity to produce economic capital. In terms of protecting the physical environment from destructive forms of development this realisation offers an opportunity for environmentalists to win the case for the protection of environmental resources, based on an economic premise. Given that much of the development process is seemingly driven by short-term financial decisions taken in a free-market system, and the 'If it doesn't pay, it doesn't stay' attitude persists, then the realisation that people will pay for experiencing physical and cultural environments offers opportunities for their protection (natural resource accounting extended to cultural resource accounting).

In her report *Ecotourism: the potentials and pitfalls* (1990:16) Boo draws attention to an economic model based around the value of tourism to the local economy, developed for the Amboseli National Park in Kenya. An economic comparison was made between the park's estimated net value for wildlife viewing and agricultural activity. The results showed that safeguarding the wildlife and the development of tourism would generate US$40 per hectare, while agricultural activities would yield US$0.8 per hectare. These potential economic benefits rely heavily on tourism being developed in a fashion that permits retention of revenues by local people. This is likely to provide a strong incentive for local people to work in harmony with planners, lessening the temptation for local people to graze their animals or to continue poaching or crop growing in sensitive areas. Such new land stewarding deals represent a chance for long-termism and sustainability to be placed on the agenda. Watson, in describing the development of the skiing industry in the Cairngorms (in Scotland), exemplifies the points made about Amboseli while also highlighting potential development conflict:

> The Cairngorms are of national importance for tourism and recreation because of their outstanding hills, snow for skiing, valley scenery, wildlife and wilderness. These qualities can be regarded as important natural resources. Unlike non-renewable oil deposits they will continue to contribute much, provided we look after them. This is not easy however, because people with differing interests give different values to these resources and wish to see different resources developed, sometimes to the exclusion of others on the same land. (1980:427)

Here we see that the inevitable link between the environment and economics is not only a phenomenon of metatourism: it applies equally to developed and developing nations. Just as for other economic activities, tourism is supported by the existence of resources on which it is based. However (a point made previously in this book), unlike other sectors, the consumer travels to the point of production where these resources are 'converted' for consumption by the tourist. These resources may be natural, consisting either of the physical environment such as beautiful beaches and mountain ranges or indigenous peoples such as the Masai Mari or Papuan Highlanders. The industry is therefore based on natural capital which can be developed and transformed into economic capital. The degree of success to which this transformation is achieved will be measured against any economic, environmental and social goals that have been decided upon as outcomes of the development process. It is therefore important to recognise the value of this natural capital as the resource base of tourism and pursue economic objectives that maintain its wealth generation possibilities into the future, as opposed to its short-term exploitation and destruction. It is also critical that we interpret the phenomenon of international tourism as having interlinked economic, environmental and social impacts. For a government to see the tourist in purely economic terms – almost as a 'commodity' or 'good' – merely as a factor in revenue generation (with the highly visible tourist forming part of the invisible trade balance) is shortsighted. Unlike a commodity or primary resource, the tourist is a discerning purchaser with a range of other options. Consequently, demand for a destination is highly vulnerable to exogenous factors including changes in fashion and consumption patterns.

The costs and benefits

Many tourism textbooks (Ryan, 1991; Cooper *et al.* 1993; Bull, 1991) will explain the benefits and costs that can be expected from tourism develop-ment. Cleverdon's seminal work of 1979 also provides an excellent account of the benefits and costs. It is not the aim of this chapter to reiterate all these points in detail. The costs and benefits are, however, summarised in the following paragraphs.

Foreign exchange and balance of payments

Tourism is an obvious source of foreign exchange and particularly useful for developing countries looking to earn hard currencies such as dollars, francs, marks and sterling. Cleverdon (1979:29) emphasises the potential of tourism to earn foreign exchange *vis-à-vis* traditional commodities:

> Commodity trade, which is the principal foreign earner for most LDCs has not provided a revenue growth to match the increase in the imports bill. Import substitution and local processing can provide a means of saving or earning FX but many LDCs run the problem of limited domestic markets or restricted access to foreign markets. In this context, tourism's advocates see it as a prime sector for encourage-ment by the government ... Demand (and expenditure) is growing faster than global inflation rates; there are few trade barriers; and FX is earned more conveniently than from manufactured goods since the customer brings himself to the point of his own expense and takes immediate delivery of the services.

While there are now major questions being asked about the 'convenience' of earning national exchequer through tourism, Cleverdon's tenet remains utterly viable and has stood the test of time.

Tourism also plays an important part in the balance of payments, helping to offset any difference between manufactured imports and exports. It is classified as part of the service sector economy and appears (as noted above) in the invisible trade balance. If the balance of payments on tourism is to be positive it is important to pursue an inbound development policy that also

139

Table 5.1 UK tourism balance sheet (£bn)

	Earnings	Expenditure	Balance
1984	4.61	4.66	(0.05)
1985	5.44	4.87	0.57
1986	5.55	6.08	(0.53)
1987	6.26	7.28	(1.02)
1988	6.18	8.22	(2.03)
1989	6.95	9.36	(2.41)
1990	7.75	9.95	(2.20)
1991	7.39	9.95	(2.57)
1992 (provisional)	7.89	11.24	(3.35)

Source: International Passenger Survey 1993.

allows for the encouragement of domestic tourism – thus retaining revenues from tourist expenditure (that residents could spend on overseas holidays) in the hosting country.

The invisible trade, of which tourism plays an increasingly significant part, is extremely important in the overall balance of payments picture in the United Kingdom. Only six times in the last two centuries (1956, 1958, 1971, 1980, 1981 and 1982) has the visible trade balance (i.e. trade in visible and tangible goods) been in surplus (Banking Information Service, 1986), with the surpluses between 1980 and 1982 mainly attributed to the economic impact of North Sea oil and gas. As Table 5.1 shows, the United Kingdom's tourism balance sheet has had a mixed performance: with the early 1980s in surplus. The earnings have continued to perform well but have been outstripped by expenditure. A surplus has not been achieved since 1985 (see Table 5.1).

Contribution to Gross National Product

The success of countries and governments are most often interpreted through percentage annual growths in GNP. Tourism can play a significant part in contributing to this through extra expenditure in the economy on goods and services. For many countries, tourism has demonstrated an ability to grow faster than, for instance, manufacturing or other economic sectors, even under generally slow conditions. For example, the contribution of tourism to Greece's GNP 'increased from 2.3% of the GNP in 1970 to 6.4% in 1990. On the contrary, the percentage of export receipts remained rather constant, 10–11%, in the 1980s' (Briassoulis, 1993:294).

Tourism income multiplier

Tourism expenditure into an economy is not solely limited to direct expenditure. The money paid by a tourist to a hotel will be used by the owners in different ways. Employees will receive wages which, in turn, they will spend in the local economy on goods and services. Hotel supplies such as food and beverages and services will be paid for out of revenue (there will, however, be a certain amount of imports within the goods and services supplied). Some of the money may be passed to banking institutions, perhaps to repay debts in the form of loans, or for savings and investment. Other money will be paid to the government in the form of personal and corporate taxation. Thus money 'leaks out' of the local economy through imports, savings, outward investment and taxation (i.e. it does not stay directly within the local economy to be spent by local people on indigenous goods or services). Meanwhile the money received by local firms supplying the hotel will be used in turn to pay for goods and will generate demand and supply in the local economy. Some of this revenue will also 'leak out' in the form of central taxation, savings, and in the case of lesser developed countries, the remittance of wages back to home countries by expatriate workers and managers. However, the tourist expenditure encourages the circulation of money in the local economy which generates further demand and expenditure. The value of this extra income to the local community will be determined by factors such as the existing level of economic development in the area, the composition of the workforce and tourism facilities ownership patterns.

Intersectoral linkages

The diverse nature of tourism means that it creates demand for a wide range of goods and services to support it. The more of these support businesses that exist locally the greater the economic advantage of tourism to the local community. The development of hotels and facilities provide opportunities for the construction and manufacturing sectors. Fishery and agricultural industries also benefit from increased tourism activity, and strong links with these will often contribute to competitive advantage through restaurants being able to claim that they use 'local produce'.

Job creation

As well as an income multiplier there is also an employment multiplier. The same processes are at work as for the income multiplier and the advantage of the job multiplier in the local area will be dependent on the nature of tourism development, the extent of outside control, the level of economic development and the skills of the locally available workforce. A generally held perception about tourism as an 'industry' is that as a service sector industry, it is labour intensive, and that employment is created at a relatively low cost when compared to (for instance) manufacturing. However, a number of commentators over a number of years (Bryden, 1973; Lea, 1988; Burns, 1994) question this simplistic approach by arguing that when cost of infrastructure and capital intensive works are taken into consideration the differences in the cost of job creation are far less dramatic.

141

Government revenues

Government revenues will be collected from increased tourism expenditure at both central and local levels. This will take the form of corporation taxes, employee taxation and in some cases direct taxation placed on the tourist; the most familiar examples would be airport arrival and departure taxes. In theory this should offer the opportunity for increased government expenditure on maintaining and improving the quality of the tourism environment.

Infrastructure development

Increased revenues from taxation should allow infrastructure development through the provision of airports, roads, electricity, water and sewerage disposal. The real value of these extra facilities to communities will depend upon the level of infrastructural development prior to tourism and the value judgement of the trade-off between economic gain and environmental (and cultural) alteration. The provision of infrastructure to any adequate level (generally meaning sufficient for western tourists) is necessary for tourism development to take place. It is therefore likely that public sector investment in infrastructure will be needed before any significant level of international tourism can be realised. This internal investment will be problematic for countries with large debt repayment problems, and may lead to further debt. There is also the dilemma to be faced about providing infrastructure for seemingly rich and hedonistic tourists when political pressure from the local level may be for more spending on health and education.

Opportunity cost

By allocating resources such as land, manpower, training and use of public and private sector funds, the opportunity for the development of other economic alternatives to tourism is reduced. It is therefore important that in addition to planning for tourism development, consideration is given to other sectors of the economy and tourism is developed as part of a balanced integrated economic development plan.

Over-dependence

If serious consideration is not given to economic alternatives and action is not taken to develop them localities can become too dependent on tourism as a form of economic activity. This makes businesses and livelihoods highly vulnerable to the determinants of tourism demand and the external influences such as recession, fluctuating exchange rates, political problems and changing consumer tastes. The high price elasticity of tourism makes it susceptible to economic recession and 'consumption–substitution' in tourist generating countries. This susceptibility to changes in consumption patterns is exampled by the decline of many British seaside resorts. Pendlebury (1993) in an article titled 'Resort that is dying for the good old days' describes the decline of Great Yarmouth, a traditional seaside town on England's east coast.

> To the strains of a palm court orchestra, thousands tea-danced the afternoon away on Britannia Pier ... this was Great Yarmouth in the four decades up to the fifties, a resort drawing millions each year. Today, those glory days are nothing but a faded memory as the resort struggles to survive. More than half its hotels and guest houses have been put up for sale ... in all, 170 of 286 establishments are on the market. Many more owners would like to sell, but the estate agents [realtors] are refusing to take any others on their books.

Thus, like many 'commodities' bought with disposable income, destinations (in terms of a 'product') may lose their perceived value for money and the tourist will seek an alternative holiday venue or decide to use the disposable income in another way.

High consumer and land prices

As tourism demand grows so will demand for suitable development sites. This leads to increases in the value of land. Some landowners will clearly profit. Others, however, clearly will not. Many in the local community may be tenants with no ownership of real estate. For them development may mean dispossession and relocation, as evidenced by the case study on the development of golf in Thailand (p.176).

Lea (1988:50) states:

> Although there are very few documented studies of how inflation due to tourism affects a host population, there is plenty of conventional wisdom to suggest some prices are linked to this cause. The more obvious instances involve increases in retail prices in shops during the tourist season, and steeply rising land values leading to a general rise in home costs and property taxes.

Lea continues this thought by citing the example of huge increases in land values in the early 1970s at Swaziland's Ezulweni Valley Tourist Centre, caused by South foreign property speculation. Cleverdon (1979:49) cites the example of land prices in San Agustin in the Canaries rising 17 times in value between 1963 and 1971. In the United Kingdom the rapid rise of house prices during the 1980s in the Lake District caused by second-home purchases (a theme explored in the context of Switzerland by Krippendorf, 1987) and retirement-home purchases meant many young local people could no longer afford to buy homes in their own community.

These market distortions then may prevent future generations of the community living in the area. Attractive prices for farmland combined with

comparatively high salaries to be made from tourism will tempt people away
from their traditional livelihoods to work in tourism.

Negative aspects of promotion

The economic impacts of tourism represent the most important facets of
tourism from a developmental viewpoint. Without a perception of the
economic benefits that tourism can bring to countries, there would be little
encouragement for tourism development by host authorities, nor would the
major world lending agencies such as the World Bank and European
Commission be willing to fund projects based around tourism development if
there were not economic gains to be made. However, the case for tourism
development is often founded on bland statistical evidence; for example, there
are 600 million international tourists in the world, a figure which is set to rise
to more than 800 million by the year 2000. This seemingly offers hope for
development but the statistics fail to tell the whole story. Although economic
figures may give indications on which to base development decisions, the wider
social and environmental impacts of any development decision must also be
considered. Often, use of natural resources may be determined on the sole
basis of economic returns between different competing economic sectors,
without wider consideration of social and environmental impacts which are
implicitly long-term.

Proponents of the tourism industry, notably tourism transnational corporations (increasingly through their pressure group the World Travel and Tourism
Council – WTTC) and major agencies such as the UNDP and World Tourism
Organisation, stress the importance of tourism as a global activity. The
emphasis given to the importance of tourism is supported by a plethora of
statistics stressing the magnitude and rapid growth of tourism's worth to
national and international economies. Indeed, the fact that tourism is truly an
international industry is demonstrated by the wish to express the extent of the
success of the industry in global terms through quantification, such as this
from a WTTERC environmental report (1993:6)

> Contributing 6 per cent of world GDP, supporting 127 million jobs,
> accounting for 7 per cent of global investment and 13 per cent of
> world consumer spending there is no doubt that travel and tourism is
> an integral part of the life of over 90 per cent of the population of
> developed countries.

Mathieson and Wall (1983:36) in their comprehensive chapter on economic
impacts state:

> The emphasis on the economics of tourism, especially its benefits,
> reflect the widespread belief among agency personnel that tourism can
> yield rapid and considerable returns on investments and be a positive

force in remedying economic problems . . . It is not surprising, then, to find that most research on economic benefits of tourism has been conducted, investigated or sponsored by such institutions.

It is, of course, not new to say that quantification does not tell us about the quality of employment opportunity or the wider social worth of the industry to those people employed in tourism. Indeed, one of the main economic indicators used for the measurement of wealth of any nation to which tourism maybe a substantial contributor, GNP, has come under attack from various sources, particularly environmental quarters as sometimes being inconsistent with the representation of the quality of life. As Pearce (1989:22) puts it:

> The tendency has been to use a measure of gross (or sometimes net) national product (GNP or NNP) as the basis for economic growth calculations. If GNP increases that is economic growth. But GNP is constructed in a way that tends to divorce it from one of its underlying purposes: to indicate, broadly at least, the standard of living of the population. If pollution damages health, and health care expenditure rises, that is an increase in GNP – a rise in the 'standard of living' not a decrease.

In tourism, measuring success of business or policy aspects based on visitor arrivals and expenditure tells us little of the improvement to the quality of life for the individual, nor does a percentage figure of tourism's contribution to foreign exchange earnings tell us how much of that money is ultimately retained in the destination or how much of it will leak from the economy at local, regional and national levels. The general statistics of tourism are impressive; however, they can be misleading and it is critically important for any student of tourism to have an understanding of the limits of these figures. It is important to understand that impressive-looking tourist statistics expressed in numbers and revenues do not necessarily relay the degree of success of tourism development. Economic benefits maybe undermined by high leakages or a political system that sees few benefits reaching the majority of the population and economic success may be achieved at a high cost to the environment and social fabric of society. Sex tourism is a big industry in Thailand with many tourists going to Thailand especially for that reason. However, it will have a costly social and economic impact on Thailand in future years as the incidence of AIDS continues to increase and the most economically productive age segment of the nation is threatened by ill health. Already for many Thai young women and girls it has meant their social exclusion from the life and community in their villages and severely limited their opportunity for marriage.

However, although there have been criticisms of the differences in methodologies of measurement of tourism statistics between countries, the growth in the industry and its increasing geographical spread is indisputable. It is the rapid growth of the industry that we observe both through our own experiences, and the availability of quantified information, that feeds its continued growth and development. Tourism offers opportunities for economic benefits at a national to local scale. Its contribution to national economies can be invaluable (sometimes acting as a catalyst for development of other economic sectors). This was the case for Spain which, in the mid-1930s before the advent of the Spanish Civil War, attracted approximately 200 000 tourists. By 1990 this had risen to 52 million visitors generating an impressive $18,593 million in tourist earnings. Between 1955 and 1963 the growth was more than 300%. During the 1960s Spain's income from tourism was enough to pay for the entire oil importation bill. Franco encouraged the development of tourism, the revenues from which were used to modernise agriculture and industry.

At a regional and local level it can provide job opportunities (even given the negative factors discussed in other chapters) and even stabilise communities where young people might tend towards urban drift. For some countries it is seen as an economic panacea. Denied the chance of undergoing an Industrial Revolution because of colonialism, the existing international political economy, domination of world markets and protective policies of trading blocs, tourism is seen as offering opportunities for both modernisation and economic success. Increasing awareness of the standard of living perceived as being enjoyed by Westerners by peoples of the developed countries makes economic development a political necessity for stability at national and international levels. As Bocock (1993:53) puts it:

> Whether it is a desire for blue jeans, pens and paper, television sets, radios, cars or travel in the aeroplane, there are things and experiences which people who are in contact with western media come to wish they could purchase, as long as the basic necessities are available to them.

Ironically, yet another paradox of postmodern tourism is demonstrated here in that we go in search of 'other' or the 'primitive' while the host community seeks the economic benefits we as tourists can bring to purchase the icons and symbols that will make them more like those that are seeking to 'get away from it all'. Tourism can therefore be an important tool for economic development of countries and in particular regions of countries. However, it is important to give consideration to the types of economic benefits that are sought and for whom they are being sought.

Tourism as 'mono-crop'

Tea, coffee and rubber plantations were initiated and developed through a world system dominated by mercantilism and colonialism. Development relied on foreign capital and expertise. Similarly, international tourism plant in

Third World countries usually relies upon overseas investment from the West for its development. As noted in Chapter 2, the following general similarities may then be drawn between the development and trade of commodities (and of plantocracies) and tourism:

- a heavy reliance upon the sale of the 'commodity' (in the sense of 'destination') in the developed world;
- need for overseas and foreign investment to develop the infrastructure and superstructure required for development;
- reliance on foreign business intermediaries to help the 'product' reach the markets;
- extreme vulnerability in terms of demand to the full range of exogenous factors;
- the 'product' (in this case the destination) originates in a country both external to and less powerful than the purchaser;
- in some senses, the 'product' is conceptualised, designed and packaged for the developed country (in the case of tourism this is primarily concerned with the selling of perception); and
- consequently its success depends upon continued western demand.

Thus we see that tourism production and consumption in the context of international political economy. It could be said the owners of production of tourism services continue to be the western countries even if the economy is moving from an agricultural to service-based economy. A functionalist viewpoint would probably interpret the relationship as a healthy one maintaining the equilibrium in North–South relationships. Developing countries receive inward investment from the North, which allows the opportunity for developing countries to improve their economics through heightened product development and greater sophistication in product positioning in the market-place. This classical economic viewpoint (as influenced by the economist David Ricardo, 1772–1823) was a cornerstone for 19th century colonialism:

> In the minds of classical, liberal economists an aggressive colonial policy was a necessary complement to the creation of a perfect international division of labour in which each area of the globe, each region or country, would specialise in what it was good at and would thus cash in on Ricardo's theory of economic advantage. (Hoogvelt, 1982:162–3)

The opportunity for western tourists to consume destinations allows for the regeneration (or recreation) of workers from the West: this facilitates the continuation of economic and social systems in the generating countries Marxists would interpret this sort of core-periphery relationship as continuing imperialism (as in 'making the empire bigger'). However, the controllers of production in tourism are no longer limited to the West: with increasing investment overseas by Japanese and other South East Asian giant companies.

147

In reality, the reliance on multinationals for investment is the only chance for many developing countries which lack the resources and expertise to develop the sector by themselves, to construct an integrated 'tourism industry'. As explained in Chapter 7, this will certainly lead to the development of metatourism and a sector continually reliant on western capital.

The expected benefits to the indigenous population will be dependent on the discredited 'trickle down' effect, as heavily promoted for domestic and international economics during the Thatcher/Reagan years: the concept of investment in large-scale projects and wealth creation at the top with the benefits working their way through the economic hierarchy to the people at the bottom. Essentially this means money working its way from higher up in the economic system to lower down. Just how well this model works will be determined by the amount of leakages from the economic systems at both macro and micro levels. Bull (1991:139–40) describes leakages as 'other calls . . . made on . . . income, which remove part of the flow from being respent in local transactions. Primarily these other calls are:

- taxation on income
- that part of extra income which people choose to save . . .
- expenditure on imports.'

The amount of leakage of money out of an economic system will be therefore partly determined by the ability of the economy to service the supply needs of the tourism industry. The higher the level of existing economic development, the greater the chance of these needs being fulfilled, as it is more likely that the closed economic system will be able to produce goods and supply the employees necessary for the tourism industry. This means that organisations are less likely to have to go outside the area for supply of goods and to attract satisfactory personnel. However, to assess the likelihood of economic leakages based purely upon an economic rationale is incomplete. Cultural influence will also influence attitudes to local suppliers and people available to work in the tourism industry.

This could be interpreted as a form of subconscious or possibly overt racism in the sense of a lack of belief in the quality of these schools and perhaps a subconscious desire to have white managers dealing with white guests. It also means that money will leak from the country through expatriate salaries to overseas bank accounts. Often this may mean wages in the form of hard currencies directly leaving the country as the hotel manager insists on payment in US dollars as opposed to local dollars: an added leakage factor. Stories of receptionists and clerks being asked to separate hard currencies from local currencies for payment of wages, although illegal, are not unknown. The extent to which the trickle-down theory works will also be determined by the political systems working in society. Where political systems are blatantly undemocratic and power, influence and wealth rest with an élite, the chances of money working its way throughout the different levels of society from top to bottom are very limited. Even in the most democratic system, the percentages of the total amount of money available for distribution will decrease through each strata of society. The implication being that the system will produce increasing disparity of wealth between different social classes as opposed to moving society toward a more egalitarian model. Disparity of opportunity of economic wealth exists in all systems. The greater the existing propensity of this 'disproportionate tourism' development based around a top-heavy approach is likely to make disparities worse. As Cleverdon (1979:106) notes:

> [planning] should even try (though this has been rarely brought about in tourism plans) to relate tourism development to the more equitable distribution of wealth within the host country.

The link between the benefits of tourism development and general development is reiterated by Ascher (1985:11): 'It is therefore becoming increasingly clear that it is not tourism that leads to development but a country's general development that makes tourism profitable'. Often the turnover of multinational companies involved in tourism development can be more than the gross national products of the countries in which tourism development is taking place.

However, from a structuralist viewpoint consumption based around symbolic processes such as the purchasing of holidays is not purely something done for psychological or physiological need. It is more complicated, including the consumption of symbols to define a certain type of lifestyle (Bocock, 1993). Baudrillard interpreted consumerism as a purchaser trying to maintain a sense of identity through the purchase of goods. Tourism is no exception to this. Thus we have designer labels such as Gaultier, designer drinks such as Sol and designer resorts such as Club Med

Conclusion

The dependency of an increasing number countries upon tourism is a result of the continuing demand for international travel from western tourists (in part motivated by an increasing desire to push the boundaries of international travel ever further) and this demand being fed by producers and destinations. It would seem the periphery for travel is pushed further and further from a dominantly western centre. North European coastlines, the European coastline of the Mediterranean, the Mediterranean coastline of North Africa, travel to the United States and the development of tourism to long-haul destinations such as Thailand, Bali, the Caribbean and southern India all represent differing evolutionary stages of the development of the tourism industry. Consumer research (widely discussed by Poon, 1993) indicates that the tourist of today wants a wider choice of destinations and activities. The pattern of consumption by tourists now extends in differing degrees to most countries of the world.

This demand offers opportunities for countries to develop international tourism markets to bring the economic benefits outlined before. In reality, development options for countries possessing limited resources, faced with rapidly rising population, massive national debt and decreasing values of primary and extractive commodities (e.g. cotton and copper) are truly limited. In economists' terms, there are opportunity costs involved in transferring agricultural land for tourism development, giving financial incentives for tourism development, and reducing or losing the traditional skills base of any community. However, as tourism has demonstrated its potential to fulfil economic goals (given well-thought-out planning backed by political will) the challenge of the opportunity cost should be met.

The success of economic development through tourism is likely to be determined by the following factors:

- the stated objectives of tourism development from the host government;
- the nature of tourism development ownership and the retention of revenues in the local economy contrasted to leakages out of it;
- the opportunities for the local people to work in the tourism industry; and
- the impact of tourism development on the environment, which may improve or detract from its quality.

Therefore the degree to which tourism development is judged as being successful in terms of its economic impacts will depend on the yardstick against which it is being measured and who is doing the measuring. Westlake (1993) commenting on the Isle of Zakynthos states: 'An islander who hires sun umbrellas on the beaches to tourists can earn in two days the monthly salary of a Greek schoolteacher'. There can be no doubt that the islander hiring the umbrellas would welcome the economic influence of tourism. However, the schoolteacher, unless very philanthropic, may not be so keen and there must be worries that well-educated people would leave their posts to join the 'tourism boom'.

The success of tourism then will largely represent a relative measurement to what has gone before in terms of development and opportunity.

CHAPTER 6

Progress: from rice paddy to golf green – environmental issues and tourism

Introduction

The objective of this chapter is to assess the implications for the environment if used as a resource for tourism development. We have identified that the physical and cultural environments of destinations are usually their main attractions. From the adventurer who decides to go to Mongolia to the mass tourist who visits to Benidorm, their perception of the environment of the potential destination is a key determinant in deciding where they will go. The importance of tourism's relationship with the environment is that the economy of a destination is dependent upon its cultural and physical wellbeing. It is therefore important to understand the impacts of both tourism development and tourists on the environment.

Ideological approaches to the environment

The significance of the need to interpret the environment as a resource central to future development, is now accepted by an increasing number of policy makers. After living in harmony with our environment for centuries we have become increasingly out of synchronisation with it, especially since the Industrial Revolution. This has been perhaps both a consequence of a mix of western religious doctrine and economic 'progress', both of which tend to ignore the intrinsic value that a pleasurable value can bring to our lives. Gosling (1990) comments on the doctrine of Christian philosophers such as Kant, who advocated humanity's need to subdue the environment, as opposed to living in harmony with it. Indeed, it could be argued that humanity's current environmental problems are rooted in the Judaic and Christian doctrine of creation, that is that the natural order was created for the sake of humanity:

be fruitful and multiply and replenish the earth and subdue it: and have dominion over the fish of the sea, and over the fowl of the air and over every living thing that moveth upon the earth. (Genesis 1, verse 28)

MacCannell (1992) believes that our guilt over our maltreatment of the environment has led to the creation of national parks, not neccessarily from a true appreciation of nature but to assuage us of collective guilt.

Since the beginning of the Industrial Revolution, the origin of which was in Northern Europe, directed by Christian philosophy, the environment has been interpreted as something there for our exploitation. As Pepper (1993:56) writes:

Modernism, then, has involved a continuous process of destruction of what went before, in pursuit of general principles that were thought to have been desirable for universal human good, for instance freedom from material want and freedom to accumulate wealth.

The phenomenon of 19th century industrial development was built upon the use of natural resources such as coal and iron ore, which are finite and non-renewable. This exploitative view was disputed by advocates of communism such as Marx and Engels, who rejected the ravaging of nature to meet the needs of capitalism (although they believed that nature would benefit from the control of humanity). Marx believed that by separating the town and the country into two completely different spheres of existence, and by applying industrial techniques to both, capitalism disrupted the ecological basis of human existence. Progressively, humans would become more alienated from their natural environment. According to Foster (1994:64): 'Marx believed that large-scale industry and large-scale agriculture both contributed to the ruining of the agricultural worker and to the exhaustion of the natural power of the soil'.

Developing the theme of our ideological approach to the environment, O'Riordan (1983) and Pepper (1993) identify two polarised ideologies which both influence our approach to our relationship with the environment and govern our interaction with it. The first, ecocentrism, interprets humanity as being part of a global ecosystem subject to ecological laws. Encompassed within this perspective is an implicit responsibility on the individual to behave ethically for the benefit of the collective mass, a form of 'personalised collectivity'. This approach characterises itself in favouritism being given to low impact development and a dislike of 'bigness' and impersonality. The concept of 'small is beautiful', as expressed by Schumacher (1973), epitomises the ecocentric approach to development.

Conversely, technocentric ideology believes in the ability of man to exploit his environment and correct negative impacts upon it through the use of, and continued refinement and advancement in, science and technology. Significantly, technocentrics place their faith in both the ability of existing institutions to accommodate environmental demands and in market forces and management techniques to control environmental problems. O'Riordan (1983:11) asserts: 'The technocentric mode is identified by rationality, the "objective" appraisal of means to achieve given goals, by managerial efficiency . . .'. Pepper (1993:33) comments:

> Technocentrism recognises environmental problems but believes either unrestrainedly that our current form of society will always solve them and achieve unlimited growth (the 'cornucopian' view) or, more cautiously, that by careful economic and environmental management they can be negotiated (the 'accommodators').

O'Riordan in Pepper (1993:34) also identifies two main typologies of technocentrics. He recognises the 'accommodaters' who are defined as having 'faith in the adaptability of institutions and approaches to assessment and evaluation to accommodate environmental demands'. Included within this category would be middle-ranking executives, environmental scientists, white-collar trade unionists and liberal socialist politicians. At the more extreme margins of the technocentric's typology spectrum are the 'Interventionists'. They have 'faith in the application of science, market forces and managerial ingenuity'. They would be typified by business and finance managers, skilled workers, self-employed workers, right-wing politicians and career-focused youth. Pepper (1993:33) says of technocentrics: 'There is little desire for genuine public participation in decision making, especially to the right of this ideology, or for debates about values.'

The type of development that is permitted in the environment is likely to be typified by the philosophy and approach of those who hold the power to control development decisions. This holds true for tourism development as well as any other type of development. Given that it is usually governments that make decisions about development, it is fair to presume that decisions will reflect a technocentric mode of thinking. This is likely to apply whether the government is to the left or the right of the political spectrum. The more right-wing the ideology of the government, the more likely it is that policy will reflect cornucopian values. The political ideology of the government will therefore be important in determining the thrust of tourism development policy and the amount of prioritisation given to environmental concerns.

Tourism: another environmentally friendly industry?

For centuries the agricultural 'community' and farmers enjoyed the reputation of being custodians of the countryside. However, as agricultural techniques became increasingly mechanised to achieve higher production, the nature of farming changed into agribusiness. To be competitive, a farmer under market conditions relied upon increasingly heavy investment in modern machinery, use of chemical fertilisers and insecticides, and the removal of natural animal habitats such as hedgerows to increase field sizes and maximise the profitability of new machinery. These points were highlighted by Shoard (1980) in her polemic *Theft of the Countryside*, which questioned widely held beliefs about agriculture being an activity that is in harmony with the environment and the existing ecosystem.

Similarly, for decades tourism has enjoyed a romantic image as a harmless and hedonistic activity that could only bring benefits to their destinations. Surely, having 'fun' can't be wrong, can it? The positive and perhaps hedonistic thinking about tourism as a form of development was demonstrated by concentration upon the economic benefits that tourism could bring. Lanfant (1980) comments:

> The evaluations of models designed to measure the impact of tourism on receiving societies were, at first, purely economic: they were restricted to the monitoring of foreign-exchange earnings, employment creation and the effects on the standard of living and on consumption. The problems of the effects of a tourist facility on the environment into which it was introduced was not elucidated because tourism was considered to be a marginal activity, operating in a closed economy, which was true enough of the tourist 'enclaves' promoted at the time.

However, Milne (1988) notes that even as early as 1961, concerns were expressed that tourism development could upset the ecological balance of Tahiti if it were not carefully regulated. Although the cultural and physical environments of tourism were given more consideration during the 1970s, a major influence on our understanding of tourism development upon the physical and cultural environments was *The Golden Hordes* by Turner and Ash in 1975. Similarly *The Holiday-makers*, by Krippendorf (1989), questioned our assumptions about the tourism industry being a friendly and harmless activity. Importantly it examined the motivations for participation in tourism and interpreted tourism as another area of consumption in contemporary society. A society based around consumption, as opposed to production, is behavioural evidence of the postmodern state. Urry (1990:91) comments upon the emergence of new middle-class groups in society:

> the heightened prestige that accrues for the middle classes not from respectability but from fashionability; the greater the significance of cultural capital to such groups and the continuous need to augment it; and a reduced functional need to maintain their economic capital intact.

As boundaries of differentiation of people based on behaviour are broken down, symbolic consumption becomes increasingly important in defining status and conveying a message about oneself, to establish a new social order.

Correspondingly, as values in societies evolve and change this progression has become a part of the tourism system. The consumption of symbolic destinations such as the Caribbean, southern India and Thailand is part of this wider process. This demand for more 'exotic' destinations is threatening the balance of many sensitive environments (from the wildlife parks of Kenya to the coral reefs of Belize) through development and tourist volume.

Significantly the increasing awareness of tourism's impacts upon destinations has coincided with a concern in western society about our relationship with the environment. Within this context, our approach to and the processes of tourism development have become increasingly analysed.

As Hudman (1991) explains, thinking about our relationship with the environment has undergone considerable change since the 1950s, when the environment was seen as a resource to 'enjoy and use'. Implicit in this philosophy was consideration of the environment as a resource that we can use freely without considering the costs or impacts that development may place upon it. It must also be remembered that in the immediate postwar period the main objective was to create wealth and prosperity, after years of attrition of living standards. Nevertheless, environmental neglect in achieving this objective supports the theory of adoption in western culture of a Kantian interpretation of our relationship with the environment. However, with the emergence of the field of Environmental Sciences and Studies in the 1960s, and the monitoring of environmental changes resulting from increasing economic growth, the philosophy of interpreting the environment as a 'free' resource was questioned. In the 1970s much of the advancement in analysis of our interaction with the environment came from the United States, which established the Environmental Protection Agency. Although concerns were primarily over visual pollutants in air and water, there was a growing awareness of hidden environmental dangers for the future, which threatened on a global scale. There was also an increasing realisation that environmental problems were not respecters of international frontiers. These problems were interlinked to a global system, where problems created in one country manifested themselves in another; for example, sulphur dioxide emissions from British power stations producing acid rain which destroys indigenous pine forests in Norway and Scandinavia. Many serious environmental problems were no longer manageable within the boundaries of international frontiers, but required international cooperation and action to provide a solution. The 1980s saw the education of some peoples of the world through global media coverage of the global and potentially irreversible environmental changes that a society based on consumption was creating. Issues such as acid rain, global warming through increased carbon dioxide emissions, ozone depletion and the resulting consequences of these phenomena such as climatic change and increased incidence of skin cancer have all come to the forefront of

155

considerations of an increasing number of peoples in the western world. This awareness has manifested itself in major policy documents about how the planet should be developed in the future. The most influential has been the United Nations publication of the *Brundtland Report* (1987), which called for the need for sustainable development of world economies. What is significant is that for the first time, major world organisations such as the United Nations, OECD and the major industrial countries recognised the need not simply to preserve the environment for aesthetic reasons, or even to preserve eco-systems, but to preserve the economic future of generations. The *Brundtland Report* is significant as the first global attempt to address environmental problems.

The Rio Summit in 1992 promoted the need to consider the environment in development decisions if the international environmental problems that had been identified in the 1980s were to be addressed. The summit certainly highlighted the differences in perspective over the need for conservation of the environment. The lesser-developed countries understood the need for environmental protection but interpreted the directives being proposed by developed countries as hindering their economic progress. There was also resentment that the biggest contributors to global environmental problems were the developed countries, who were now trying to impose directives upon less-developed countries. There was, perhaps, also a suspicion that these directives may be a back-door route to limiting global competition and reinforcing the economic dominance of the developed countries.

The relationship between tourism development and the environment must therefore be set within the context of wider global debate. A shift in emphasis toward community planning (Murphy, 1985; Haywood, 1988); ecocentrism (O'Riordan, 1983; Pepper, 1993) and alternative tourism, is apparent and is increasingly debated as the future of tourism development. These concepts are discussed in Chapter 8. Probably in no other revenue-generating activity, with the exception of farming, is the symbiotic relationship between an economic activity and the environment more significant and important to its future sustainability than in the case of tourism.

Development and the environment

The title of this chapter implies a transformation from a primarily agricultural community to one of a postmodern type based around services and consumption of leisure. For many destinations the golf course represents the icon of modernisation and development and is symbolic of a successful and prosperous community. This transformation may happen very rapidly as golf courses are developed at a rapid rate across South East Asia. Pleumaron (1992:2) comments that Malaysia plans to double its number of courses from the present 91 by the year 2000, the Philippines has at least 12 new courses being constructed and many more planned, while Thailand built 160 courses between 1989 and 1994. Other countries developing golf courses include Indonesia, Singapore, India, Cambodia, Sri Lanka and even China, where golf is officially denounced as a 'decadent sport'. However, these courses are not of the type generally seen in Europe. They are considerably larger, more like 'golf cities', consisting of perhaps up to three championship golf courses, luxury hotels, housing estates and leisure and shopping facilities. The courses are often designed by companies belonging to world-class golfers such as Jack Nicklaus. The golf course represents the chance to attract Japanese business and conference tourism, and offer 'proof' of a modernising economy and society. The development processes that underpin these courses and the impacts they are likely to have raise key questions about the role of tourism in society. For a more detailed analysis and discussion of these impacts refer to the case study 'Golf development in Thailand', Chapter 5.

The economic benefits searched for by lesser developed countries and communities from tourism go hand-in-hand with a perceived sophistication to modernise their society into one more familiar with the western world and economic and political success; see, for example, Richter's (1989) account of the development of five-star luxury tourism under Marcos in the Philippines being used to symbolise the modern organised state to world bankers.

However, the development process raises key questions concerning the nature, suitability, sustainability and profitability of development schemes and to whom these benefits are targeted. The type of development process that is implemented will be a key determinant of the impacts of tourism development upon a destination. It is certain that any development decision will lead to economic, environmental and social changes. A key determinant, deciding the extent to which such changes are viewed as either being positive or negative, will be who retains control and influence over these changes and the pace at which they occur. Another determining factor will be the suitability of the proposed development for the environment in which it is being placed.

Tourism takes place in a tremendous diversity of landscapes. Although the majority of mass tourism occurs around coastal areas, tourism landscapes also include mountain areas and river valleys, wetlands and deserts and in a variety of climatic zones, from arctic to tropical. In fact, tourism by its very nature is often attracted to fragile areas. All of these locations will have ecosystems which have taken thousands of years to establish and are extremely sensitive in their tolerance of development before change is induced. In many areas indigenous cultures have become an integral part of this ecosystem. Tourism has been introduced into fragile ecosystems such as coral reefs and wildlife parks inducing negative environmental changes. Many ecosystems have already been affected by human activity such as farming, mining and settlement and therefore may be more tolerant of tourism development. From an environmental perspective it is therefore important to develop tourism in such a way that respects the stage of the development of the ecosystem in which it is

157

placed, and does not induce negative changes. This requires environmental planning using techniques such as environmental impact analysis, carrying capacity analysis, government legislation offering protection from development and zoning of areas for land uses.

Frequently, tourism development in Third World countries has been characterised by large-scale development, based on investment from transnational corporations including major development banks, and reliance upon the 'trickle-down effect' to bring the economic benefits as explained in Chapter 5. However, this economic and political push for tourism development has often been at great expense to the environment and democractic rights. A 'top-heavy policy' of tourism development underlined by centralised direction, overseas investment, grandiose schemes and absence of development control may not be the best way to develop tourism. Although this may produce quick and spectacular results (as long as the developers do not become bankrupt during the development process), the development is likely to be totally inappropriate in safeguarding a harmonic relationship with the environment. This form of metatourism increases the dependency of the periphal nations upon the core.

The impact of tourism upon the environment is not limited to where there is development of facilities. Incorporated into the system of tourism is the movement of the tourist between their home and their destination, a transit zone. In the debate concerning the authenticity of the tourism product in Chapter 2 one of the major differences highlighted between tourism and a manufactured good, and a point worth reiterating, is that the tourist must come to the point of production to consume. Both the zones of transition and destination will experience varying degrees of environmental impacts, from tourist pressure to infrastructure and superstructure development to serve the tourists. Some of these impacts will also have global implications. However, tourist-generating regions also face negative environmental impacts. The removal of countryside for airport construction, residents living under flight-paths and increased volumes of traffic on roads around airports are all examples of negative impacts associated with the environmental aspects of the tourism systems in source areas.

The transition period

The transportation of hundreds of millions of tourists around the world in the international tourism system adds to other, more general, environmental impacts being experienced globally. Elkington and Hailes (1991:35–51) explain the impact of this mass movement of tourists in consuming the resources of the environment. The most obvious means of transport for medium- to long-haul travel is by aeroplane. The constantly rapid growth in air traffic means a need for expanding air terminal capacity at destinations around the world. This expansion involves the use of extensive areas of rural land, disruption to local communities, perhaps even destruction of natural habitats to accommodate the extra expanse needed for airport development. Noise is also a major problem for local communities that have to suffer the arrival and departure of aircraft, even though technology has produced 'quiet' engines.

Once the tourists are airborne they continue to consume resources vociferously. Two of the major emissions from jet engines are nitrogen oxides and carbon dioxides, both being gases which contribute to major global environmental problems. The increase in concentration of carbon dioxide into the earth's atmosphere leads to augmented absorption of infra-red radiation, the major cause of global warming. In the United States, where air traffic is particularly high owing to the vast distances to be covered and the deregulation policies of the Carter government in the 1980s, the estimated contribution of aircraft to US carbon dioxide emissions is 10%. Globally, airlines account for 2% of emissions of CO_2 and NO_2. However, the World Travel and Tourism Environmental Research Centre (WTTERC, 1993: 16) says: 'this sector has been the focus of attention because emissions are often at high altitudes where they may have greater effect than emissions from other forms of transport'. There are major environmental implications for the economies of tourist destinations from global warming, including:

- Devastation of the economies of marginal ski resorts, such as Scotland, Greece and some of the European Alps.
- Increased growth in algae, making coastal resorts less popular, for example the Adriatic Riveria in 1989 and 1990.
- Flooding of low-lying areas, such as the Maldives Islands.
- Destruction of coral reefs caused by changes in sea temperatures.

The emission of nitrous oxygen adds to the contribution of oxides already in the environment, which ironically leads to the breakdown of the ozone layer, the part of the atmosphere which protects sunbathers from cancer. WTTERC (1993:18) state:

> Some scientists believe that a 1 per cent decrease in the ozone layer could result in a 2 per cent increase in human skin cancer. Whilst such statistics can be debated, it is known that very small percentage reductions in the ozone layer will result in considerable increases in the amount of ultraviolet radiation reaching earth.

However, some companies within the airline industry are taking steps to reduce air and noise pollution associated with tourism movement. British Airways has issued an environmental strategy and has created the post of a senior environmental manager. The essential elements of this strategy are:

- taking account of environmental issues in British Airways' commercial decision-making;

- working constructively with organisations concerned for the environment;
- promoting our environmental activities with British Airways staff and customers, and letting them know of our concern and care for the environment;
- observing rules and regulations aimed at protecting the environment;
- providing support and advice on environmental matters relating to our operations; and
- using natural resources efficiently. (Source: *British Airways Environmental Review*, 1990:3)

It is not only the airline industry that causes pollution problems. For short-haul travel within Europe the most popular means of travel is by car, with mass migration in summer of tourists from the north of Europe to the playgrounds of the south of Europe. Cooper *et al.* (1993:183) state: 'Trips by car account for 90 per cent of the pleasure/personal and business trips taken by Canadian and US residents and for almost 83 per cent of total passenger kilometres in Europe.' Unfortunately the car, measured in terms of negative environmental impacts, is the worst means of transport available both in terms of local and global impacts. The obvious signs of environmental impact experienced by tourists and the host community in destinations include traffic congestion, noise and poorer quality air. There are also ever-present problems in terms of potential death on the roads; even crossing to gain access to the beach can be a major problem in many places, especially where there has been a lack of integrated planning for tourism. (CO_2 and NO_2 emissions also contribute to global warming and ozone depletion.) In the United Kingdom the car causes approximately 19% of carbon dioxide emissions and 45% of nitrogen oxide emissions (ETB, 1990:25). Both these gases are major constituents of acid rain and smog. Growth in road traffic is also being related to respiratory diseases such as asthma. A survey of recreational trips to the countryside in the United Kingdom showed that 80% of trips were made by the car (ETB, 1990).

The pressures of development

For many destinations, development pressure leads to careless consumption of the environment through inappropriate strategies and plans, targeting financial and economic gains at the expense of environmental and cultural factors. Paradoxically for many tourism destinations it is the presence of these physical and cultural assets that provides the attraction base for it to develop. For example, obvious links between a tourism product and the environment range from the exotic, including safari-tourism in Kenya and visiting corals and rain forests in Belize to the more mundane pursuits such as walking in a National Park in England or Wales. As Wood and House (1991:30) poignantly put it,

The phrase most often used by tour operators and holiday-makers alike when describing an attractive resort is 'unspoilt' [i.e. get there before the tourists]. We all want somewhere untouched by man it seems. So the environment is the most important factor in deciding if a resource is attractive or not.

Examples of negative environmental impacts from tourism development are easy to find. From the pollution of the Mediterranean to the destruction of coral reefs of the coastlines of Belize, Kenya and Australia, tourism is partly to blame.

Environmental destruction may also take place in destinations promoting so-called 'alternative forms' of tourism, often promoted as being more environmentally friendly than development normally associated with meta-tourism. Cater (1992:20) comments on the growth of tourism to Belize which heavily promotes itself as an ecotourist destination:

> Already the Hol Chan Marine reserve is showing signs of black band disease, a killer algae which attacks corals that have been knocked and broken. Researchers have also found a marked decline in the population of commercial species such as conch and lobster due to overfishing in Belize, partly to satisfy tourist demands.

One of the major problems faced in the Mediterranean basin is the pollution of the sea, the main resource of tourism to the area. It is estimated that in 1992 that more than 100 million visitors went to the Mediterranean coastline. Pollution of the waters has come from a variety of industries that use the sea as a free waste disposal unit. However, industries such as the oil industry, chemical industry, automobile industry and others have begun to invest a share of their profits into environmental protection. Tourism contributes to the pollution of the Mediterranean through the dispersal of human waste into the sea. It is estimated 70% of waste waters are led directly into the sea without purification or treatment. This waste courses faecal pollution and is environmentally damaging to beaches and sea. It is also economically damaging to those communities whose livelihoods are virtually dependent upon tourism. It poses a direct health risk upon the tourists themselves through the possibility of outbreaks of cholera, typhoid, hepatitis and dysentery. It is estimated that only 4% of shellfish from the area are fit for human consumption and periodic increases in algae can be expected. The economic effects on destinations can be marked as reported by Bayswater (1991). In her article, entitled 'Prospects for Mediterranean beach resorts: an Italian case study', she examines the impact of the algae scare which was given much media coverage in 1989 and also in 1990, on tourist arrivals to the Italian Adriatic Riveria. The algae had proliferated to the extent that it was impossible to swim in the water and use the beaches of certain Adriatic resorts. Bayswater comments

... in most resorts along the Adriatic Riveria hotel bednights were down by a quarter and sometimes a third in the summer season of that year (with non-Italian visitors staying away in much larger numbers than Italians). The decline in individual resorts in that year varied between 19.7 per cent in Lido di Jesolo and 30.4 per cent in Bibione.

In a leading British quality newspaper coverage was given to the pressures on resources from tourism development on the environment of Goa. Nicholson-Lord (1993), commenting upon the role of tour operators and their relationships with hotel developments the article, states:

> British Airways and Cox and King both send tourists to new complexes such as the Taj holiday village and the Fort Aguada beach resort. These are guaranteed water 24 hours a day. Yet the pipeline that supplies them passes through nearby villages that asked for between one and two hours' use of the pipe each day but were refused and have to rely on wells ... Hotels, many foreign owned, receive subsidised water and electricity. Yet one five-star hotel consumes as much water as five villages and one 'five-star' tourist consumes 28 times more electricity than a Goan.

These examples illustrate some of the developmental issues involved in tourism. The competition for resources between developers and local people is a key issue. Sometimes this competition leads to the loss of environmental resources that people have traditionally taken for granted. Perhaps part of the problem over use of resources is the consequence of Judaic doctrine, which has meant the environment has been largely seen as a free resource, certainly where ownership is not defined, and so liberated of normal market or legal constraints. This perspective may well bring conflict between western developers and other cultures, who may have differing interpretations of the environment.

Developing the ideas of Mathieson and Wall (1982) the environmental consequences of tourism development may be categorised into the following groups.

- Loss of aesthetic value, through the altering and removal of natural habitat, and the building of amenities in a global architectural style.
- Noise and air pollution, especially during peak season. This impacts upon the host community, wildlife and the tourists themselves. Ultimately it results in the loss of the tourist and recreational value of a site.
- Excedence of the physical carrying capacity of an area leading to impacts such as overcrowding, littering, trampling and erosion. A key element for any destination will be to try to establish its physical carrying capacity, and balance the supply and demand functions. Klamm's (1992) account of the development of the Languedoc-Roussillon, in the south of France,

outlines an attempt to do this. The project, which has been developed over the last 30 years, changing 'this formerly backward, declining and mosquito ridden area of south-west area France into the French Florida', had a defined carrying capacity of 800 persons maximum per hectare on the beach.

- Water pollution caused by the overloading of existing infrastructure facilities through the peak holiday seasons. In resorts where the population may possibly double during the holiday season this represents a major problem. In countries where the main attraction is a coral reef this may cause extra problems. Very often the development of accommodation along coastal frontage causes both beach erosion and the destruction of coral reefs through poor sewage disposal and tourist behaviour (e.g. the breaking of coral for souvenirs and walking on the coral, killing it, as witnessed off the Mombasa coast). Extra nutrient enrichment from sewage leads to eutrophication, causing the proliferation of algae. Besides posing a threat to bathers through skin rashes and gastrointestinal upsets the algae will spread, overgrowing and killing the reef. Combined with the effect of local people selling coral in shops, a coral reef can be quickly depleted as a tourist resource. Extra pollution comes from the dispersal of lead and toxic substances from the use of waterboats and speedboats.

- Disruption of animal breeding patterns and habitats is another major problem. This has been a particularly publicised problem in the Serengeti Wildlife Park in Kenya. Although tourism plays a vital part in protecting wildlife by offering another source of economic revenue to local people other than poaching and further grazing of wildlife areas, it also has disruptive effects. The over-use of the Masai Mara and Amboseli Park by minibuses and the wish of drivers to take the tourists close to the animals for observation and photographs has led to many of the animals being constantly disturbed, causing problems in eating and breeding habits. The problems in the Amboseli Park have been compounded by other environmental changes, which are threatening the tourism economy. According to Thomas (1993) the Amboseli Park, which overlooks Mt Kilimanjaro, was teeming with wildlife in the 1960s and 1970s. Today it is virtually barren, with the ecologists warning that unless urgent action is taken it will turn into an environmental wasteland. Ecologists believe that the death of vegetation and absence of wildlife may be due to ecological change. At the present time trees are dying because of increasing salinity in the soil caused by the water table rising. Although the changes have not been caused by tourism, the effects upon the tourism industry have been enormous. As Thomas says:

> Many tour companies now avoid Amboseli in favour of better-endowed parks where the 'big-five' – lions, elephants, giraffes, rhinos and buffalo are still to be found. The declining tourist

industry has hit local industries that depend upon tourism. Hotels and lodges reported a 30% fall in room occupancy during the last peak season.

- Deforestation in Alpine areas and in the Himalayas is also a problem. Lean and Keating (1992) state:

> Scientists say that the mountains around Albertville, Savoy, will never recover from the 1 billion francs for the Games, which have scraped the soil from fragile alpine pastures to make smooth-running pistes. Officially protected forests have been violated and rare marsh-land damaged . . . One of the resorts playing host to the Olympics, Les Arcs, has already suffered a catastrophe. In 1981, 60 people died when a landslide of 300,000 tons of rock and broken trees crashed into chalets and roads. Tree-felling and the bulldozing of pistes was blamed.

ski resort

- In Nepal the problem is of deforestation to accommodate the needs of the growing market of western tourists who trek there. Owing to the lack of electricity or gas supplies all the cooking and heating of water has been done by firewood. Western tourists demand a hot shower at the end of a hard day's walking and also their meals must be provided for. This has lead to rapid deforestation of Nepal's forests and associated environmental problems of increased run-off and landslides.
- Impact on vegetation through the collection of flowers, plants and the destruction of dunes and parks through excessive pedestrianisation and vehicular traffic.

Here today, gone tomorrow?

Tourism is by definition a transitory activity. As tourists we stay in a destination for perhaps up to two weeks of our lives and will probably never return there. Within that contextual setting, is it not normal that we may have less respect for the environment of our hosts than for our home environment?

A parallel may also be drawn to tour operators, who are largely free to move to other destinations if they so wish, and developers who use prime sites for short-term return. The impact of development will be decided by certain interlocking environmental and political factors, including:

- scale of planned development and growth targets;
- fragility and sensitivity of the landscape, for example wetlands will be more much susceptible to changes in the ecosystem from development than more man-made environments;
- sensitivity of the development in terms of its integration with the local environment and culture;

164

- the political environment of development: the more *laissez faire* the attitude to development, the greater the danger of environmental damage. Where planning restrictions do not exist or are not enforced and the more development is determined by market forces, searching for short-term financial gain and a quick payback, the greater the likelihood of spontaneous uncontrolled development, as witnessed in the Costa Brava, Spain;
- range of developmental incentives and the importance attached to tourism by national or regional government; and
- the cultural attitudes of local people to the environment. Where land is held as being sacred there may be opposition to development for tourism. Conversely, if the environment is interpreted as a resource for exploitation without consideration of the sustainability of the resources less respect will be given to its wellbeing.

The relationship between the tourist and the environment will depend upon:

- the typology of tourists attracted to the destination and their associated characteristics of behaviour;
- the availability of information to educate the tourist, for example, tourist codes;
- volume of tourists using the destination; and
- physical robustness or fragility of the landscape to different types of tourist behaviour.

Building on these considerations it is possible to categorise tourism's relationship with the environment into three broad categories after the work of Mathieson and Wall (1982:96).

Neutrality

In this scenario tourism development does not greatly infringe upon the natural environment and there is little interaction between the tourist and the natural environment. In reality this position is likely to be maintained for relatively little time, if indeed at all, owing to the pressure for development and its encroachment upon the environment.

Opposition

This is the most widely commented upon and experienced situation where the interests of tourism development and conservation of the environment are in opposition to each other. It has usually been the situation that tourism has developed destroying natural resources, as opposed to concern for the conservation of natural resources preventing tourism development.

Harmony or symbiosis

In this situation positive benefits are provided by tourism development to the environment and vice versa. The most likely case will be that revenues from tourism allows the preservation of a fragile ecosystem that would otherwise be developed and used for other purposes because of resource pressure.

The position of neutrality between tourism development and the environment is unlikely to endure for a long time. We would expect to find the position of neutrality in the very early stages of the tourism development lifecycle where tourists are categorised by the allocentric and explorer typology types. Tourist numbers will be very small and travellers likely to lodge in the houses of the existing indigenous population. It is likely that a genuine interest in the culture and lack of need for any additional facilities to those already existing at the destination means the impact of these tourists is virtually zero in environmental terms. However, if tourist numbers increase then development is also likely to increase and extra pressure will be placed upon the environment from extra accommodation and other tourist facilities. If the financial profit motive becomes the dominant motivatory force within the destination system and there is a lack of planning legislation or an unwillingness to either force or enforce it the relationship between tourism development and the environment may quickly become one of opposition.

Much of the academic, technical and general writing on the way in which tourism and the environment interact has been overshadowed by negative aspects of tourism as the villain. However, there are examples of tourism being used to protect wildlife habitats and conserve environments from other forms of development. The key to achieving these symbiotic and beneficial relationships is the realisation that carefully planned tourism incorporating local participation and providing direct financal benefits will negate the pressure of other usage of natural resources for activities such as logging, mining and agriculture.

Boo (1990:16) and Sherman and Dixon in Whelan (1991:121) draw attention to an economic model developed by Western and Henry in 1979 for the Amboseli National Park in Kenya. The model illustrated was that an individual lion would generate US$27,000 per annum from tourism and an entire elephant herd was estimated to be worth approximately US$610,000 per annum. It was also estimated from the park in 1973 that revenues from protected tourism areas where big game animals would be left relatively undisturbed (apart from by tourists) would raise more than US$40 per hectare compared to the most optimistic results of projected returns for agriculture of US$0.8 per hectare.

These figures provide a strong basis for support of an economic rationale for tourism development over other forms of development. The EIU (1991: 79) points out:

Kenya's human population rose from around 14 million in 1970 to a current total of 25 million. It will reach around 35 million by 2000. Thus the pressure on land will become even more acute, including the land on which the wildlife depends, and which in turn is the centre for much of the tourism that is so vital to the country's development.

The Kenyan Wildlife Service (KWS) realise that the protection of the parks cannot be achieved without the cooperation of local people who may lose possible earnings from activities such as agriculture and livestock rearing. The KWS therefore sets out the following guiding principles to revenue sharing.

- To pay people who live in wildlife areas adjacent to national parks and who, in the national interest, tolerate wildlife and bear consequent costs . . . the costs borne may be in the form of damage caused by wildlife or of opportunity costs – potential income foregone by, for example, not cultivating or fencing the land.
- To win the moral and practical support of people living near a protected area for the conservation of that area by assisting their development.
- To demonstrate at national and district levels that protected areas can contribute significantly to rural development. (EIU, 1991:84)

However, even seemingly symbiotic relationships may also contain problems. Negative impacts from tourism in the Masai Mara Park such as disruption to wildlife breeding and migration habits, killing of animals from tourism debris around lodges, encroachment of the building of lodges within the park and erosion of the park are well documented (EIU *Travel and Tourism Analyst*, 1991; Whelan, 1991).

Boo (1990:xiv) draws attention to how tourism can offer a more symbiotic relationship with the environment:

Existing studies show several benefits at the national level from ecotourism. From a conservationist standpoint, nature tourism can provide an economic justification for conservation of areas that might not otherwise receive protection. In East Africa, for instance, a preservation of native wildlife for tourist viewing has proved a successful economic argument for conservation. In Rwanda, where Parc des Volcans not only protects mountain gorilla populations but also prevents deforestation of the local watershed and safeguards agricultural production, tourism to the park has become the country's third largest source of foreign exchange.

Steele, in *Tourism in Focus* (1993:6) explains further

A trained guide accompanies each group of six tourists who can spend a maximum of one hour with a gorilla troupe. As tourist demand has risen, admission fees have risen sharply from $14 in 1980 to $170 by 1987. This allows the park to make very large profits, whilst keeping tourists restricted at 6000 a year. The profits can be reinvested in park management so that the gorilla population has risen from 254 in 1981 to 294 in 1986.

However, as positive and symbiotic as this relationship may seem, Ryan (1991:97) draws attention to West, a gorilla expert at Bristol Zoo:

> Too many visits from tourists could prevent gorillas from breeding. They live in a fragile habitat, and the damaging of footpaths and the lighting of camp fires will stop them from living their normal lives. We have to regard the gorilla population in Rwanda as one that is going extinct. As gorillas are closely linked to humans they can pick up human ailments such as colds, flu, pneumonia and measles – a disease like measles can kill a gorilla. Before tourists can get close to gorillas they ought to be screened for infection.

The choice for future planners of tourism is not therefore necessarily going to be a straightforward one. Faced with encroaching pressures from increasing population on limited land resources there are likely to be many pressures on fragile ecosystems. Opening these areas to tourism may offer a degree of salvation and may be infinitely preferable to the alternatives. However, any tourism activity will impact upon the environment and it is the management of these impacts that is the key to the longevity of the environment as a natural resource for tourism.

The impact of the tourist in the system

Stay at home?

This may be the only option if the negative impacts upon the environment from tourism development are ever to be fully eradicated. Of course, the reality in a society where a holiday is regarded as a necessary purchase, and socioeconomic indicators such as higher disposable incomes and more holiday leave encourage tourism, tourism demand will continue to grow. At least the travel industry is beginning to respond to concerns over the environment. As the *Economist* (23 March 1991) puts it: 'The link between tourism and the environment is now, probably, the matter that most exercises long-term planners in the travel industry'. There are examples of where major players in the industry are examining ways of making their operations more environmentally efficient. As previously mentioned, British Airways have undertaken an environmental review, Thomsons have appointed an environmental director, Thomas Cook have a green mission, Steinenberger hotels are undertaking environmental audits and TUI, the German tour operator, undertakes hotel and destination audits. However, only time and results will reveal the genuine commitment of particularly the tour operator industry to environmental improvement of destinations. Most tour operators do not have direct investments in destination areas. Putting direct investments into resorts for hotel or general destination improvement, as Thomsons have done in Majorca, demonstrates a genuine commitment. Suspicion remains about whether these initiatives mark the beginning of a new era with the emergence of the philanthropic tour operator, or whether they represent a marketing ploy. From the viewpoint of destination planning, strategic options linked to achieving goals must be developed to maximise the positive impacts of tourism and minimise the negative. This point is expanded upon and fully discussed in Chapters 7 and 8.

Elitist or protectionist?

The growing realisation that traditional economic methods of calculation of development decisions is leading to environmental destruction has led to an emerging emphasis on the inclusion of 'environmental worth' in economic calculations. Pearce (1989) emphasises the new approach to calculating the worth of our environment. The work of Pearce to develop economic methodology to support sustainable development decision-making has influenced the economic criteria used by major world lending agencies such as the United Nations.

Economic methodology which will help to protect the environment is now being used in tourism. Both Sherman and Dixon in Whelan (1991) and Steele (1993) describe and explain the various policy instruments available to protect the environment.

Underlying the basis of environmental economics (which believes the users and polluters of natural resources should pay) is the essay by Hardin (1968) entitled 'The tragedy of the commons', encompassing economic and ethical values. The theme of the essay concerns the use of 'free' (in a financial sense) use of natural resources, that is, the commons. If the commons is used by herders for grazing their cattle a farmer could decide to put an extra cow on the commons to provide an enhanced financial return. The costs of doing this would be absorbed by his neighbours and would be unlikely to create a notable imbalance in the replenishment of the grass on the commons. The ethical argument becomes one of 'individualism' against 'collectivism'. While the impact of one farmer putting one extra cow onto the commons may remain minimal, if the farmer decides to put more than one cow onto the commons, or his neighbours decided they wished to do the same thing, this would lead to a usage imbalance of the natural resource and ultimately the destruction of the commons as a natural resource.

While 'individualism' may bring initial benefits to the developers of natural resources, if this is pursued at the expense of 'collectivism' it will ultimately lead to short-term wealth creation, removing the possibility of using the resource as a means of creating monetary wealth. It is therefore imperative that resources are used in a sustainable way to ensure that their use for wealth creation exists for future generations.

The same principle applies to tourism development. A beautiful bay attracts the entrepreneur who develops a tourist lodge. Seeing their success other entrepreneurs decide to develop and the development cycle has started which may ultimately lead, if not monitored and controlled, to the environmental and economic destruction of the resort.

A key theme, then, in introducing environmental rationality into the field of economics is how the environment as a resource is addressed. A central concept is the idea of 'rent'. Steele (1993:4) says: 'This refers to the scarcity value that certain items have – when something is scarce people will pay more'. He continues: 'So just as countries charge foreign mining companies for extracting their oil and other minerals, so foreign tourists should be charged for extracting the benefits of an ecotourist site'. It is critical to find ways of making sure that the environment is no longer interpreted as a free resource. In the case of tourism, not only should the tourists have to pay for the use of environmental resources but the developers of accommodation units etc. must be made to pay the full costs of measures necessary for environmental maintenance.

Another key issue is how to control access to areas, especially fragile areas, such as those increasingly used for ecotourism. Indeed, an ethical question can be asked as to whether it is right to put often unique ecosystems into the marketplace as a commodity for financial gain? Paradoxically it must also be remembered that in some cases it may be the only chance to save these areas from internal pressure generated by population growth and pressure.

Land ownership will be an important factor for controlling access. In more fragile areas, as Steele points out, access can be controlled using two basic components: 'First, some agency has to be given responsibility for reducing open access and secondly, the most suitable policy instruments must be chosen'. Management options include state ownership and legislation giving specific status to an area or region which offers it a degree of protection from development.

Policy controls must therefore be decided upon which will restrict open access to both the tourist and the developer. The two main measures are 'quantity' control and 'price' control. This is a choice between limiting numbers through legislation and control (quantity control) or by making it so expensive that only a certain number of tourists will be able to visit the site (price control). In an ideal world neither is a palatable option. Both will deny freedom of access to the individual and it can be argued that price control is highly élitist and puts what have previously been regarded as common and free resources beyond the reach of all but a privileged few. However, to maximise the 'rent' of the site it would make sense to use a price control mechanism, compared to a quantity control mechanism where potential revenues may be lost.

To protect the environment will unfortunately involve difficult decisions which have to be restrictive and may therefore be deemed to be either authoritarian or élitist. If resources are to be protected in a world where capitalist economic theory is dominant then they may be only be able to be protected through their economic worth in the marketplace.

Development issues concerning the use of the environment are illustrated in the following four case studies:

TOURISM DEVELOPMENT IN JAVA

Java forms the principal island of the Indonesian archipelago, which straddles the equator between the continents of Asia and Australia. It consists of nearly 14 000 islands, half of which are inhabited. Although less well known than the neighbouring island of Bali for its tourism Java is a significant business and commercial centre. Much of its activity is centred on Jakarta, the capital city of Indonesia.

The politics and consequently all political parties in Indonesia are governed by the philosophy of *Pancasila*. Pancasila translates as five principles and is the name given to the philosophical basis of the Indonesian Republic. They are as follows.

- Belief in one and only God.
- A just and civilised humanity.
- The unity of Indonesia.
- Democracy guided by the deliberations of its representatives.
- Social justice for all Indonesian people.

The dominant sectors in the economy are smallholder agriculture, export-orientated state agriculture and mineral and oil exploration. Major exports include oil and products, wood and products, natural gas, textiles and garments, rubber and products and coffee. In the early 1980s the government started a programme to encourage economic diversification and to decrease the reliance on revenues from oil and gas exports. Tourism development is to play an important role in this strategy.

Foreign investment is actively encouraged by the Indonesian government. This has been encouraged by reforms in customs regulations, simplifying the taxation system and streamlining regulations relating to foreign investment. Foreign investment is also encouraged by:

- free exchange of currency allowing repatriation of profits;
- a large workforce;
- low labour rates;
- lack of labour unrest; and

- a relatively stable political situation.

Major investors in the economy have come from Japan, followed by Hong Kong, the United States, West Germany, The Netherlands and Thailand.

TOURISM TO INDONESIA

Tourism grew in importance to the Indonesian economy throughout the 1980s. The growth in the last four years of the 1980s was more than 20% per annum and this growth has continued into the early 1990s. The top five source markets in order of importance are Singapore, Japan, Australia, Malaysia and the United Kingdom.

The continuing increase in world tourism arrivals and the gains in the worldwide market share of the East Asia and Pacific region indicate a potentially strong future for the tourist industry in Indonesia. However, there are certain problems faced by the tourism industry and the Department of Tourism including:

- lack of an effective marketing programme and budget with a particular lack of prepared information about destinations;
- lack of tourism resorts; and
- comparatively low aircraft seat capacity and restrictions on night-time flying owing to a shortage of airport facilities.

TOURIST DEVELOPMENT ON JAVA

Fanga Ltd are a Japanese fish-farming community who are seeking to diversify into the tourism industry. They have chosen Java as a likely investment site because they already have offices located in Jakarta and are encouraged by the attractive financial investments offered by the Indonesian Government, who have prioritised both Japanese investment and development of the tourism industry.

Fanga have identified a 300-hectare site for development. They already own 25% of the site and are absolutely certain that the landowner of the other 75% will sell the land to them. The site is in an attractive rural area 30 minutes by helicopter and 2 hours by road from Jakarta. Fanga have employed a team of consultants to conduct a feasibility study of the site for them and establish the most probable profitable concept. The consultants suggest two five-star hotels and two top-quality golf courses as the most financially profitable concept. These facilities would be the key to establishing a large conference market for Japanese businessmen, who are usually obsessed by golf and conduct much of their business on the golf course.

At present the site is occupied by 50 families who are tenants on the land. They survive by small-scale fish farming from the lake on the site and from banana, rice and cotton plantations. There is also a small restaurant which is used to serve passing road traffic. The consultants state in their report, 'Villages are mainly linear settlements along the adjacent roads. The consultants understand that the proposed development will mean the resettlement of a number of families'.

TOURISM IN LANGKAWI

Langkawi is an area forming a small archipelago of 99 islands off the west coast of peninsular Malaysia, situated on the latitude of the Thailand and Malay border. The islands are very attractive with high mountains, sandy beaches and jungle-covered outer islands.

The total population of Langkawi was estimated to be approximately 35 400 in 1990; 94% of the population are Malays, 3% Chinese and 3% Indians and others, including Thais. The majority of the islanders earn their living from small-scale agriculture such as rice growing, fishing and rubber tapping. Eighty per cent of the people still live in villages and a distinctive feature of village life is *gotong royong*, in which the village people group together to perform services for each other or for the community as a whole.

Bird (1989), referring to the development of Langkawi, explains how development plans for the island had been forged by the end of the 1970s by federal government without consultation local people or even local leaders. Bird states:

> giving increasing attention to the tourist industry as an option
> for development the government was conscious that Malaysia
> did not have any particular destination or attraction that could
> serve as a major drawing point for tourists. It was felt that
> Langkawi had the potential to fulfil this role.

One of the most ambitious parts of the overall development planned for the island was a decision to build a $3 billion Langkawi resort to be situated on 3500 acres of land around a beautiful bay known as Tajung Rhu. Bird states: 'this area was known for its numerous casuarina trees, its beach front "carpeted with white flowers", its crystal clear lagoon and waterways, and its magnificent limestone hills'.

Although most of the land required for the project was state-owned, a large proportion belonged to local villagers. This land was compulsorily reclaimed by the state government, resulting in the 'splitting up of a long established community, damage to the anchovy industry and loss of livelihood for many villagers'.

173

The development company was a public limited company known as Promet, its largest shareholder being Singaporean. The federal and state governments would give direct financial support to the project by providing the necessary infrastructure for its development, including an international airport, roads, water and electricity supply.

Initial construction work began on the project in 1984. However, by 1985 Promet was put into receivership and the 400 construction workers on the site had either lost their jobs or walked out over pay disputes. Today Tanjung Rhu is an area of devastation.

To describe it as a wasteland or moonscape, an area reminiscent of china clay mining, is the closest visual description of what is left. Jungle and mangrove swamps have been completely cleared, the sand has disappeared from the beach to be used in construction and the water is silty and unclear. The full ecological cost is unknown without money being made available for research and evaluation.

GOLF IN THAILAND

Cohen (1994) describes the impacts of golf course development in South-East Asia on communities that literally earned their livelihoods from the tending of paddy fields. Commenting upon the attraction of golf to businessmen and politicians in Thailand he writes: 'The main seduction of golf is quite simply this: golf equals power; golf is status; golf is the passport to fast-track corporate, political, and military career promotion.' Golf has become the world's fastest growing sport, and golf course development the fastest expanding property sector. In the last decade the number of courses in Europe has risen by 74%, whilst in Thailand between 1989 and 1994, Western and Japanese investors, in partnership with local developers, have developed 160 courses, mainly on agricultural terrain. The development of a golf course is not only an icon of belonging to the postmodern, leisured world, but is also paradoxically a breeding ground of influential business contacts and political influence. Many of these developments are 'golf villages' with condominiums, conference centres, and other leisure facilities. Whereas a typical European golf course may cover an area of sixty-four hectarses, a Thai golf city can be up to eighty times that size. However, the use of a golf course is not purely for fresh air and business. Cohen reveals the story of Laem Chabang Country Club, situated between Pattaya and Bangkok. The course was developed on fertile land where families had tended to their rice paddies for generations. The families had rented the land from a rich Chinese land owner. In 1991 the region 'opened its floodgates to rampant capitalism and tourism', encouraged by 'cheap labour, exotic locations, good weather, pliant people – the co-operation extended by army generals and politicians (many of whom are co-investors) was unprecendented.' Consequently, the hundred families who farmed the land were told they must leave, as the land was going to be developed for a golf course.

Development tactics will depend upon the pattern of landowner-ship. Sometimes it may be a straightforward financial investment. The small number of farmers who own land and have the right to refuse to move and choose to do so may find another tactic is to buy up the land on the periphery of their settlement to encircle them. They are then told they will need to buy a helicopter to leave their land, as every time they pass through the developers' lands, they will be sued for trespass. Other tactics may be less covert. In the Philippines the military were mobilised to evict more than 1000 families; in Indonesia 1329 families were forcibly removed from their lands.

However, golf course development does not mean job opportun-ities are not provided for locals deprived of their lands. Returning to the Laem Chabang Country Club, Cohen recounts the story of Oy. Oy's family were dispossessed of their livelihood when the land they tended was redeveloped. However, Oy has found work as a caddy on the course. In fact, the course is a labour-intensive employer of caddies; all female as well. It is normal for each player to have three female caddies, the first, by convention the ugliest, to carry your clubs; the second for your parasol and folding chair; and a third to hold your drink and massage your back between holes.' However, there are social conventions. It is not etiquette to assume the automatic right to fondle your caddy, indeed you must flatter her. Ninteenth-hole activity is likely to cost another 1000 baht (28), the equivalent to a month's earnings that the caddies will earn from purely golfing duties. Caddies earn on average 90 baht (3) for caddying 18 holes. Oy refuses to be drawn into prostitution, and the activity carries a high social stigma, but she says women are forced into it because of the appalling wages. Oy's family have also been employed on the golf course: her mother is another caddy and her father is employed to mow the grass. They live with fellow workers just outside the fairway, in a ramshackle and airless house. The village headman is now an executive manager of the golf course, living in a newly constructed double-storey house, with its own putting green and surrounded by a high perimeter fence, guarded by a bad-tempered dog. The villagers say it was given to him, to ensure that the transition went smoothly.

However, it is not just the villagers who are dispossessed of their land who may suffer from golf course development. Golf courses are users of large amounts of water and often will illegally block off streams or take water from reservoirs, so denying it to villagers. The massive

175

amounts of chemicals used in the courses, in the form of fertilisers and pesticides, also contaminate the water, soil and air. One chemical that is used to encourage grass growth is aeolite, which is carcinogenic, whilst another which is used as a soil-coagulating agent, Acrylamid, is extremely toxic. As Pleumaron (1992:3) says: 'Neither of the substances can be removed in water treatment plants. Golf courses located in upper water catchment areas are particularly dangerous because the toxins are washed down and can contaminate fields and residential areas.'

CHAPTER 7

Planning: retrospection, interventions and approaches

Tourism planning: a retrospective view

Introduction

One of the problems that occurs with tourism as an industry is that its complexity is not acknowledged by many of those whose mainstream work does not directly interface with it (Krippendorf, 1987, preface). In this category could be included government economists, official planners and politicians. This lack of understanding is due perhaps to the ephemeral aspects of tourism's nature, the fact that its product is the provision (as some see it) of pleasure and holiday experiences for foreigners, and that it is a relatively novel economic sector for many countries. One consequence of this has been that tourism planning might be perceived as simply the allocation or zoning of certain areas, providing a number of hotel rooms and ensuring a steady flow of tourists through the provision of airline capacity. The results of this simplistic attitude towards tourism are to be found all around the world: Benidorm, parts of Miami, Tahiti, and, more recently, some coastal areas of Turkey; for example, the town of Bodrum on the Aegean has suffered from rapid over-development (see Burton, 1991:152). Each of the examples has followed what appears to be an inevitable pattern of discovery and over-development leading to eventual decline. Based on early work by Cleverdon (1979) Lea developed three questions that arise for tourism administrators (Figure 7.1).

Butler (1980) developed a deterministic theory (i.e. whereby a process is perceived as predetermined, or inevitable) that seemed to be saying that a cycle of evolution could be traced for resorts, and in a sense this could be the key weakness of lifecycle models applied to tourism: that they tend to reflect back on past visitor arrivals, without offering much hope of scientific prediction of when (or even if) the 'purchase' or popularity curve will begin to fall. Plog's (1973) paper on 'Why destination areas rise and fall in popularity'

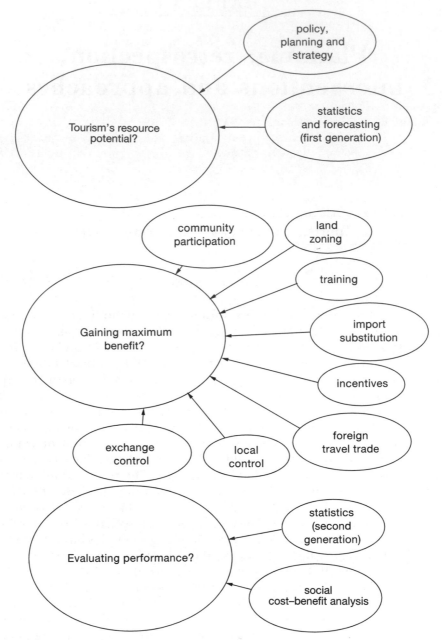

Figure 7.1   Three major questions in tourism administration, after Cleverdon (1979).
Source: Lea (1988:76).

put forward the rather obvious idea that the personality type of the tourist follows a pattern that could be plotted on a lifecycle curve: allocentric types ('trailblazers' or travel adventurers) will visit a destination during the early stages of its development. When the particular destination has been 'discovered' by the package holiday industry, and has been developed along lines that offer familiarity to holiday-makers from the main generating markets, then the psychocentric type (those who seek familiarity, comfort and non-challenge from their destinations) will arrive. The weakness of Plog's work lies not only in its limited value in predicting future events, but also in that it fails to define clearly what exactly is meant by 'destination,' or 'resort': is it a specific geographic location? Are locations monodimensional (i.e. having only a single set of attribute types)? Are these destinations clearly 'undiscovered' or 'discovered'? It could be argued that many destinations are multifaceted, with aspects that cover a range of familiar and unfamiliar places. Bradley (1991:389), in discussing 'brands', asserts that while products, services and brands do mature and have a lifecycle, with the possibility of reaching a fairly static position in the market, the notion of 'lifecycle', especially the decline stage, should be under management control: 'the life cycle is a dangerous self-fulfilling concept'. This thinking must be taken on board by tourism planners. Butler's work has been influential, but there are clear dangers in it. What remains interesting about Plog's work is that it reminds us that destinations change over time, and that the type of tourists attracted will change, and that the different types of tourists will, by their various sets of behaviours, have differing effects on the destination. In many instances this is linked to product price. For instance, Bali attracts different types of tourist from its different generating markets. Australians see Bali in terms of a cheap beach holiday. Britons see it as an exotic long-haul culture destination often as part of a multiple stopover vacation which would include a 'shopping stopover' in Hong Kong or Singapore. Political troubles in Sri Lanka during the decade of the 1980s caused them to make dramatic cuts in their accommodation and airline prices. As a consequence, the country is perceived in many of its main markets, especially the United Kingdom and Germany, as a cheap destination. Yet for the Japanese, for whom it is a new holiday venue, no such prejudices exist. Once more we have the uniqueness of tourism as a product and its relationship with the markets demonstrated.

Planning approaches

Planning approaches have their roots in town planning, land-use planning and architectural/landscape design for one-off luxury resorts in places such as Hawaii, Florida and Bermuda. Such resorts predated mass tourism. With their general reputation for exclusivity and excellence they may well have attracted further investment and generally 'put the destination on the map'. Many of these early resorts, such as Kaanapali in Maui, Hawaii, the Fijian Resort Hotel on Fiji's Coral Coast and (somewhat later) the Rarotongan Resort in the Cook Island, were also significant in that their opening clearly acted as a catalyst for further development. Historically, tourism developments were undertaken in the prevailing attitudes of the time: such attitudes barely registered the notions of 'sustainability' or 'environment'.

These early developments were, of necessity, fairly substantial. A certain critical mass was required in order to justify international marketing investment and start-up costs. These would include preparation of standard operating procedures and training as well as other costs associated with luxury accommodation and infrastructure. On this theme of investment, speed of development and impacts, Peck and Lepie (1989) developed a typology of touristic development based upon their observations of three North Carolina coastal towns (Table 7.1), their hypothesis being:

> that both the rate (magnitude and speed) of development and the amount of community involvement and control (power) over the change would affect the amount of distribution of payoffs and tradeoffs associated with increased tourism. We further suspected that of the two, power would be the more crucial factor. (Peck and Lepie, 1989:204)

While it is certainly important to note that Peck and Lepie's article is placed

Table 7.1 Typology of touristic development.

Rate of change	Power basis	Payoffs and tradeoffs – effects on lifestyle of community
Rapid growth	'Bedroom' communities Summer residents Specialised commerce (outside financing)	Rapid change of local norms New power structure and economy
Slow growth	Individual developments Local ownership Expanding local commerce (local financing)	Slow change of norms Stable power structure Expanding local economy
Transient development	Pass-throughs Weekenders Seasonal entrepreneurs (local financing)	Stable norms Individual mobility within power structure and economy Little overall change in local economy

Source: Peck and Lepie (1989:204).

within the 'Tourism in Complex Societies' section of Valene Smith's (1989) volume, it is a model that has transferability. We can see that while such planning can certainly work for large developments it is, in a paradoxical sense, the smaller developments that can create the real eyesores. In Nusa Dua, on the Indonesian island of Bali, a classic example of an integratively planned and carefully targeted resort zone, small developments, some of dubious standards, have sprung up since about the late 1980s when planning restrictions effectively faded. These new, locally owned and financed developments provide a sharp contrast with the well-established luxury resorts such as Sheraton Lagoon and the extraordinary Bali Hilton. The paradox for students of tourism is that these low-priced locally funded and run establishments are what many tourism theorists (Murphy, 1985; Farrell 1982) have been asking for! Yet they probably do not meet the expectations of the majority of visitors to Nusa Dua, with its reputation for the highest level of luxury. This leads us to the central dichotomy of tourism planning: who is it for?

In asking this question, another is begged: what is the purpose of tourism planning? A similar set of responses can be tabled for both questions:

- tourism planning is for the local residents conducted within a framework set by the agents (i.e. the planning authorities) of their elected officials (i.e. the politicians);
- *but* it is also for the developer who wants to know what else is going to be built in the immediate locale (in terms of competition and suitability) and to ensure optimum land usage;
- tourism planning will optimise land use beyond the needs of one particular developer and beyond the needs of a particular set of shareholders; and
- tourism planning can insist on long-term environmental planning, and awareness of social/cultural sensitivities (a kind of psychological conservation for the residents).

Such measures will also act to preserve the long-term viability of tourism by protecting the components that make up the attraction of a particular area from over-use. In this sense it should be emphasised that tourism plans should be only a single component of overall regional or national development plans, and subservient to them. This is much more likely to produce a mixed, diverse and stable economy. Many diverse countries have discovered that to rely heavily on tourism places them in a vulnerable position within this fragile and tenuous industry; for example, the United Kingdom, which suffered from the fear (by its major market, the United States) of terrorist attacks, Florida in the United States (by Britons mindful of criminal attacks on tourists) and Fiji, which suffered from both political problems which, through bad publicity in the Australian press, and through natural disasters such as tropical cyclones, and Australia, which in 1989 suffered a devastating pilots' strike on its domestic airline routes.

181

The actors in planning

The players usually involve developers, the visitor industry (including invest-ors, management corporations and potential operators), government and local residents. Experiences from Hawaii, if not a paradigm then certainly a sort of living laboratory for tourism development and planning, seem to indicate that successful completion of tourism ground-plant projects, that is, those delivered on time, within cost and to the satisfaction of local community, local government and tourists, are those with close (and above all, early) collaboration with the relevant planning authorities. These might take place at local, regional or national according to the local political set-up.

The concerns of the players can usefully be summarised as:

- *economic development* to ensure stability and wellbeing of the area;
- *the provision of jobs* so as to provide financial security, and personal satisfaction of individuals and families;
- *visitor satisfaction* so that tourists will enjoy their vacation, return and recommend the destination to friends; and
- *profit* for the visitor industry.

The priority given to each of these will vary according to the attitude of elected politicians. However, the axiom to be drawn from the above is that tourism will only exist if the visitor industry finds it profitable. Given that political representatives are in the business of looking after the interests of their constituents, one of the challenges for them is to ensure that tourism planners develop schemes to encourage long-term commitment based on operating profits rather than inflated property prices or land speculation, neither of which brings advantage to the majority of residents. One of the major criticisms of the initial introduction is that it inflates land prices to a point where local trading in property and traditional land usage patterns are distorted. This also happens in the context of 'second homes' purchases, where cottages and other residential dwellings are bought as holiday homes by more affluent outsiders. Failure to achieve the right balance between profitability and maintaining cultural and social integrity can result in bad community attitudes and resentment of tourism. Tourists and the tourism industry become the focus of hostility and blame is placed on them for a range of societal problems; cultural fatigue sets in. In the context of Hawaiian tourism (although unique in some aspects as a State of the United States, rather than an independent Island Nation) thinks that excellence is the key issue: 'create the quality and the cash flow looks after itself' (Farrell, 1982:109). In another context, that of reminding us that slow development is not only more preferable in terms of helping the local residents cope with change, but is also much more likely to lead to a more successful tour product, Farrell remarks that 'human instigated change is antagonistic to natural ecological change' (1982:189) carrying capacity/critical overload.

Carefully judged and far-sighted planning and regulation (at reasonable politically acceptable levels for all players) which involves early and frequent consultation with residents can ensure that 'the tourism product is created, distributed and consumed in a manner which benefits the community best' (Chuck Gee in Farrell, 1982:318). Given tourism's reliance and consumption of public place and space, it is an economic activity that cannot be regulated by market forces alone: planning is essential if tourism is to 'sow the seeds of its own destruction'.

Causes and results of poor planning

One of tourism's many paradoxes is the difficulty in defining what is meant by 'success'. This can be linked to the different interests of the players listed above. Having a dream holiday at the right price could be the tourists' definition. Generating profits that encourage investors and shareholders could be another. Tourism that causes minimum disruption to the local residents is certainly one of the key components of successfully managed social planning. Increased government revenues and political stability might well be a government definition of success. If success is measured only in financial returns and employment generation then a resort destination such as Pattaya (Thailand) must be judged a success because both these success criteria have been achieved. The paradox for tourism planners is that Pattaya 'developed totally without planning or regulation' (Richter, 1989:91). Clearly, Pattaya is not a 'success', and this serves to illustrate that qualitative as well as mere quantitative criteria must be set.

Causes of poor, inadequate or inappropriate planning can be categorised under three general headings.

1. *Briefing failure.* Officials or other clients have prepared an inappropriate brief for the consultant planners, or have over-ambitious plans for tourism. This may in itself be caused by a failure of officials to grasp the complex nature of tourism (perhaps Euro Disney's financial failures immediately following its opening was, in part, due to misreading the sociocultural attitudes and spending patterns of Europeans versus North Americans).
2. *Technical failure.* The consultants fail in one or more areas of expertise. This may be in the form of inappropriate advice regarding markets. Poor methodology resulting in wrong quantitative projections (see Bryden's (1973) chilling analysis of the Zinder Caribbean Tourism report).
3. *Social failure.* The consultants fail to take account of the social dimension pertinent to the specific location under study. The tourism planning *per se* is technically correct, but social disruption becomes inevitable (see Farrell's (1982) account of tourism development in Hawaii).

183

The impacts of deficient planning are categorised by Mill and Morrison (1985:288) under five groups: physical impacts; human impacts; marketing impacts; organisational impacts (related to lack of coordination between public and private sector in creating structures to monitor and advance the visitor industry); and 'other impacts' which include problems of seasonality, lack of attractions, lack of maintenance and poor information-giving services.

CASE STUDY: TOURISM AND THE ENVIRONMENT 1973 STYLE

The Belt, Collins and Associates 1973 Tourism Development Programme for Fiji

This plan stands as a model of the dominance of World Bank metatourism approach of the 1960s and 1970s. It is very similar in nature to the plan prepared several years before (by more or less the same team of consultants) for Ceylon (Sri Lanka) and for several other Pacific Islands (notably French Polynesia). Belt, Collins and Associates, 'a company which has probably been associated with more major developments in the Pacific than any other group of planners' (Farrell, 1982: 91) wrote the plan over a period of 14 months, consisting of a detailed 230-page large-format volume which comprised 16 chapters and 4 appendices. Chapter six, 'The Environment for Tourism', was contained in 10 pages (pp. 55–65). The four sub-headings were:

- environment for tourism;
- the Physical Setting;
- Climate; Historical Influences;
- The People; Land Tenure; and
- Infrastructure Considerations

What this demonstrates is that at the time, a completely different interpretation of the word 'environment' existed. The chapter commenced by stressing what it considered to be the two most important factors for successful tourism:

> ... An attractive, clean and safe environment is essential or visitors will not enjoy their tour, not recommend Fiji to their friends and the country will soon acquire an unfavorable overseas image. Generally, Fiji's environment is clean and atractive although the appearance of some villages and town buildings could be greatly improved through better building design and landscaping. Littering is not now a major problem nor is water and air pollution but vigorous action will be

required by Government and private enterprise to assure that the littering and pollution are controlled as the country urbanizes and industrializes. Fiji is also a relatively safe and convenient place to tour but improved transportation facilities, higher traffic control standards and better utility services will need to be implemented as the country develops. Most importantly, there needs to be the attitude on the part of the local citizens to want to have and work towards an attractive, clean and safe environment . . .

. . . Just as essential as a pleasant physical environment is the need for a receptive cultural environment. The visitor wants to feel that he is welcomed by the local people as a guest in their country, and that he receives a positive and cooperative response to his social overtures. Visitors do not enjoy being treated as a meal ticket for the hotel owners and employees, even though this is one of the reasons for developing tourism. Fiji is well known for its warm, friendly and hospitable people with interesting lifestyles and this trait is one of the major attractions of the country. This courteous and hospitable attitude needs to be maintained for both the vitality of Fiji's society and the success of tourism . . .

The plan did recognise the potential dangers of tourism and in chapter two, 'Objectives, Opportunities and Problems' (p. 10), under the section on 'Problems', concern was noted about several negative issues, including: possible speculative land dealings; the temptation for over-reliance of tourism at the cost of a balanced economy; over-commercialisation and lack of quality in many existing hotels; and generally poor infrastructure. However, dominating the whole plan seems to be the notion that Hawaii can serve as an ideal model, and several mentions are made of this throughout. There is little evidence of meaningful consultation and no evidence of consultation at community level. This is clearly a top-down plan that was to be imposed on a subservient population. While some members of Government supported it the plan was not 'of the people' and there was not only limited support, but little interest in this plan drawn up by outsiders. Cynics at the University of the South Pacific dubbed it the 'Disneyfication of Fiji'. In the final analysis certain aspects of the plan pertain even to the present time, especially some of the tourist zones they recommended. The plan was over-ambitious and inappropriate to the needs of the vast majority of the people of Fiji, rooted in neocolonialism (a sense of 'we know what is best for the natives' pervades), and failed to attract the necessary investment needed. This pattern was repeated with many similar plans in developing regions of the world. Visitor arrivals predictions taken from the plan are shown as illustration of how misguided many parts of the plan were.

Public sector interventions in tourism

Introduction

For the purpose of this section, the 'government' mainly applies to national or federal governments, but could also apply to state or regional tiers of government. Actions by governments shape the sociopolitical climate: they have generally provided the legal framework and conditions for tourism to operate.

Tourism policy-making

Edgell (1990:105) offers a model for the tourism policy development decision-making process which integrates what Poon (1993:35) refers to as 'frame conditions' (others may refer to them as the 'external environment'), goals and objectives and resources (Figure 7.2). Bull illustrates the political and economic conditions briefly referred to in the introduction by overtly-linking the general tourism policies with general economic policies (Figure 7.3). Developing tourism policies involves legislation, the creation of a favourable financial climate and the necessary infrastructure and market research. There are six specific areas in which governments of all kinds may operate in order to plan, promote and regulate the development of international tourism:

- the creation of a legal framework that will include travel visas, labour laws, foreign investment, consumer protection, building and planning regulations;
- the provision of national and regional transport infrastructure with a focus on airports and seaports;
- the provision of general infrastructure and support services such as water, power, communications and emergency services;
- the provision and/or zoning of suitable land for resort or other tourist development facilities;
- the provision of financial and fiscal incentives including tax breaks, preferential energy tariffs, grant aid and soft loans; and
- the provision of market intelligence and promotional activities such as

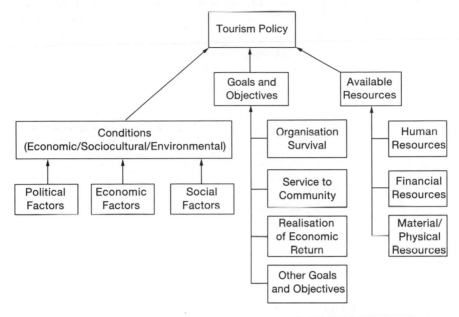

Figure 7.2 The tourism policy development/decision process.
Source: Edgell (1990:105).

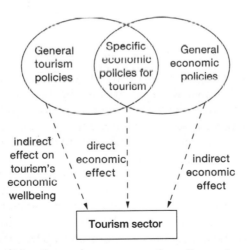

Figure 7.3 Government economic policy and tourism.
Source: Bull (1991:199).

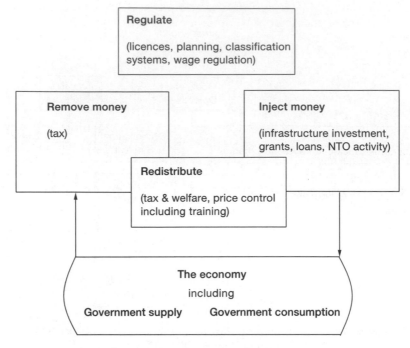

Figure 7.4 The roles of government in tourism.
Source: Bull (1991:200).

statistical analysis of the industry's performance, technical assistance through training, destination brochures and coordination of joint marketing efforts.

Bull (1991) illustrates the five areas in which national governments have various roles to play (Figure 7.4).

Figure 7.4 demonstrates the breadth of tourism as an industry: a point made throughout this book. Even given this illustration of the government's role, increasingly planning will overtly encourage the involvement of private finance and public–private sector partnerships, such as happened with the France–UK Channel Tunnel which was completed in January 1994. The private sector has traditionally provided the accommodation and attractions through entrepreneurship and company enterprise. The range of amenities developed privately might include hotels and resorts, theme parks, restaurants, clubs and cinemas. To some extent, the private sector also provides the transport systems (although this is complicated by the various stages and levels of state ownership of buses, airlines and railways). The private sector will also conduct its own promotionals and marketing initiatives. These could be stand-alone or in conjunction with other operators to give economies of scale. The rapid political changes to the command economies of Eastern Europe and the former Soviet Union have been accompanied by an equally rapid decline in state ownership: privatisation is seen as the key to operating profitable, and thus sustainable, tourism enterprises.

Government intentions in tourism planning

While not all governments have tourism plans as such, most will have an 'official position' towards tourism. There will be common factors to most statements of government intentions concerning, or philosophy about, tourism that will define the characteristics of that destination's tourism. These are likely to encompass the following:

* visitor arrival targets;
* the importance of having a clear idea as to the purpose of tourism; and
* planning, building and/or zoning rules and regulations.

There must be close cooperation between the numerous players involved in the local industry, that planning should recognise the symbiotic link between tourism and the host community and, finally, that local people should, in a sense, be seen as shareholders in the industry with regular reports from planning authorities on progress and future plans. Proper planning of the physical, legal, promotion, finance, economic, market, management, social and environmental aspects will help deliver the benefits of tourism development.

AUSTRALIAN NATIONAL TOURISM: GOALS AND POLICIES

In Australia, responsibilities for tourism promotion and development are divided between the States/Territories and the Commonwealth (i.e. Federal) Government. The States and Territories have responsibility for marketing and promoting their own attractions and matters directly relating to the development and regulation of their visitor industry such as zoning and licensing. The Commonwealth Government has prime responsibility for the international aspects of tourism and the formulation and implementation of national goals and policies. In general, Australia has provided what it sees as a favourable economic climate best suited to the free operation of the industry in the marketplace. The most significant move in this direction has been the deregulation of Australia's domestic aviation. Tourism goals for Australia cover four areas:

Economic   to improve the competitiveness of the tourism industry, minimise constraints on development and provide an

	appropriate economic environment in which the industry can optimise its contribution to national income, employment and balance of payments.
Environmental	to develop the tourism potential of the natural and cultural heritage while preserving and protecting it through sensitive, balanced and responsible management.
Social	to facilitate the operation of tourism activity in the public interest and encourage increased participation in tourism with the view to enhancing the quality of life for all Australians.
Support	to ensure that the necessary planning, coordination, research and statistical support is provided for effective policy formulation and the integrated development of the tourism industry.

A number of consultative bodies exist to ensure communication between the various government departments and between Commonwealth Government and State/Territory Governments. These include: Tourist Ministers' Council, comprising Commonwealth, State and Territory Ministers responsible for tourism; the Australian Standing Committee on Tourism, comprising heads of Commonwealth and State/Territory tourism authorities; and the Tourism Advisory Council, comprising representatives of the tourism industry and relevant trade unions. Other bodies include Great Barrier Reef Ministerial Council and Consultative Committee, the Tasmanian World Heritage Area Ministerial Council and the National Tourism Industry Training Committee. Other government departments such as Local Government and Ethnic Affairs, Transport and Communication, Immigration and Industry, Technology and Commerce. These are supported by such agencies as the Australia Bureau of Statistics and the Bureau of Industry Economics. These are noted to emphasise not only the eclectic nature of tourism, but the absolute importance of coordination, clear lines of responsibility and communication.

This integrated effort is underpinned by a tourism policy with the following aims:

- to increase recognition of the characteristics and importance of tourism and the contribution it can make to the national economy and Australian Society;
- to identify and analyse the major factors which fall within the Commonwealth Government's area of responsibility and which influence the industry's performance and growth prospects; and
- to delineate a coordinated policy towards tourism, integrating the diverse elements which constitute the industry and outlining

appropriate consultative machinery to ensure that tourism objectives are adequately considered in the formulation of Government policies.

All the parties involved clearly recognise that without professional and sustained international promotion, tourism will not be successful. The Australian Tourist Commission (ATC) is the statutory authority charged with this task. Up until the late 1980s the ATC also promoted domestic tourism. This role has now been given over to the States/Territories. The ATC now has a clear focus on the international marketing.

The Commonwealth Government also encouraged increased investment in tourist facilities. This included, during the mid- to late 1980s, better depreciation rates for hotel buildings and equipment. At the same time, the government also relaxed restrictions on foreign investment, allowing foreign ownership of resorts and hotels without the former requirement of 50% Australian equity.

The increasing number of tourists highlighted the need for more consistent standards and a better trained workforce. As a short-term measure, in addition to the efforts made to increase the numbers being trained through the formal education and training system, arrangements were made to allow fast-track immigration of skilled tourism workers (Figure 7.5).

Goal setting

Perhaps the most important role that governments of whatever nature play is that of goal setting. It is the goals set by government that define the purpose of and aspirations for tourism. In order to be achievable, these goals should take account of existing and potential touristic resources and markets. These tourism goals will be subservient to the broader set of national goals: tourism as a tool to achieve a variety of sociopolitical and economic national goals, not tourism planning for the provision of a nice destination for holiday-makers! In reality, the driving forces are likely to be the achievement of macro-economic goals and entrepreneurial spirit, and as David Edgell (1990) reminds us, policy-makers themselves are influenced by the prevailing sociocultural conditions (Figure 7.6).

In general, specific goals for tourism are likely to focus on the needs of:

- potential visitors;
- investors and entrepreneurs; and
- social, environmental and economic needs of specific locations, regions and at a national level.

The way in which these goals are prioritised and codified will be a direct

191

reflection of the political climate of the particular destination. For example, the Papua New Guinea Five Year Tourism Development Plan states quite clearly that 'The principal objective of the National Government through the department of Culture and Tourism is to maximize the socio-economic benefits derived from tourism.' The plan goes on to stress the importance of an acceptable economic rate of return on the resources employed. The Australian plan, too, recognises this: 'As the government continues its policy of facilitating structural change within the economy by encouraging less industry

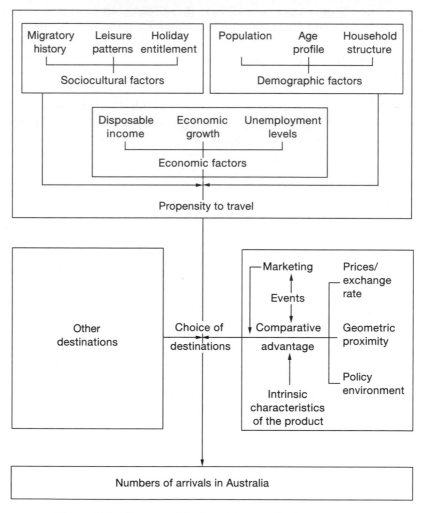

Figure 7.5 Factors affecting visitor arrivals in Australia.
Source: Faulkner (in Theobald, 1991:235).

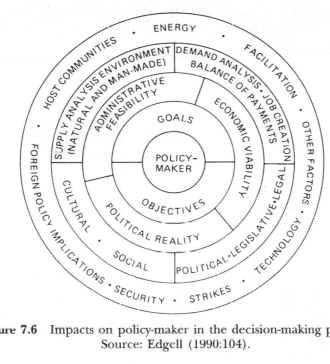

Figure 7.6 Impacts on policy-maker in the decision-making process.
Source: Edgell (1990:104).

reliance on protection and assistance, the tourism industry will surely emerge as a major catalyst for economic growth.' The two case studies, Australia and Papua New Guinea, demonstrate two approaches to government intervention in tourism.

CASE STUDY IN GOVERNMENT TOURISM PLANNING: PAPUA NEW GUINEA

Introduction

The Papua New Guinea (PNG) Five Year Development Plan (1990–5) was conceived at the first National Symposium for Tourism held in early 1987. The plan was written by the Department of Culture and Tourism in cooperation with the Travel Association of PNG. It briefly analysed the tourism situation at the time and identified constraints. Its main function was to set goals and define strategies for achieving these goals. Visitor arrivals for the years 1982–6 inclusive averaged just over 32 000. However, 'purpose of visit' statistics indicated that 'visiting friends and relatives' accounted for about 20% of traffic and the 'business, officials, conference' category some 40%. In terms of 'holiday' visitors, the arrivals declined from 9739 in 1982 to 8439 in 1986. The five-year plan set a target of 60 000 visitors for the year 1993.

Objectives

To achieve this target figure in line with the general philosophy of minimising negative impacts, the Plan detailed 13 principal objectives which, broadly speaking, consisted of a range of statements concerning:

- greater participation in the industry by Papua New Guineans;
- encouragement of tourism projects through investor incentive packages;
- encouragement of linkages between tourism and other sectors of the economy;
- development of training and education opportunities;
- encouragement of village tourism through technical and financial help; and
- dissemination of information through public awareness campaigns.

Policies and strategies

The plan then makes 12 statements which specify the actual tourism policy; in summary, these were:

- improving quality of services (including inspections);
- equitable geographic spread of tourism;
- promoting local produce over imported commodities;
- attracting foreign investment;
- development of infrastructure;
- reducing imports for the industry;
- encouraging more flexible air transport system and cheaper fares; and
- assisting operators with promotional activities.

Several strategies for achieving the tourism objectives were developed. These were (in full):

- To attract national and foreign investments in tourism, the National Government will consider the introduction of investors' incentive packages.
- The National Government through the Department of Culture

and Tourism in consultation with Government financial institutions like the Agricultural Bank and PNG Banking Corporation will set up National Tourist Assistance Scheme to help nationals set up and manage tourism related activities and related industries.

- The Government through the Department of Civil Aviation and Transport will continue to make available funds for development of additional infrastructure facilities in order to accommodate increased visitors.
- The Government will encourage linkages between tourism and other sections in order to maximize local goods and services particularly from the entertainment and agricultural sector. This will have the effect of reducing imports and avoiding leakages and to generate additional employment.
- The National Government will adopt a more liberal access transport policy to encourage the operations of more international air services and increased revenue from landing fees, tourist expenditure etc.

Problems affecting the industry

The plan identified certain constraints on the industry. These included the law and order situation; the general lack of support for tourism from previous governments; the limited amount of money available for tourism promotion; the high cost of staying and travelling in PNG; poor access; overseas competition; lack of entertainment after dark; and the total dependence on the private sector for overseas promotion.

Product development

The plan defines the tourism product as:

> [meaning the] physical and natural attractions that [PNG] has to offer in terms of spectacular scenery, landscape, seascape, historical and cultural activities, and as well as special interests. It also includes accommodation, transport (air and surface) and facilities. All of the above items are the components which are put together by tour operators to form the Papua New Guinea holiday or product.

The product was categorised under three key components: accessible transport; availability of accommodation; and amenities.

Marketing and promotion

The section on marketing described how the government intended to market PNG. The focus was to be through overseas travel marts and trade fairs. The rationale underpinning the marketing efforts was described thus:

> The marketing and promotional objectives of the Department of Culture and Tourism are the creation of a positive image for Papua New Guinea so that it becomes a desirable holiday destination for potential tourists from our main source markets.

> Statistics released by the National Statistics Office for 1986 indicated that 40% of holiday visitors to PNG came from Australia and 31% came from USA. Other important source markets are West Germany, Japan, United Kingdom and New Zealand.

Tourism investors incentive package

The government developed a number of financial incentives to be offered to exploit the full potential of tourism and its ability to contribute to the foreign currency reserves of the country. Tourism's high labour requirements were also referred to as an important reason for encouraging the development of tourism. Specifically, the incentives focused on three categories of investment:

- operations with more than 50% national equity would qualify for a five-year tax break, tax-free importation of capital equipment;
- new foreign investment worth more than Kina 5 million and with a national equity holding of at least 20% would, in the first year, qualify for 30% write-off for building costs and 60% write-off if the construction was from local materials. If the taxable income was less than the investment allowance, the allowance could be carried forward to the following years; and
- investments with 20% initial national equity were allowed exemption of taxable income in line with other export industries and exemption from land rent for the first five years.

Three other incentives offered were:

- all tourism accommodation buildings having local architectural designs symbolising Papua New Guinea cultures qualify to write off 2% of the building costs;

- repatriation of profits on original investments guaranteed for foreign investors; and
- boats purchased solely for tourism activities were allowed exemption from duty.

The role of Provincial Governments

The Provincial Governments were identified as having a key role in developing and monitoring tourism. The following areas were designated as being the responsibilities of the Provincial Governments.

Identify and document tourism products in the Provinces that could be an attraction to visitors and tourists. The Department will assist the Provincial Government by providing services.

Identify prime sites for hotel development (site should preferably be on Government land to avoid land disputes). Developers locally and internationally can be found by the Department of Culture and tourism.

To provide tourism information centre.

To maintain closer liaison with the Department of Culture and Tourism by providing information on standards of the accommodation and availability of beds, on a regular basis.

Maintain a standard of accommodation that is acceptable on an international level with inspections by the Provincial Tourism Officers on a regular basis.

Maintain a calendar of events within their Provinces.

Contribute a percentage of the bed tax to a trust fund for use in marketing of their area abroad.

In some senses, Papua New Guinea plan reflects Farrell's (1982:134) feelings that government agency plans are 'symbolic rather than practical, rhetorical rather than truly reflective [with] many remain[ing] unimplemented'. The targets set for tourism in the five-year strategic plan were not achieved, and many of the measures remain unimplemented.

Incentives

There is often a need on the part of countries at all levels of development to encourage investment in industry. For instance, in the United Kingdom, national government and regional development agencies offer incentives to potential investors. At a national level the government has promised to 'wage

Table 7.2 Tourism development incentive categories.

Direct financial commitments	Which would include grants, loans or equity holding from government sources such as a national development bank
Financial arrangements	Comprising loan backing and exchange rate guarantees
Fiscal incentives	Including tax breaks on profits, preferential services and energy tariffs, duty exemptions for plant and equipment, tax exemption on reinvested profits
Indirect/supplementary	The options here include cheap or free access to technical training for staff, promotional and marketing assistance, profit repatriation guarantees liberal work permit policies

a war on red tape', in other words freeing entrepreneurs from the restrictions of regulatory control concerning say, employment practices and export administration. Regional development has been encouraged through offering factory sites free or at very low cost. As in the case of manufacturing or any other type of business, tourism incentives can be categorised under four headings (Table 7.2). The range of incentives on offer will be a reflection of two things: the attitude of government towards tourism as a legitimate and important industry, and the level of need for the government to encourage inward investment. It demonstrates political action as opposed to political rhetoric.

Conclusions

The philosophy underpinning this chapter has been the recognition of the importance of close cooperation between the numerous players involved in the industry, that planning should also recognise the symbiotic link between tourism and the host community and finally that local people should, in a sense, be seen as shareholders in the industry with regular reports from planning authorities on progress and future plans. Proper planning of the physical, legal, promotion, finance, economic, market, management, social and environmental aspects will help achieve the goals set by government for tourism and thus deliver the benefits of tourism to all those who should benefit.

If the purpose of good government is to lead nations to a successful and a secure future, then government intervention must be of a type that will help the people towards successful participation in a healthy industry. Some countries, it could be said, have not managed this balanced development. The tourism industry in Guam, for instance, is owned almost exclusively by Japanese interests. Much of Fiji's tourism industry is owned by foreigners (increasingly the Japanese) and grave concerns have been raised over the pattern of ownership in the tourism industry in Queensland, Australia, where again it is the Japanese who appear to have the dominant controlling interest. Further afield, many of the hotels in certain parts of East Africa are owned by British companies (Wyer and Towner, 1988, discuss a range of topics related to UK ownership and control patterns in Third World hotel and tourism operations).

Tourism can play a very important part in earning foreign exchange, but governments have to take account of the power of tourism. Unplanned tourism will swamp economies and cultures as it has done in Thailand, Saipan, Tahiti, Hawaii and so on. However, given proper control and a carefully planned, integrated approach to development, tourism can be effective in giving returns to investors while helping achieve national social, economic and environmental goals. In the case of developing countries this will include developing strategies to minimise potential losses through expatriation of profits and salaries or through the high importation costs of goods and services that enable the industry to function to the various styles and levels required by a broad range of clientèle.

Approaches to tourism planning

Introduction

That tourism differs from manufacturing in that consumption takes place at the place of production is a point made before in this book. The implication for tourism producers is that the supply-side requires a complex range of facilities and attractions that are in a fixed location: the 'distribution' of a tourism product entails bringing the consumer to the product rather than the product to the consumer. This is a fundamental difference between tourism and almost any other form of economic production–consumption pattern.

Complexities of planning for tourism

Failure to recognise these complexities is at the heart of many of tourism's planning failures or inadequacies. Such failures are discussed by Choy (1991) who identifies three types of 'market failure' (i.e. failure of the markets to fully account for the totality of impact: where governments have to intervene such as in the case of pollution, this does not mean 'project' or financial failure). Choy continues:

199

The first [market failure] involves the public interest in products and services which are consumed collectively such as parks, highways, historic sights, and public beaches. The second type encompasses external effects both positive and negative, which affects persons not directly involved in an activity. For example, construction of a resort may restrict access to beaches and fishing areas ... The third type involves costs and benefits which are not reflected in market prices such as the value of open space, costs of social impacts and benefits from environmental preservation.

Choy is cynical in his view of government planning, seeing it as almost doomed to failure if it tries to do anything other than 'resolving issues involving the three types of market failure, leaving the private sector to assume the ... risks of tourism projects'. (A view borne out in the 1973 Fiji tourism plan's inability to accurately project visitor arrival numbers.) Even so, Choy's viewpoint fails to recognise the potential value of good planning: each of the three cases he examines (Hawaii, French Polynesia and the Cook Islands) has achieved different levels of success and failure, the failures of French Polynesia being based on the failure of their consultants to 'get it right'. Hawaii's State Tourism Plan (STP), while making inaccurate predictions for some of the islands, seems broadly correct in its predictions of about 6.4 million visitor arrivals for 1990. The new Cook Islands Tourism Master Plan set targets for visitor arrivals that were fulfilled. While each destination will have different needs in so far as tourism planning is concerned, perhaps the overriding characteristic of successful planning is that it is based upon clearly defined tourism policy and tourism goals that are agreed to after consultation with residents. This strategic approach is spelt out by Faulkner (1994), who sees four essential ingredients:

- 'a comprehensive and integrated plan of action for an enterprise organization.
- A clearly enunciated set of goals and objectives which provide the focus for the plan of action ...
- The establishment of systems for monitoring and evaluating progress towards goals and objectives.
- An approach to planning which explicitly reconciles the inherent competitive advantages and limitations of the organisation (or its product) with the challenges (opportunities and threats) of the environment.'

Clearly, Choy is wrong to assign planning failure (especially in developing countries with a lack of expertise) as being inherently associated with detailed (Master Plan approach) government planning failure: the plans themselves may have been wrong, but that should not colour the attitude towards the value and use of tourism planning for destinations. Countries as diverse as

Mauritius and New Zealand have demonstrated the benefits of planning to manage tourism.

Types of planning

Gunn (1988:214) describes three levels for overall tourism planning:

- *continuous tourism planning* focusing on collaboration between all players in the public and private sectors;
- *regional strategic planning* providing guidelines and concepts in both physical and programme development; and
- *local tourism planning* which avoids sporadic developments that fail to integrate with broader objectives and planning.

Contemporary approaches to planning

The foremost concern of contemporary planners is not only the integrative approach, but also to ensure a strategic framework for tourism. Gunn develops this by linking goals setting with research and synthesis which then feeds into the tourism planning concept stage (looking at alternatives in both physical and systems planning) and finally the recommendation phase (Figure 7.7). While Gunn allows for feedback between goal setting (or objectives setting as Gunn refers to it) and planning concept formation, there seems to be no overt route for results of the recommendations to be fed back to the goals: in a sense, goals should allow a level of flexibility to enable results and *realpolitick* to be taken into account.

Farrell, quite rightly, puts the planning concerns in characteristically humanist style:

> to ensure the continued health of the industry and the State, planning needs to take into consideration such additional important factors as the social effects of tourism, the social and cultural health of its people, the protection of our Aloha Spirit and the protection of our precious environment. (Farrell, 1982:313)

Attempts at reaching synthesis between humanistic concerns and 'efficient' planning have been made. The 1990–4 Trinidad and Tobago plan is an interesting example.

TRINIDAD & TOBAGO PLAN 1990–4

The Trinidad and Tobago strategic plan 1990–4 was based on a 1988 document produced by the former Trinidad and Tobago Tourist

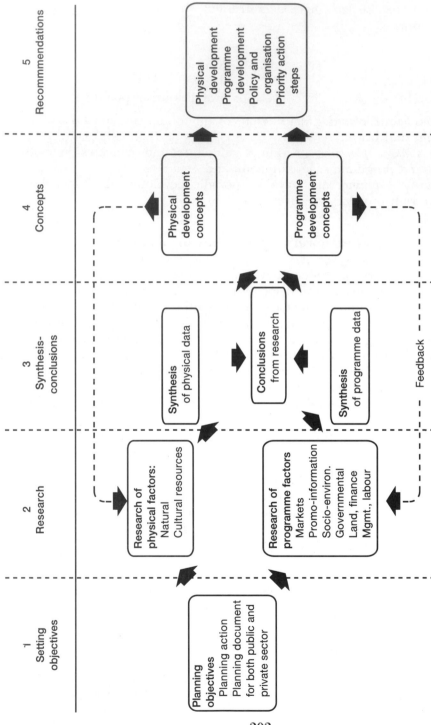

Figure 7.7 Strategic planning process. Periodically, it is necessary for a region to engage in a specific strategic planning process whereby market–plant match can be accomplished. However, this five-step process should be closely integrated with continuous and community planning for tourism.
Source: Gunn (1988:266).

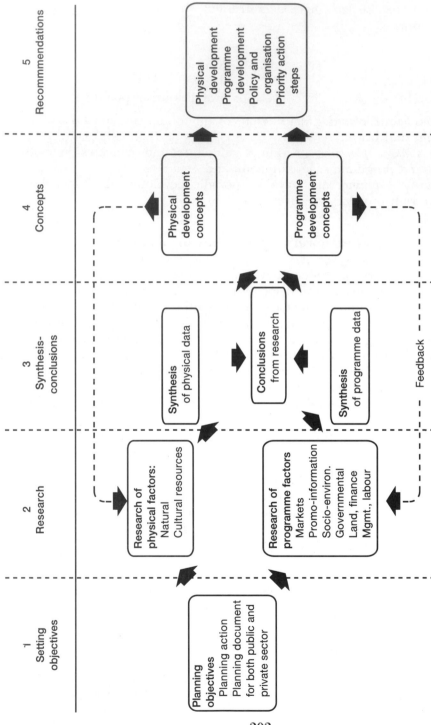

Tourism

Board (TTTB). In 1989 the TTTB was reorganised, refocused and redesignated to become the Trinidad and Tobago Tourism Development Authority (TDA). The new organisation was given more autonomy, and a brief to be proactive in providing support and direction for the nation's tourism. Its corporate mission statement was 'To increase the value and volume of tourism flows; to develop the highest skills and professionalism in the industry and related areas; to create a greater public awareness, appreciation and understanding of tourism; to operate in a manner that reflects national aspirations.'

It provided the framework for detailed plans covering: organisation of TDA; marketing; development and financial aspects. The strategic plan was based on an analysis of the current position and likely outlook for international travel, the competitive position of Trinidad and Tobago as a destination, and a SWOT analysis of the

Table 7.3 Objectives of the Trinidad and Tobago plan 1990–4.

Economic objectives	Social objectives
• Generation of substantial foreign exchange earnings	• The encouragement of those cultural forms and expressions that are distinctly national in origin and development
• Provision of direct employment at all levels within the industry	
• The provision of additional sources of income (profits, wages, rents, fees, etc.)	• The development of new attractions based on the diverse social and cultural heritage of Trinidad and Tobago in order to provide residents and visitors with more leisure activities
• The generation of linkages with other sectors of the economy, e.g. agriculture, manufacturing, handicraft, sport, culture, various art forms and construction	• Fostering of greater national awareness and pride by attention to the preservation, restoration and promotion of historic sites, cultural festivals, etc.
• The projection of a positive image and awareness of Trinidad and Tobago to the outside world, thereby opening up further opportunities for trade	• The protection of physical and social territorial rights of residents
	• Ensuring, as far as possible, that all sections of the national community benefit from tourism
	• The discouragement of the importation of undesirable trends in lifestyles and social behaviour

Table 7.4 Selected strategies and actions by TDA in relation to tourism policies.

Policy (summary)	Focus of short-term strategies
Market focus on resort tourism; activity tourism and cruise ship tourism	Marketing emphasis on: cultural heritage; natural resources and history with a view to optimising use of existing plant and to generate demand for new accommodation. Expand attractions to include: incentive travel; sporting, cultural and educational events. Develop higher profile for Port of Spain in cruise ship traffic. Develop inter-island day trips
Match *existing product profile* with markets that make the best economic and social contribution to the country	Concentrate on: 'general' holiday-maker; special interest visitor, and incentive travel. Prepare clearly defined and quantified targets for each generating source, and each activity, this will provide performance targets. Priority generating markets (in order) will be: Europe; North America, Caribbean and Latin America. Broaden seasonality. Move demand upscale
Given the limited *marketing budget*, concentrate resources on markets with highest returns	Overall objective of maximising foreign tourism revenues. Development of clear trade/consumer targeting with minimum office/administrative costs. Increase industry participation in marketing cost-sharing.
Product and *infrastructure* developments in line with needs of tourists and social objectives of government	In acknowledging quality constraints, the underlying strategy is to: develop new accommodation in Tobago; upgrade all product areas through incentives and licensing/classification of hotels; to ensure profitable conditions for operators; encourage at least one international 'brand name' property for Tobago. Water-based activities, gold and shopping also targeted for growth and promotion
Further development of *cruise ship industry* with emphasis on 'home-porting' of vessels. Make Trinidad and Tobago the hub for Southern Caribbean cruise ships	To ease bureaucratic burdens for cruise ship tourists and operators; to actively market Port of Spain to operators, especially the new Tobago port of Scarborough. Promote Port of Spain as the home port for all vessels with Southern Caribbean/South American destinations with particular reference to mid-week turnarounds which would create opportunities in bunkerage, water supply and locally manufactured goods

To adopt a more independent, positive and critical approach to *air access*	Link specific needs of tourism industry to national air policies; ensure government regulations do not favour national carrier at the expense of tourism, encourage direct international access to Tobago. Increase seat capacity; encourage 'open skies' policy for charters but not at the expense of scheduled routes; move from consolidator fares to promotional fares; encourage hub activities to help develop direct non-stop capacity
Develop *public awareness programme* that sensitises the importance of tourism and the need to project a positive image and attitude	Develop a programme specific to the needs of Trinidad and Tobago. Launch this in schools. Other measures include: attract business sponsorship; inculcate positive attitude in welcoming visitors; undertake proactive media campaign; encourage good relations through entrepreneurial activity
To promote *economic linkages*	Encourage and support investment activities that serve to promote linkages; identification of import substitution
To extend the *season* from peak to off-peak	Given that niche-marketing and price promotional are powerful tools, expand demand through identification of new markets, greater use of promotionals, incentives to tour operators and for Trinidad, create new demand from cruise line traffic and conferences

Source: Trinidad and Tobago Tourism Development Authority Strategic Plan 1990–4 (July 1990).

nation's tourism product and processes. Two sets of objectives were set: economic objectives and social objectives (see Table 7.3). The overall mission for the TDA was summarised as 'increasing significantly tourism's contribution to GDP and social and cultural development while controlling its negative effects'. Table 7.4 shows selected strategies and actions by TDA in relation to tourism policies.

Table 7.5 Tourism development strategies.

Mass tourism	Green tourism
Development without planning	First plan, then develop
Project-led schemes	Concept-led schemes
District level planning only	Regional coordination of district plans
Scattered development	Concentrated development
Building outside existing settlements	Development within existing settlements
Intensive development in areas of finest landscapes	Fine landscape conserved
New building and new bed capacity	Re-use existing buildings – better utilisation of bed capacity
Building for speculative unknown future demand	Fixed limited to development
Tourism development everywhere	Development only in suitable places, and where local services already exist
Development by outside developers	'Native' developers only
Employment primarily for non-natives	Employment according to local potential
Development only on economic grounds	Discussion of all economic, ecological and social issues
Farming declines, labour force into tourism	Farm economy retained and strengthened
Community bears social costs	Developer bears social costs
Traffic 'plan' favours cars	Traffic 'plan' favours public transport
Capacity for high season demand	Capacity for average demand
'Natural' and historical obstacles	'Natural' and historical obstacles retained
Urban architecture	Vernacular architecture
High technology and mechanised tourist installations	Selective mechanised development – 'low-tech' development favoured

Source: Butler (1992: 36).

While issues concerning sustainability are central to tourism planning, they are explored elsewhcrc in this book. However, in the planning context it is useful to examine some tourism development strategies, Butler (1992) has identified strategies that pertain to mass tourism and green tourism (Table 7.5). Here Butler is comparing the strategies that create different styles of tourism and serves to illustrate, if we take it within the context of the Trinidad and Tobago plan, that academics and planners should be feeding into each other's work: the Trinidad and Tobago plan did not give clear indications that theoretical aspects and thus impacts were fully taken into account.

CHAPTER 8

Alternative and sustainable tourism development – the way forward?

Introduction

The objective of this chapter is to introduce and analyse the various concepts and terminology incorporated under the generic title 'alternative tourism'. More specifically it concentrates particularly on the terms 'sustainable development' and 'ecotourism'. It discusses the advantages and disadvantages of considering alternative forms of tourism as a policy means of achieving sustainable tourism development.

> Development never will be, and never can be, defined to universal solution. It refers broadly speaking, to desirable social and economic progress, and people will have different views about what is desirable. Certain development must mean improvement in living conditions, for which economic growth and industrialisation are essential. But if there is no attention to the quality of growth and to social change one cannot speak of development. (Brandt, 1980:48)

The era of the 'alternative'

The concept and dynamics of 'mass tourism' with its associated problems as portrayed in *The Golden Hordes* (Turner and Ash, 1975) have been interpreted as phenomena in need of critical analysis. In the search to minimise the problems thrown up by mass tourism and for a conceptual framework which is more destination friendly (Weiler and Davis, 1993) new ideas of what tourism should be have emerged. These ideas are often given the generic title of 'alternative tourism' and have in part been embraced by the private sector, in response to the demands of a wider society in the 1990s for greener and environmentally friendly products. These ideas have also increasingly found favour in postmodern societies, in search of 'the alternative' as a means of giving new meaning and values to social order, and a form of self-identification. The notion of the new 'consumer with a social and environmental conscience' extends to buying holidays, as well as buying toilet paper or cosmetics. There is little doubt that the tourism market has become greener in response to this trend in society of heightened environmental awareness and environmental concern. Wright (1993) states that the consumer market is 'becoming greener or more environmentally sensitive' and a recent poll demonstrated that 85% of the industrialised world's citizens believe that the environment is the number one public issue facing the world today. In the United Kingdom a survey carried out by Crown-Burge (Smith and Jenner, 1989) found that 40% of the population expressed concern about the destruction of the environment, almost as many as were worried about AIDS. Consumers are demanding alternative forms of products and this has presented the opportunity and need for the tourism industry to respond to this market-led approach.

Alternative tourism also implies that a form of tourism is being developed which is more environmentally friendly, in both its physical and cultural form, than the mass tourism that went before it. Sometimes the alternative forms merge together to be represented as the new form of tourism that will make its development sustainable, through minimising damage to resources and allowing for their future replenishment. Under this generic form of alternative, we can introduce a number of other tourism terminologies including eco, green, rural, farm, sports and adventure. Within them, there seems to be an implicit assumption that such forms of tourism offer a better social and environmental balance than the existing model of mass tourism. The implication is that by promoting forms of 'alternative tourism' or calling ourselves 'alternative tourists' we are encouraging a type of tourism that is 'better' and more 'sustainable' than what has gone before it. Butler (in Smith and Eadington, 1992:38) summarises the comparisons of conventional or 'mass tourism' with alternative tourism in Table 8.1.

Cater (1993:85) describes most of the characteristics of alternative tourism as being in direct contrast to those of conventional mass tourism. She states: 'Activities are likely to be small scale, locally owned with consequently low impact, leakages and a high proportion of profits retained locally. These contrast with the large-scale multinational concerns typified by high leakages which characterise mass tourism'.

An important difference about alternative tourism, *vis-à-vis* mass tourism, is that it is smaller scale. For example, in place of the International Hilton or the Hyatt, smaller hotels and pensions would be developed. The actual supply of beds and rooms may total the same number as a grand hotel but, by implication, ownership is likely to be of a more local and indigenous nature. In turn this should mean a higher retention of revenues locally, employment of more local people, and a higher demand for locally produced goods and services.

Alternative tourism therefore poses a threat to, or at least offers another variety of, metatourism. Although destinations may still be dependent upon the core for their tourist markets, the ownership will be more local than in the

more traditional forms of metatourism dominated by transnational corporations. By implication, this form of alternative tourism development will require
a high input of planning and regulation so as not to replicate the spontaneous
development seen around the Mediterranean coastline and other areas of the
world, where local ownership may be high, but many destinations have
suffered the 'boom–bust' experience.

Sustainable development – tourism's benefit?

Closely linked to the idea of alternative tourism is the concept of sustainable
development. Since the appearance of the United Nations' *Brundtland Report*
(1987) and the 1992 Earth Summit Conference in Rio de Janerio, the concept

Table 8.1 Principal agents of change relating to types of tourism.

	Conventional tourism		Alternative tourism	
	Short term	Long term	Short term	Long term
Tourists				
Numbers	Small, rapid growth	Large, perhaps decline	Small, slow growth	Small, consistent
Behaviour	Sedentary	Sedentary	Explorer	Explorer
Location	Limited/resorts	Resorts	Communities, households	Widespread, households
Time	Short	Short, definite	Long, indefinite	Medium, definite
Contact	Some, economic	Great, shallow	Some, intensive	Intensive
Similarity	Little	Little	Very little	Very little
Resource				
Fragility	Possible pressure	Possible ruination	Little pressure	Pressure
Uniqueness	Possible pressure	Possible ruination	Little pressure	Pressure
Capacity	Problem	Probably exceeded	Minor problem	Problem
Economy				
Sophistication	Some	Developed	None	Very little
Leakage	Some	Some	Maybe lots	Maybe lots
Political				
Local control	Some	Little	Most	Some vulnerable
Planning extent	Some	Little/reactive	Little	Little

Source: Butler (in Smith and Eadington, 1992:38).

of sustainability has been central to informed discussion on development. This conference, organised by the United Nations on the subject of Environment and Development, aimed to focus on protection of the environment and making development less harmful to it, a central paradox here being that development takes place in the environment. As previously mentioned, although many developing countries realise and accept the need to protect their own environments and alleviate international environmental problems, such as depletion of the ozone layer and global warming, they lack the resources to be able to do this. Many of the practical measures proposed to alleviate international environmental problems originate and are directed by developed countries. As Adams (1992:1) puts it:

> To an extent, concern over Third World environments simply reflects the growing integration of the global village, and environmental pressure is at least in part an extension of traditional concerns about environmental quality in that village's new countryside, in the Third World.

The analogy of the Third World being the global village's new countryside is highly prevalent to tourism, as long-haul travel becomes more popular and the pleasure periphery is pushed further outwards. This sentiment acknowledged the pragmatic view that safeguarding and protecting biodiversity in the developing world is essential to the environmental and economic wellbeing of the West. Coupled with this is the realisation that the environment and economics need to be supportive of each other for sustained wealth, as opposed to being mutually exclusive.

Blaikie (1992:87) states:

> Poverty and environment are linked in a close and complex way. Poor people live in and suffer from degraded environments, and very often they create environmental degradation because their poverty forces them to do so. It is obvious, but worth repeating, that farmers in the highlands of Ethiopia or Nepal do not farm steep and eroded hillsides through perversity but through necessity.

This is also the case in the Philippines or Brazil, where some poor actually live in the rubbish dumps, surviving by foraging through the less poor's detritus, that is, less symbolic than actually living in rubbish.

The term 'sustainable development' is now increasingly referred to in the wider economic world as a desirable goal to achieve through economic policy. In the business sector some organisations are considering sustainable development as a way of securing their long-term futures and also introducing a higher component of ethical considerations into their operations. One of the leading pioneers of this trend in the United Kingdom is The Body Shop, an international skin and hair company with more than 700 stores worldwide.

Environmental and social considerations have always been at the forefront of their decision-making.

In *The Green Book* (1992:5) the policy of the Body Shop is declared thus:

> The Body Shop has always had a clear, top-level commitment to environmental and social excellence. Because of this, we make sure we include environmental issues in every area of our operations.

In particular, on p. 16, in reference to product development, the theme of sustainability is addressed directly:

> We strive to obtain raw materials from unities who want to use trade to protect their culture and who practise traditional and sustainable land use.

Although the company received a great deal of criticism in 1994, focused on the actual quantity of raw materials purchased from indigenous peoples, the high profile and associated business success enjoyed through the pursuit of this policy is significant. The indication to all business sectors, including tourism, is that there is a considerable consumer base willing to pay higher prices for what they consider to be an ethical investment to purchase a product.

This concern for the 'sustainable profile' of companies' products is also found in a few leading tourism organisations (however, it must be stressed these companies unfortunately are in the minority). Chapter 6 includes reference to British Airways' environmental policy, aimed at improving the use of resources and reducing waste and unnecessary pollution. Thomas Cook have a 'Green' Mission: 'The Thomas Cook Group endeavours to demonstrate a responsibility to the environment in all its worldwide activities'; and Thomsons, Britain's largest tour operator, have an environmental director. TUI, Germany's largest tour operator, has an environmental department while Steinenberger, the German hotel group, have been initiators of the concept of hotel audits, as have Grecotels in Greece. In the private sector environmental directives usually take the form of audits connected with the company's product. Usually these are hotel or destination based. Hotel audits usually incorporate factors such as waste disposal, water usage, energy usage and noise pollution, etc. A typical accommodation audit is shown in Figure 8.1. Destination audits adopt a more macro perspective of environmental quality and include similar criteria to accommodation audits, although based on a wider spatial scale. Typical factors to be taken into consideration are shown in Figure 8.2.

However, the meaning of sustainable development is not clear, and consequently open to varying interpretations. Just as people will have different views of development and what is desirable, varying interpretations of exactly what the term 'sustainable development' means is common. However, there has been a popular consensus of hope that sustainable development (provided

HOTELS, CLUBS, HOLIDAY APARTMENTS

TUI Environmental Checklist 1992

Destination _____ Town _____ Object _____ Date _____

	Very good	Good	Satis-factory	Not good	Unsatis-factory	Comments + Explanations
1) Hotel management						
a) **Waste water treatment** — Connection with waste water treatment plant, own waste water treatment plant (which technique: mechanical, biological etc. keeping clean of waste water etc.)	☐	☐	☐	☐	☐	
b) **Waste disposal** — Waste avoidance (no small packages and separation of waste for recycling, composting, gathering of special waste)	☐	☐	☐	☐	☐	
c) **Water supply** — Lowering of water-consumption/water economy measure, use of ground water etc.	☐	☐	☐	☐	☐	
d) **Energy supply** — Energy saving, alternate energy production (solar or wind energy) etc.	☐	☐	☐	☐	☐	
e) **Management** — Detergents, insect pest control, food etc.	☐	☐	☐	☐	☐	
2) Noise protection in/at hotel — Traffic abatement, other noise protection measures	☐	☐	☐	☐	☐	
3) Gardens of hotel — Arrangement and maintainance of garden water economy measures/use of purified waste water, pesticides etc.	☐	☐	☐	☐	☐	
4) Architecture and building materials of hotel — Building style and materials typical of particular region, problematic building material etc.	☐	☐	☐	☐	☐	
5) Environmental information and environmental offers of hotel — Information leaflets, bicycle rental, courses and guided tours etc.	☐	☐	☐	☐	☐	
6) Location and immediate surroundings of hotel grounds — Surrounding landscape, buildings around hotel, traffic etc.	☐	☐	☐	☐	☐	
7) Sea- and poolwater and beach quality in hotel area — Cleanliness/hygiene, natural state etc.	☐	☐	☐	☐	☐	
8) Other aspects of hotel either causing concern or being particularly environment-friendly						

Criteria and Hints for 1992 TUI Environment Reports

Destination: _

Location: _

Period covered: _

DESTINATIONS

Suggestions for background

1) Sea and shoreline

Quality of water for bathing and of the beaches (water for bathing — sea, lakes, rivers), assessments based on appearance, smell, or survey findings where available; cleanliness and care of beaches = refuse collection, type of beach cleaning, Blue Flags, etc.

2) Waste Water Disposal

Filtration plants (technology, capacity, function); drains; other forms of waste filtration; where waste water diverted; re-use, etc.

3) Garbage Disposal

Garbage collection; avoidance of waste in built-up areas and in the countryside; separation and recycling; depots, rubbish incineration, etc.

4) Atmosphere and Noise

Air pollution by industry, traffic, use of incinerators at rubbish dumps; measure for cutting down noise (traffic, discos, machinery, etc.)

5) Surroundings

Architecture/building density/concrete; traffic and traffic reduction measures; green spaces, parks, public grounds, etc.

6) Landscape and Nature

Scenery; extent of building on the coast, nature reserves; protection of plants and animals; measures to preserve the landscape, etc.

7) Power Sources

Power generation (type of fuel used); alternative forms: wind and solar energy, etc.

8) Water Supplies

Sources/springs of drinking water; ground water; desalination, etc.; quality of drinking water; measures to reduce consumption of ground water by use of used water (e.g. filtered waste water), etc.

9) Environmental Briefing/ Environmental Facilities

Briefing material issued by local authories, local information points, possibilities for obtaining information, notice boards, posters; tracks for walkers and bicyclists, guided tours, excursions, etc.

10) Environment Awareness

Awareness among the populace and the authorities/our partners/suppliers; behaviour generally, treatment of environmental protection in the media, schools, etc.; willingness to provide information and extent of efforts made by the authorities; environmental legislation; tourism planning, etc.

that agreement can be reached on what this truly means) in tourism may be achieved through promoting forms of tourism alternative to mass tourism.

Sustainable development is defined by the United Nations' *Brundtland Report* (1987) as: 'development that meets the needs of the present without compromising the ability of future generations to meet their own needs'. The report includes the proviso:

> that sustainable development is not a fixed state of harmony, but rather a process of change in which the exploitation of resources, the direction of investments, the orientation of technological development and institutional change are made consistent with future as well as present need.

It is therefore important to clarify that sustainable development does not necessarily mean no development. One of the main problems with the concept of sustainability is its inherent vagueness, which allows varying interpretations by different interested parties. Indeed, McKercher (1993), commenting on the possible dangers of 'sustainability' to tourism, picks up this theme and outlines the contrasting interpretation of the meaning of sutainability between the pro-development and conservationist bodies. First he outlines the approach to sustainability from the development orientated camp. The basis of their argument is the concept of 'constant wealth'. Within this concept, wealth is based on the aggregate value of both natural and man-made capital, and while the total assets should grow between generations the reserves of natural assets may be permitted to decline, provided that their use generates wealth. This approach will therefore favour prioritisation of activities that can generate most wealth over activities that produce less wealth. It also allows the natural resource base to be exploited in any fashion providing it generates wealth. Referring to the pioneering work of Pearce (1989) on an environmental approach to economics, McKercher quotes Pearce as stating:

> Therefore in areas where tourism development is one development activity out of a choice of many, it is quite possible that alternative activities such as mining or logging may offer a higher financial rate of return on investment. This will therefore mean that tourism development that would have taken place will be pushed out by other forms of activity such as mining or logging.

Sherman and Dixon (1991:89) draw attention to the same scenario:

> Consider a tropical rain forest somewhere in Central America. Though it is presently inaccessible, an extension of national highway will soon open up the area. Various potential users of the resource become interested in the possibilities. A campesino considers the area's potential for agricultural development and sees dollar signs. A logger looks at the timber resources and also sees money to be made. A nature tourism operator reaches the same conclusion ... each

215

potential user of the previously inaccessible resource seeks monetary benefits from its exploitation and use. Their different visions, however, are likely to conflict. Some uses will preclude others, though certain combinations of uses can exist.

The second threat to tourism development, based on the premise of sustainability, comes from conservationists, who support the argument that tourism and other activities should not be allowed in areas which are 'environmentally sensitive' (another terminology which is open to wide interpretation!). Tourism development could therefore be halted by con-servationists because of their desire to establish more protected areas through legislation, which prohibits their use especially by any form of commercial tourism.

A more intergrated planning approach, sharing the use of resources with other sectors to provide optimal benefit and reduce over-dependecy on any one activity, would seem a sensible policy to pursue. Although McKercher's view may be interpreted as being slightly polemic, it nevertheless highlights the dangers of assuming that sustainable development policies are necessarily going to favour tourism as an activity. Tourism advocates should therefore be very cautious, especially those in the industry, of believing that by encouraging sustainable development (with the advantage of being seen to be ethical), especially in areas where different developmental activities are competing for resources, that tourism activities will necessarily be given preference over other forms of development.

Nor, critically, should it necessarily be assumed that members of the local community will always favour protection of the environment for the purposes of tourism. An article entitled 'Up the estuary without a paddle' (McGregor, 1994) describes such a case. The St Lucia Wetlands in South Africa is an area containing coral reefs, turtle beaches, high afforested dunes, freshwater swamps, grasslands and estuaries. She explains the dilemma over its future development. Rio Tinto Zinc, the global mining company, wish to mine the more abundant dunes for titanium dioxide slag. The company claims that after mining it will 'reconstitute and regenerate the dunes and the ecosystems of the area will be assured'. Despite these assurances and a white South African culture, which has always favoured mining as a wealth-producing activity in the past, Justice Ramon Leon, the head of a review panel established to investigate alternative development scenarios, favours tourism development. In McGregor's article Eddie Kock of the Group for Environmental Monitoring states:

> This breaks a mindset that has dominated the country's political economy since the turn of the century, encapsulated in mineral affairs minister, George Bartlett's statement that 'mining is what this country has always done and always will do'. It reflects a growing awareness that tourism based on the protection of wilderness areas is fast becoming a

more effective way of generating the economic growth this country needs.

However, surveys among local people, mainly Zulus, show support for the mining development option as opposed to tourism. McGregor explains why:

> RBM (a subsidiary of Rio Tinto Zinc) has always paid relatively high wages and sponsored schools, clinics and other facilities. The titanium mining project also offered another 59 jobs in the area. Natal Parks Board on the other hand, which runs the St. Lucia Wetlands and the surrounding game reserves, pays relatively low wages and is perceived to be implicated in the seizure of conservation land from local people in the sixties and seventies.

This case study illustrates the key point made in Chapter 5, that revenue retention by local people of tourism expenditure and perceived financial benefits over other alternative development options, will be a major determinatory factor in the protection of natural resources. It also illustrates the need for consultation and participation with the local people in development decisions, if the sustainability of fragile ecosystems is to be maintained in the face of resource pressures.

As previously mentioned, the tourism industry has not been immune from having to respond to environmental concerns and the 1987 *Brundtland Report*. Not least is the realisation that physical resources, placed into a tourism system that 'consumes' landscapes, far from being renewable are finite if not managed properly. The number of destinations that can be environmentally exhausted (as in open-cast mining) through tourism development, to the extent where tourists no longer want to go there, is not inexhaustible. However, this realisation, or willingness to respond to it, is still in its initial stages, particularly in the tour operating sector, where short-term financial considerations still overrule longer term environmental concerns. Unfortunately for the future of many destinations sunlust tourism based on extremely cheap prices is not sustainable. Nor are the cheap prices (particularly present in the United Kingdom's outbound market) sustainable indefinitely to the tourist. Eventually the tourist will be faced with picking up the bill to pay for the necessary environmental improvements after years of neglect in the destinations. Many areas of Spain built on cheap tourism in the 1960s are now discovering that they are faced with the need to implement environmental improvements in response to problems caused by tourism development. This point was emphasised in a recent article in a British newspaper. Entitled 'Prices to rise 20% on Costas', the article explains how Spanish hoteliers are planning to raise their prices by up to 20% in 1995. The reason given for these rises is the belief by the Spanish that they are necessary for investment and upgrading of properties (*The Times*, 11 June 1994).

Noel Josephides, the Managing Director of Sunvil Holidays and ex-Chairman of the Association of Independent Tour Operators (AITO), gave a fascinating insight into the role of tour operators in destination development and the creation of environmental problems, at the conference 'Tourism: Hosts and Guests Partners in Development?' held at the Commonwealth Institute on 22 March 1994. He explains how destinations become fashionable for tour operators, for example the Algarve in 1987, Turkey in 1988 and Cyprus in 1992. Encouraged by heavy pre-payments from operators, hoteliers build extra rooms to accommodate increasing numbers of tourists. Eventually, however, this building boom leads to over supply and capacity as demand fails to keep pace with increased supply. This then leads to discounting of room rates and tariffs by hotels. The infrastructure has failed to keep pace in its development to accommodate the increased number of tourists and the destination begins to experience environmental problems. These problems may begin to receive increasing coverage in the press and the destination will begin to experience an image problem. This image problem, combined with the need for discounting, will drive prices downwards for the hotel owners. Discounting will attract a less affluent client and the destination will find that it is forced to accept lower-spending tourists brought in by less reputable/fringe tour operators who are searching for a quick financial kill. The destination has now developed a down-market image with visitors likely to be arriving predominantly from one country.

It can be deduced that the differing interpretations of the meaning of 'sustainable development' are likely to lead to confusion and conflict over the usage of resources. It is also possible that tourism proponents will not necessarily benefit from jumping onto the sustainable bandwagon, especially if the concept of 'constant wealth' is adopted as the philosophy of planning authorities. The next section therefore outlines some of the guiding principles that have been established for sustainable tourism development.

Components of sustainable tourism development

Murphy (in Theobold, 1994:272) gives an extensive and detailed list of the components of sustainable development in Table 8.2. Although the components apply to all forms of development they can be adapted to tourism development. Indeed, the link between these components and the guiding principles for sustainable tourism development developed by the United Kingdom's Department of the Environment (1991:15) are axiomatic. These guiding principles are as follows.

- The environment has an intrinsic value which outweighs its value as a tourism asset. Its enjoyment by future generations and its long-term survival must not be prejudiced by short-term considerations.
- Tourism should be recognised as a positive activity with the potential to benefit the community and the place as well as the visitor.
- The relationship between tourism and the environment must be managed

Table 8.2 Sustainable development components.

1 Establishing ecological limits and more equitable standards	'Requires the promotion of values that encourage consumption standards that are within the bounds of the ecological possible and to which all can reasonably aspire'
2 Redistribution of economic activity and reallocation of resources	'Meeting essential needs depends in part on achieving full growth potential and sustainable development clearly requires economic growth in places where such needs are not being met'
3 Population control	'Though the issue is not merely one of population size but of the distribution of resources, sustainable development can only be pursued if demographic developments are in harmony with the changing productive potential of the ecosystem'
4 Conservation of basic resources	'Sustainable development must not endanger the natural systems that support life on Earth: the atmosphere, the waters, the soils, and the living beings'
5 More equitable access to resources and increased technological effort to use them more effectively	'Growth has no set limits in terms of population or resource use beyond which lies ecological disaster ... But ultimate limits there are, and sustainability requires that long before these are reached the world must ensure equitable access to the constrained resource and reorient technological efforts to relieve the pressure'
6 Carrying capacity and sustainable yield	'Most renewable resources are part of a complex and interlinked ecosystem, and maximum sustainable yield must be defined after taking into account system-wide effects of exploitation'
7 Retention of resources	'Sustainable development requires that the rate of depletion of non-renewable resources foreclose as few future options as possible'
8 Diversification of the species	'Sustainable development requires the conservation of plant and animal species'
9 Minimise adverse impacts	'Sustainable development requires that adverse impacts on the quality of air, water, and other natural elements are minimised so as to sustain the ecosystem's overall integrity'
10 Community control	'Community control over development decisions affecting local ecosystems'
11 Broad national/ international policy	'The biosphere is the common home of all human-kind and joint management of the biosphere is prerequisite for global political security'
12 Economic viability	'Communities must pursue economic well-being while recognising that [government] policies may set limits to material growth'
13 Environmental quality	'Corporate environmental policy is an extension of total quality management'
14 Environmental audit	'An effective environmental audit system is at the heart of good environmental management'

Source: Murphy (in Theobald, 1994:272).

so that the environment is sustainable in the long term. Tourism must not be allowed to damage the resource, prejudice its future enjoyment or bring unacceptable impacts.

- Tourism activities and developments should respect the scale, nature and character of the place in which they are sited.
- In any location, harmony must be sought between the needs of the visitor, the place and the host community.
- In a dynamic world some change is inevitable and change can often be beneficial. Adaptation to change, however, should not be at the expense of any of these principles.
- The tourism industry, local authorities and environmental agencies all have a duty to respect the above principles and to work together to achieve their practical realisation.

Central to the implementation of these principles is that consideration be given in the development process to the model shown in Figure 8.3. The emphasis in this model is for a movement towards integration of the physical environment (place), the cultural environment (host community) and the tourist. The implication is that in future planning of tourism, greater efforts need to be made to incorporate community representation into the planning process (although great difficulties may be experienced in defining the true meaning of community because of its diversity and complexity of social construction) and achieving universal agreement of such wide representations of interests may be difficult. As Haywood (1988:105) puts it:

> Tourism planners are now being asked to be more responsive to a broader set of economic and social needs. If this is to occur local governments should recognise that they will have to become more responsible to the local citizens whose lives and communities may be

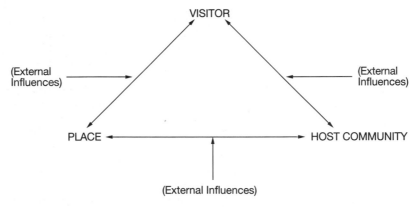

Figure 8.3 Model for sustainable tourism.
Source: ETB (1991:10).

220

affected by tourism ... Local residents obviously become part of the tourist product attracting tourists through their culture and hospitality, and consequently the resident, as a community member, is affected by tourism in all its positive and negative manifestations.

Let's go eco – let's be alternative!

The two key questions arising are how tourism policy and development may be changed in such a way as to allow it to incorporate the principles of sustainability, and how is this to be achieved? Other issues raised are:

- Does sustainability exclude large-scale development of tourism plant or facilities, or will the use of audits and emphasis on issues such as recycling and making plant more green and efficient be enough to satisfy the requirements of sustainable development? or
- Does sustainable development mean that we must all become ecotourists who use small-scale facilities planned with the physical and cultural environment uppermost in consideration and ourselves full of environmental philosophy?

Ecotourism, like sustainability, has become a buzz-word of the 1990s as a form of alternative tourism which countries should pursue as being more environmentally friendly and minimising the negative environmental impacts of tourism.

Ecotourism has been defined by the Ecotourism Society (1992) as:

purposeful travel to natural areas to understand the cultural and natural history of the environment, taking care not to alter the integrity of the ecosystem, whilst producing economic opportunities that make the conservation of natural resources financially beneficial to local citizens.

However, it is a rapidly growing segment of the tourism market, as portrayed by Mackay in *The Times*, 17 February 1994. In an article entitled 'Ecotourists take over', she states that research from the International Centre for Ecotourism Research at Griffith University in Queensland, Australia, found that ecotourism is the fastest growing subsector of the international tourism industry. It has a growth rate three times that of tourism overall.

'Americans travel overseas for nature-related travel each year'. Using the definition of ecotourism from the Ecotourism Society it is possible to make certain assumptions about the sort of tourist who is likely to participate in ecotourism. The definition includes 'purposeful travel', the inference being on education either before or during the holiday to permit understanding of the cultural and natural history of the environment. We should also expect that ecotourism is an alternative form of tourism to 'mass tourism', which will permit the sustainability of the ecosystem for use by future generations, that is, reference to taking care not to alter the integrity of the ecosystem. The ecotourist should also be someone who is willing to forego (indeed who does not expect) accommodation standards equivalent to those offered by the large transnational hotel groups. By accepting the living standards of the local community the ecotourist will create a climate in which it is possible for indigenous cultures to provide accommodation and retain the economic benefits of tourism.

Ecotourism would therefore seem to offer a form of tourism development for the future which would not only be capable of encompassing the principles of sustainability, but which also offers real market opportunities for developing countries who often possess many of the attractive resource bases for this type of tourism. As Cater (1993:85) points out:

> Ecotourism, as a particular variant of alternative tourism, has been eagerly seized upon by Third World destinations as the answer to the classic impasse that they find themselves in: the need to capitalise on their tourism resources to earn badly needed foreign exchange without, at the same time, destroying those resources and thus compromising sustainability.

She continues: 'it [ecotourism] is not a substantially different hybrid from conventional tourism unless it is carefully planned for and managed'.

Owing to the variety of definitions of tourism, the type of tourism product that forms an ecotourism product is debatable. Safari tourism in Kenya, which takes place on a large scale and with the use of tour operators who service the mass industry, fulfils the original criteria, as does trekking in the Himalayas. It is therefore extremely difficult to present the characteristics of the ecotourist. Mawforth (1993:2) proposes three typologies of ecotourists:

- The rough ecotourist: young to middle-aged; travels individually or in small groups; independent organisation; cheap hotels; buses, eats, locally; sport and adventure tourism.
- The smooth ecotourist: middle-aged to old; travels in groups; tour orientated; three–five-star hotels; luxury restaurants; nature and safari tourism.
- The specialist ecotourist: young to old; travels individually; independent or specialist tours; a wide range of hotels, transport and eating places; scientific investigation or pursuit of interest.

Poon (1993) observes the evolution of a new tourist typology in the 1990s with different behaviour, values and expectations than the tourists before them. These are shown in Table 8.3. While the table perhaps presents something of a stereotypical (even idealised) version of the two sets of tourists, it does display a movement of attitudes of increasing numbers of tourists from

Old tourists	New tourists
Search for the sun	Experience something new
Follow the masses	Want to be in charge
Here today, gone tomorrow	See and enjoy but do not destroy
Show that you have been	Just for the fun of it
Having	Being
Superiority	Understanding
Like attractions	Like sport and nature
Precautions	Adventurous
Eat in the hotel dining room	Try out local fare
Homogeneous	Hybrid

Source: Poon, 1993.

those of believed supremacy, intolerance and transience to those of accept-ance, tolerance, understanding and a wish to be educated.

According to Mackay (1994), the industry itself divides ecotourists into three categories: big 'E', little 'e' and soft adventure. The industry believes that most tourists fall into the little 'e', which indicates that the tourist wants to know that his hotel, resort, airline or tour operator has acceptable environ-mental standards. Big 'E' travellers are more like Cohen's (1974) explorers who head off into the wilderness with a backpack and a compass for days at a time. The 'soft adventurer' likes to visit wilderness areas, wanting to experi-ence them in comfort, but also to know these areas are not being 'exploited': unfortunately a very ambiguous term.

Participation in this alternative form of tourism often relies upon the exploitation of new virgin areas for tourism rather than visiting those areas already developed as tourist destinations. There is a desire to be alternative which, by definition, involves being different to the masses who visit other areas. The proponents of these ideas seldom address the ways in which ecotourists might become the 'trail-blazers', opening up virgin territory to the very 'Golden Hordes' that they disdain! The assumption and judgement of mass tourism as something that is worthy of disdain has been criticised as being selective and élitist. This élitist viewpoint, which is supported by the relatively high prices charged for ecotourism, has been heavily criticised by Wheeller (1993a, 1993b) and renamed egotourism. It is certain that the concept of ecotourism, which is focused around selectivity and attracting higher-spending tourists, does raise ethical questions about restricting access to fragile areas to a wealthy minority of tourists who are best able to afford the high prices. It also introduces a high amount of subjectivity in the form of value judgements, made to encourage the 'politically correct traveller', while discouraging the uncouth 'mass traveller': a far cry from the 1960s, when the advent of cheap package holidays bringing international travel to the masses was heralded as social advancement, the 'debourgoisment', of international travel. The transition in the marketplace, expressed in terms of the products that are being offered within it, are very much demand-driven. However, the extent to which tourists will be willing to pay more for their holidays in aid of environmental protection has still to be tested. The 'ecotourism' market still only constitutes around 5% of the international tourism market (Blaza, 'Hosts–Guests: Partners in Development' Conference, 1994) and the extent to which this form of tourism will penetrate the market has still to be established. If tourist products are 'manufactured' and consumers manipulated into buying such products, and if there is seen to be no money in it, then the big operators will not 'produce' it . . . therefore it will not take off!

Although in the short term there may seem to be benefits, such as little pressure on resources and of retention of local control in decision-making resulting from encouraging alternative forms of tourism, in the long term without proper planning these benefits may be lost.

Without attentive planning and management control, the development cycle for ecotourism is not likely to be any different from that of beach-based tourism. Development of an infrastructure to allow easy access to remote areas: leaving development to market forces without planning controls; neglecting environmental management techniques: the familiar 'boom–bust' cycle has been re-invented. The pressure for development scenario is not unfamiliar to that which exists for mass tourism. It is therefore far from certain that ecotourism will necessarily present a form of tourism that can be developed in a sustainable fashion; nor do the benefits of ecotourism necessarily offer any more lucrative benefits to local people than conventional tourism, if these tours use airlines and hotels that are foreign-owned.

There are no reasons why tour operators or governments should not be driven by the financial benefits of ecotourism, just as for any other form of tourism. Given that the environment must be seen as a resource for tourism, if the dynamics of development are dominated by short-term economic, social and political objectives, then mal-exploitation is almost inevitable. Increasingly in a world where market forces seem dominant and the creation of economic wealth is still a paramount objective, and where entrepreneurial activity is encouraged with minimalist intervention from the state to achieve this aim, then natural wealth, both physical and cultural, will be exploited for its full potential in turning it into economic wealth.

It is clear that alternative forms of tourism will not, in the long term, necessarily lead to the development of tourism in an alternative manner. Although alternative forms of tourism are generally presumed to be less harmful than mass tourism, without proper planning control, and if left to the consequences of short-term economic gain, the exploitation of an eco or green resource will be no different to any other form of development, nor will it necessarily bring less impact. The dangers of accepting more 'environmentally friendly' mass tourism are that very fragile ecosystems may be being put at the mercy of market forces. If these areas are seen as a resource for development, then the likely dynamic is that they can be used for the creation of economic wealth to meet the needs of future generations. The key to utilising resources to maximum effect for the benefit of existing or future generations is the careful application of management and environmental planning techniques, and developing concepts and dynamics of tourism that are framed by long-termism and sustainability.

References

Adams, W.M. (1992) *Green Development: environment and sustainability in the Third World*, London: Routledge.

Alpert, W.J. (1986) *The Minimum Wage in the Restaurant Industry*, New York: Praeger.

Angell, D. *et al.* (1990) *Sustaining Earth: response to the environmental threat*, London: Macmillan.

Ankomah, P. (1991) 'Tourism Skilled Labor: the case of Sub-Saharan Africa', *Annals of Tourism Research* 18, pp. 433–42.

Ascher, F. (1985) *Transnational Corporations and Cultural Identities*, Paris: UNESCO.

Atkinson, R.L., Smith, E. and Hilgard, E.R. (1990) *Introduction to Psychology*, Orlando: Harcourt, Brace, Jovanovich.

Bagguley, P. (1987) 'Flexibility, restructuring and gender: changing employment in Britain's hotels, Lancaster Regionalism Group' in *Hospitality Industry Labour Trends: British and international experience*, Wood, R. (ed.), Tourism Management, pp. 297–304.

Banking Information Service (1986) *Trade Report*, London.

Bayley, S. (1991) *Taste: the secret meaning of things*, London: Faber & Faber.

Bayswater, M. (1991) 'Prospects for Mediterranean beach resorts: an Italian case study', *Tourism Management* 5, pp. 75–89.

Bello, W. and Rosenfeld, S. (1992) *Dragons in Distress: Asia's miracle economies in crisis*, London: Penguin.

Belt, Collins and Associates (1973) *Fiji's Ten Year Tourism Master Plan*, Washington DC: World Bank.

Biddlecomb, C. (1981) *Pacific Tourism: contrasts in values and expectations*, Suva: Pacific Conference of Churches.

Bird, B. (1989) *Langkawi: from Mahsuri to Mahathir: tourism for whom?* Kuala Lumpur: INSAN.

Blaikie, P. (1992) in *Green Development: environment and sustainability in the Third World*, Adams W. (ed.) London: Routledge.

Blaza, A. (1994) *At the symposium. Tourism – Hosts and guests: partners in development*, Commonwealth Institute, London.

Boas, F. (1955) *Primitive Art*, New York NY: Dover Publications.

References

Bocok, R. (1993) *Consumption, London:* Routledge.

Body Shop (1992) *The Green Book,* West Sussex: Body Shop International.

Boniface, P. and Fowler, P. (1993) *Heritage and Tourism in the 'Global' Village,* London: Routledge.

Boo, E. (1990) *Ecotourism: the potentials and pitfalls,* Baltimore: World Wildlife Fund.

Bowen, J. and Basch, J. (1992) 'Strategies for creating customer-oriented organisations' in *International Hospitality Management: Corporate Strategy in practice,* Teare, R. and Olsen, M. (eds), London: Pitman.

Bradley, F. (1991) *International Marketing Strategy,* Hemel Hemstead: Prentice Hall International.

Brandt, W. (1980) *A Programme for Survival, North–South,* London: Pan.

Briassoulis, H. (1993) 'Tourism in Greece' *Tourism in Europe: structures and developments,* Pompl, W. and Lavery, P. (eds), Wallingford: CABI.

British Airways (1990) *Environmental Review: Heathrow and Worldwide Flying Operations,* London: British Airways.

Britton, R. (1979) 'The image of the Third World in marketing', *Annals of Tourism Research* 6(3) pp. 313–29.

Britton, S. (1982) 'The political economy of tourism in the Third World', *Annals of Tourism Research* 9 pp. 331–58.

Brown, J. (1964) *Freud and the Post Freudians,* London: Penguin.

Bryden, J. (1973) *Tourism and Development: a case study of the Commonwealth Caribbean,* Cambridge: Cambridge University Press.

Buck, R. (1978) 'Towards a synthesis in tourism theory', *Annals of Tourism Research* V (I) pp. 110–11.

Bull, A. (1991) *The Economics of Travel and Tourism,* Melbourne: Pitman.

Burkart, A.J. and Medlik, S. (1989) *Tourism: past, present and future* 2nd edn, Oxford: Heinemann.

Burns, P. (1994) *Tourism and Employment: reflections, problems and prospects with case studies from two developing countries,* London: University of North London Press.

Burns, P. and Cleverdon, R. (1995a) 'The Cook Islands: a destination on the edge', in *Issues in Island Tourism,* Conlin, M. and Baum, T. (eds), Wiley, in press.

Burns, P. and Cleverdon, R. (1995b) *Tourism Planning, Problems and Prospects: case studies from the Pacific,* London: University of North London Press, in press.

Burton, R. (1991) *Travel Geography,* London: Pitman.

Butler, R.W. (1980) 'The concept of a tourism area cycle of evolution: implications for management of resources', *Canadian Geographer,* 24, 5–12.

Butler, R.W. (1990) 'Alternative tourism: pious hope or Trojan horse?' *Journal of Travel Research* xxviii, 3.

Butler, R.W. (1992) 'Alternative tourism: the thin end of the wedge', in *Tourism Alternatives: potentials and problems in the development of tourism,* Smith, V. and Eadington W. (eds), Philadelphia: University of Pennsylvania Press.

Butler, R.W. and Waldbrook, L.A. (1991) 'A new planning tool: the tourism opportunity spectrum', *The Journal of Tourism Studies* 2 (1) pp. 2–14.

Cater, E. (1992) 'Profits from Paradise', *Geographical Magazine* 3, 3, pp. 16–21.

Cater, E. (1993) 'Ecotourism in the Third World: problems for sustainable tourism development', *Tourism Management* April pp. 85–90.

Chambers Twentieth Century Dictionary (1972), Bath: Pitman Press.

References

Choy, D. (1991) 'Tourism planning: the case for "market failure" ', *Tourism Management* December 1991.

Clarke, J. and Chritcher, C. (1985) *The Devil Makes Work: leisure in capitalist Britain*, London: Macmillan.

Cleverdon, R. (1979) *The Economic and Social Impact of International Tourism on Developing Countries*, London: EIU.

Cleverdon, R. (1992) *Assessment of Netherlands Outbound*, unpublished ms.

Cohen, E. (1974) 'Who is a tourist: a conceptual clarification', *Sociological Review*, 39 pp. 164–82.

Cohen, E. (1985) 'The Tourist Guide: Origins, Structure and Dynamics of a Role', *Annals of Tourism Research* 12, 1.

Cook Islands (1982) *Development Plan 1: 1982–1985*, Rarotonga: Planning and Economic Development.

Cook Islands Master Tourism Plan (1992–2001) Funded by Asian Development Bank, undertaken by RTP/ESG Consultants (London) for Government of the Cook Islands.

Cook Islands Tourist Authority (CITA) (1994a) *Tourism marketing Update: January*, Rarotonga: Cook Islands Tourist Authority.

Cook Islands Tourist Authority (CITA) (1994b) *Tourism marketing Update: February*, Rarotonga: Cook Islands Tourist Authority.

Cooper, C. (ed.) (1989) *Progress in Tourism Recreation and Hospitality Management*, London: Belhaven Press.

Cooper, C., Fletcher, J., Gilbert, D. and Wanhill, S. (1993) *Tourism Principles and Practices*, London: Pitman.

Cox, R. (1994) 'Global restructring' in *Political Economy and the Changing Global Order*, Stubbs, R. and Underhill, G. (eds), Basingstoke: Macmillan.

Crocombe, R. (1989) *The South Pacific: an introduction 5th edn*, Christchurch: Institute of Pacific Studies, USP.

Crossland, D. *The Times*, 29 June 1993.

Dann, G. (1981) 'Tourism motivation: an appraisal', *Annals of Tourism*, vol. 8, (2) 187–219.

de Kadt, E. (1979) 'Social planning for tourism in the development countries, *Annals of Tourism Research* 6(1) pp. 36–48.

Department of Environment (1991) *Tourism and the Environment: maintaining the balance*, London: HMSO.

Donaldson, L. (1993) *Decolonising Feminism*, London: Routledge.

Doxey, G. (1975) 'A causation theory of visitor – resident irritants: methodology and research inferences', *Proceedings of the Travel Research Association*, 6th Annual Conference, San Diego, California.

Ecotourism Society (1992) *Definition and Ecotourism Statistical Fact Sheet*, Alexandra, Va: Ecotourism Society.

Edgell, D.L. (1990) *International Tourism Policy*, New York: Van Nostrand Reinhold.

EIU (1991) 'Managing Tourism and the Environment – a Kenyan Case Study', *Travel and Tourism Analyst*.

Elkington, J. and Hailes, J. (1991) *Holidays that don't Cost the Earth*, London: Gollancz.

Elliot, M. 'Travel and tourism – the pleasure principal', *The Economist*, 23 March 1991.

228

References

English Tourist Board (ETB) (1990) *The Green Light: a guide to sustainable tourism*, London: ETB.

English Tourist Board (1991) *Tourism and the Environment: maintaining the balance*, London: ETB.

Enloe, C. (1989) *Bananas, Beaches and Bases: making feminist sense of international politics*, London: Pandora/Unwin.

Evans, G. 'Tourist rush for kill a seal pup holiday', *Evening Standard* (London), 5 July 1993.

Ewert, A. (1989) *Outdoor Adventure Pursuits: foundations, models and theories*, Colombus: Publishing Horizons.

Farrell, B. (ed.) (1977) *The Social and Economic Impact of Tourism on Pacific Communities*, Santa Cruz: Center for Pacific Studies.

Farrell, B. (1982) *Hawaii: The Legend That Sells*, Honolulu: University of Hawaii Press.

Faulkner, H. (1994) 'Towards a strategic approach to tourism development: the Australian experience' in *Global Tourism: the next decade* Theobald, W. (ed.), Oxford: Butterworth–Heinemann.

Finnish Tourist Board (FTB) (1993) *Key Goals and Strategies for 1993–95*, Helsinki: FTB.

Fitzsimmons, J. and Fitzsimmons, M. (1994) *Service Management for Competitive Advantage*, New York: McGraw–Hill.

Foreign Affairs Committee (1983) *Turks and Caicos Islands: Airport Development on Providenciales*, London: HMSO.

Foster, B. (1994) *The Vulnerable Planet: a short economic history of the environment*, New York: Monthly Review Press.

Fukuyama, F. (1992) *The End of History and the Last Man*, London: Penguin.

Gabriel, Y. (1988) *Working Lives in Catering*, London: Routledge.

Gamble, W. (1989) *Tourism and Development in Africa*, London: John Murray.

George, S. (1989) *A Fate Worse Than Debt*[???].

Gill, R. (1967) *Evaluation of Modern Economics*, New Jersey: Prentice Hall.

Gill, S. and Law, D. (1988) *The Global Political Economy: perspectives, practices and policies*, Hemel Hemstead: Harvester Wheatsheaf.

Goodall, B. (1991) in Cooper, C. (1991) *Progress in Tourism, Recreation and Hospitality Management* vol. 3 London: Belhaven Press.

Gosling, D. (1990) 'Religion and the environment', in *Sustaining Earth: response to the environmental threat* Angell, D. *et al.* (eds), London: Macmillan.

Gourevitch, P. 'In the holocaust theme park', The *Observer* Magazine, 30 January 1994.

Graburn, N. (1989) 'Tourism: the sacred journey' in *Hosts and Guests: the anthropology of tourism* 2nd ed., Smith, V. (ed.), Philadelphia: University of Philadelphia Press.

Graburn, N. (1984) 'The Evolution of tourist arts', *Annals of Tourism Research*, 10(1): 9–33.

Greenland Tourism Development Plan 1991–2005, Copenhagen: Hoff and Overgaard.

Greenwood, D. (1989) 'Culture by the pound: an anthropological perspective on tourism as cultural commoditisation', in *Hosts and Guests: the anthropology of tourism* 2nd edn, Smith, V. (ed.), Philadelphia: University of Pennsylvania Press.

Gunn, C. (1988) *Tourism Planning*, New York: Taylor and Francis.

References

Hall, C. (1992) in *Special Interest Tourism* Weiler B., and Hall, C. (eds), London: Belhaven.

Hardin, G. (1968) 'The tragedy of the commons', *Science* 162 pp. 1243–8.

Harrison, D. (1993) Letter to Editor, *In Focus* Spring.

Harrison, P. (1993) *Inside the Third World: the anatomy of poverty* 3rd edn, London: Penguin.

Haywood, M. (1988) 'Responsible and responsive tourism planning in the community', *Tourism Management,* June.

Hibbert, C. (1987) *The Grand Tour,* London: Thames Methuen.

Hoogvelt, A. (1982) *The Third World in Global Development,* Basingstoke: Macmillan.

Hudman, L. (1991) 'Tourism's role and response to environmental issues and potential future effects' *The Tourist Review* 4, pp. 17–21.

Hudson, R. and Townsend, A. (1992) 'Tourism employment and policy choices for local government', in *Perspectives on Tourism Policy* Johnson, P. and Thomas, B. (eds), London: Mansell.

Hughes, R. (1980) *The Shock of the New: Art and the Century of Change,* London: British Broadcasting Corporation.

Hutt, M. (1995) in Solwyn, T. (ed.) *The Tourist Image: Myth and myth making in tourism,* in press.

Inskeep, E. (1991) *Tourism Planning: an integrated and sustainable development approach,* New York: Van Notrand Reinhold.

Jafari, J. (1977) Editor's page, *Annals of Tourism Research* V, 1.

Jenkins, C. (1991) 'Tourism policies in developing countries' in *Managing Tourism* Medlik, S. (ed.), Oxford: Butterworth–Heinemann.

Jenks, C. (1993) *Culture: key ideas,* London: Routledge.

Johnston, M. (1992) in *Special Interest Tourism* Weiler, B. and Hall, C. (eds), London: Belhaven.

Jones, P. (1993) 'Operations management issues' in *The International Hospitality Industry: organisational and operational issues* Jones, P. and Pizzam, A. (eds), London: Pitman.

Jones, P. and Pizzam, A. (eds.) (1993) *The International Hospitality Industry: Organisational and Operational Issues,* London: Pitman.

Josephides, N. (1994) *At the symposium. Tourism – Hosts and guests: partners in development,* Commonwealth Institute, London.

Kincaid, J. (1988) *A Small Place,* London: Virago.

Klemm, M. (1992) 'Sustainable tourism development: Languedoc and Roussillon, thirty years on', *Tourism Management* June pp. 169–80.

Krippendorf, J. (1989) *The Holiday-makers: understanding the impact of travel and tourism,* Oxford: Butterworth-Heinemann.

Lanfant, M.F. (1980) *Tourism in the process of internationalisation, International Social Science Journal,* xxxii 1.

Lea, J. (1988) *Tourism Development in the Third World,* London: Routledge.

Lean, G. and Keating, M. (1992) 'Rare habitats ruined as gas masks issues', London: *Observer* (9 February).

Lizaso-Urrutia, L. (1993) 'General Issues and Considerations on the Anthropological Study of Societies, Culture and Tourism', Unpublished thesis, University of North London.

Lockwood, A., Gummesson, E., Hubrecht, J. and Senior, M. (1992) 'Developing and maintaining a strategy for service quality' in *International Hospitality Management: corporate strategy in practice* Teare, R. and Olsen, M. (eds), London: Pitman.

Long, C. 'Britain's hidden army of illegal migrant labour', *Observer,* 4 October 1992.

Macauley, F. and Hall, S.J. (1992) 'Ethics, the internal customer and quality', Paper delivered at the second annual conference on human resource management in the hospitality industry 8 December (Brighton University).

MacCannell, D. (1976) *The Tourist: a new theory of the leisure class*, New York: Shocken Books.

MacCannell, D. (1989) *The Tourist* 2nd edn, London: Macmillan.

MacCannell, D. (1992) *Empty Meeting Ground: the tourist papers*, London: Routledge.

Mackay, A. (1994) 'Eco tourists take over', *The Times*, London, 17 February.

Marshall, B. (1992) *Teaching the Postmodern: fiction and theory,* London: Routledge.

Maslow, A.H. (1984) *Motivation and Personality,* New York: Harper.

Mathieson, A. and Wall, G. (1982) *Tourism: economic, physical and social impacts*, Harlow: Longman.

Maurer, J.L. (1981) *Tourisme dans le Tiers Monde: mythes et réalités*, Geneva: Centre Europe-Tiers Monde.

Mawforth, M. (1993) 'In search of an ecotourist', *Tourism in Focus,* 9 pp. 2–3.

McElroy, K. (1990) 'Tourism, the driving force of spectacular growth', *Guardian,* 25 May.

McGregor, L. (1994) 'Up the estuary without a paddle', *Guardian* (29 April).

McIntosh, R. and Goeldner, C. (1984) *Tourism: principles, practices, philosophies*, 4th ed., Columbus, Ohio: Grid Publishing.

McKercher, B. (1993) 'Can tourism survive "sustainability"?' *Tourism Management* April.

Medlick, R. and Middleton, V. (1973) 'Product functioning in tourism', *Tourism and Marketing* 13, AIEST (Berne).

Middleton, V. (1988) *Marketing Tourism*, Oxford: Heinneman.

Mill, R. (1990) *Tourism: the international business*, London: Prentice Hall.

Mill, R. and Morrison, A. (1985) *The Tourism System: an introductory text*, New Jersey: Prentice Hall.

Milne, S. (1988) *Pacific Tourism: environmental impacts and their Management*, Paper presented to the Pacific Environmental Conference, London 3–5 October.

Minerbi, L. (1992) *Impacts of Tourism Development in Pacific Islands*, San Francisco: Greenpeace Pacific Campaign.

Murphy, P. (1985) *Tourism: a community approach*, London: Routledge.

Murphy, P. (1994) 'Tourism and sustainable development' in Theobold, W. (ed.) *Global Tourism: the next decade*, Oxford: Butterworth–Heinemann Ltd.

Nash, D. (1979) 'The rise and fall of an aristocratic tourist culture, Nice 1763–1936', *Annals of Tourism Research* 6 pp. 61–75.

Nash, D. (1989) 'Tourism as a form of imperalism' in *Hosts and Guests: the anthropology of tourism*, Smith, V. (ed.) Philadelphia: University of Pennsylvania Press.

Nash, D. and Smith, V. (1991) 'Anthropology and tourism', *Annals of Tourism Research* 18(1) pp. 12–25.

Nicholson–Lord, D. (1993) 'Mass tourism is blamed for paradise lost in Goa', *Independent*, 27 January.

Nigeria Advertisement Supplement, *Observer,* 27 March 1994.

Nuñez, T. (1989) 'Touristic Studies in Anthropological Perspective', *Hosts and Guests:*

the anthropology of tourism 2nd ed., Smith, V. (ed.) Philadelphia: University of Philadelphia Press.

O'Grady, R. (1981) *Third World Stopover,* Geneva: World Council of Churches.

O'Hear, A. (1980) *Karl Popper,* London: Routledge & Kegan Paul.

O'Riordan, T. (1983) *Environmentalism,* London: Pion.

O'Rourke, D. (1987) *Cannibal Tours* (film), Canberra: O'Rourke and Associates.

O'Sullivan, T., Hartley, J., Saunders, D., Montgomery, M. and Fiske, J. (1994) *Key Concepts in Communications and Cultural Studies,* London: Routledge.

Olsen, M. and Merna, K. (1993) 'The changing nature of the multinational hospitality firm' in Jones, P. and Pizzam, A. (eds.) (1993) *The International Hospitality Industry: Organizational and Operational Issues,* London: Pitman.

Packard, V. (1957) *The Hidden Persuaders,* New York: McKay.

Pearce, D. (1987) *Tourism Today: a geographical analysis,* Harlow: Longman.

Pearce, D. (1989) *Blueprint for a Green Economy,* London: Earthscan Publications.

Pearce, P. (1982) *The Social Psychology of Tourist Behaviour,* Oxford: Pergamon Press.

Pearce, P. (1993) 'Fundamentals of tourist motivation' in *Tourism and Research: critiques and challenges* Pearce, D. and Butler, W. (eds), London: Routledge.

Peck, J. and Lepie, A. (1989) 'Tourism and development in three North Carolina coastal towns' *Hosts and Guests: the anthropology of tourism* 2nd edn, Smith, v. (ed.), Philadelphia: University of Philadelphia Press.

Pendlebury, R. (1993) 'Resort that is dying for the good old days', Daily Mail, 10 November.

Pepper, D. (1993) *Eco-Socialism: from deep ecology to social justice,* London: Routledge.

PKF (1993) *International Hotel Trends: a statistical summary,* San Francisco: PKF International Consulting.

Pleumaron, A. (1992) 'The golf war', *Tourism in Focus,* 5 pp. 2–4.

Plog, S. (1973) 'Why destination areas rise and fall in popularity' *Cornell Hotel and Restaurant Administration Quarterly* pp. 55–8.

Pompl, W. and Lavery, P. (eds) (1993) *Tourism in Europe: structures and developments,* Wallingford: CABI.

Poon, A. (1993) *Tourism, Technology and Competitive Strategies,* Wallingford: CABI.

Rajotte, F. and Crocombe, R. (eds.) (1980) *Pacific Tourism as Islanders see it,* Suva: Institute of Pacific Studies.

Redwing Holiday (1989–90) *Go Places,* SunMed Holidays, November 1989–October 1990, West Sussex: Redwing Holidays.

Richter, L. (1989) *The Politics of Tourism in Asia,* Honolulu: University of Hawaii Press.

Riley, M. (1991) 'An analysis of hotel labour markets' in *Progress in Hospitality Management* Cooper, C. (ed.) Vol 3, London: Belhaven.

Riley, M. and Jones, P. (1992) 'Labor strategy in international hotel management' in *International Hospitality Management: corporate strategy in practice* Teare, R. and Olsen, M. (eds), London: Pitman.

Ritchie, J. and Zins, M. (1978) 'Culture as a determinant of the attractiveness of a tourist region', *Annals of Tourism Research* 5 pp. 252–67.

Ritzer, G. (1993) *The McDonaldization of Society,* Newbury Park: Pine Forge Press.

Robertson, R. (1992) *Globalization: social theory and global culture,* London: Sage.

RTP-ESG (1991) *Cook Islands Tourism Master Plan,* London: Economic Studies Group.

232

References

Ryan, C. (1991) *Recreational Tourism: a social science perspective*, London: Routledge.

Said, E. (1978) *Orientalism: western concepts of the orient*, London: Routledge & Kegan Paul.

Salmon, R. (1977) 'Development of tourism in French Polynesia: promises and problems' in *The Social and Economic Impact of Tourism on Pacific Communities* Farell, B. (ed.), Santa Cruz: Center for Pacific Studies.

Schumacher, E. (1973) *Small is Beautiful*, London: Sphere Books.

Selwyn, T. (1992) 'Peter Pans in South-East Asia', *Tourism in South East Asia*, London: Routledge.

Selwyn, T. *ECOMOST (European Models of Sustainable Tourism)*, Brussels: EC.

Sherman, P. and Dixon, J. (1991) in *Nature Tourism: managing for the environment* Whelan, T. (ed.), Washington DC: Island Press.

Shoard, M. (1980) *Theft of the Countryside*, London: Maurice Temple Smith.

Sinclair T. (1991) *The Tourism Industry: An International Analysis*, Wallingford: CABI.

Smith, C. and Jenner, P. (1989) *Tourism and the Environment*, Occasional Studies EIU no.5.

Smith, V. (1989) *Hosts and Guests: the anthropology of tourism* 2nd ed, Philadelphia: University of Pennsylvania Press.

Smith, V. & Eadington, W. (1992) *Tourism Alternatives: potentials and problems in the development of tourism*, Philadelphia: University of Pennsylvania Press.

Stanton, M. (1989) 'The Polynesian cultural center: a multi-ethnic model of seven Pacific cultures' in *Hosts and Guests: the anthropology of tourism* Smith, V. (ed.) Philadelphia: University of Philadelphia Press.

Steele, P. (1993) 'The economics of ecotourism', *Tourism in Focus* 9 pp. 4–6.

Stubbs, R. and Underhill, G. (eds) (1994) *Political Economy and the Changing Global Order*, Basingstoke: Macmillan Press.

Teare, R. and Olsen, M. (1992) *International Hospitality Management: corporate strategy in practice*, London: Pitman.

Theobold, W. (ed.) 1994 Global Tourism: the next decade, Oxford: Butterworth–Heinemann Ltd.

Thomas, M. (1993) 'Kenyans seek killer in dying park', *Panoscope* 37 pp. 8–9.

Timberlake, L. & Thomas L. (1990) *When the Bough Breaks . . . our children, our environment*, London: Earthscan.

Tourism Council of the South Pacific (TCSP) (1992) *Western Samoa Tourism Development plan 1992–2001*, Suva: Tourism Council of the South Pacific.

Tourism Council of the South Pacific (TCSP) (1993) *Annual Report*, Suva: Tourism Council of the South Pacific.

Tourism Council of the South Pacific (TCSP) (1990) *Solomon Islands Tourism Master Plan*, Suva: United Nations Development Project.

Trinidad and Tobago Tourism Development Authority, (1990) *Strategic Plan 1990–1994*, Tobago.

Tse, E. and West, J. (1992) 'Development strategies for international hospitality markets' *International Hospitality Management: corporate strategy in practice*, Teare, R. and Olsen, M. (eds), London: Pitman.

Turner, L. and Ash, J. (1975) *The Golden Hordes: International Tourism and the Pleasure Periphery*, London: Constable.

Tylor, E.B. (1871) *Primitive Culture*, London: John Murray.

References

United Nations (UN) (1987) *World Commission on Environment and Development, Our Common Future (the Brundtland Report)*, Oxford: Oxford University Press.

United Nations Development Programme (UNDP) (1992) *Master Tourism Plan for Sri Lanka 1992–2001*, New York United Nations Development Programme and Horwarth Consulting.

United Nations Environmental Programme (UNEP) (1979) *Report on Tourism and the Environment*, New York: United Nations.

United Nations/International Labour Organization (UN/ILO) (1986) *Building the attitude of Hotel Personal*, Phuket, Thailand.

Urry, J. (1990) *The Tourist Gaze*, London: Sage Publications.

Uzzell, D. (1984) 'An alternative structuralist approach to the psychology of tourism marketing' *Annals of Tourism Research* 11 pp. 79–99.

Vidal, J. 'Money for old hope', *Guardian* (Environmental Section), 7 January 1994.

Walker, J. (1983) *Art in the Age of Mass Media*, London: Pluto Press.

Wallerstein, I. (1979) *The Capitalist World Economy*, Cambridge: Cambridge University Press.

Watson, A. (1980) 'Conflict in the Cairngorme', *Geographical Magazine*, LII, 6, pp. 427–445.

Weiler, B. and Davis, D. (1993) 'An exploratory investigation into the roles of the nature-based tour leader', *Tourism Management* April.

Weiler, B. and Hall, C. (1992) *Special Interest Tourism*, London: Belhaven.

Westlake, J. (1993) 'Tourism and the environment, the case of Zakynthos', *Tourism Management* April, pp. 137–41.

Wheeller, B. (1991) 'Tourism's Troubled Times: responsible tourism is not the answer', *Tourism Management*.

Wheeller, B. (1993a) 'Sustaining the ego?' *Journal of Sustainable Tourism* 1(2).

Wheeller, B. (1993b) 'Willing victims of the ego trap', *Tourism in Focus* 9.

Whelan, T. (1991) *Nature Tourism: managing the environment*, Washington: Island Press.

Wolf, C.P. (1977) 'Social impact assessment: the state of the art updated', *SIA Newsletter* 29 pp. 3–23.

Wood, (1984) 'Ethnic Tourism, the state of cultural charge in Southeast Asia, *Annals of Tourism Research*, 11(3), pp. 353–74.

Wood, K. and House, S. (1991) *The Good Tourist*, London: Mandarin.

Wood, R. (1992) *Working in Hotels and Catering*, London: Routledge.

World Tourism Organisation (WTO) (1992) *Tourism Trends to the Year 2000 and Beyond* Research report presented at EXPO Seville, September 1992, by Robert Cleverdon.

World Tourism Organisation (WTO) (1994) *Global Tourism Trends*, Madrid: World Tourism Organisation.

World Tourism Organisation (WTO) (1994a) *Tourism in 1993: highlights*, Madrid: World Tourism Organisation.

World Tourism Organisation (WTO) (1994b) *Global Tourism Forecasts to the Year 2000 and Beyond: Vol. 4 – East Asia and the Pacific*, Madrid: World Tourism Organisation.

World Tourism Organisation (WTO) (1994c) *Global Tourism Forecasts to the Year 2000 and Beyond: Vol. 2 – Africa* Madrid: World Tourism Organisation.

References

World Travel and Tourism Council (WTTC) (1994) *Annual Report*, Brussels: World Travel and Tourism Council.

World Tourism and Travel Environment Review Committee (WTTERC) (1993) *World Travel and Tourism Environment Review*, Oxford: OCTALS, Oxford Brookes University.

Wright, P. (1993) 'Ecotourism: ethics or eco-sell?' *Journal of Travel Research*, Winter.

Wyer, J. and Towner, J. (edited by Millman, R. and Hutchinson, A.) (1988) *The UK and Third World Tourism: a report for the Third World Tourism European Ecumenical Network*, Tonbridge: TEN Publications.

Index

Index